Qualitative
Reading
Inventory–II

Qualitative Reading Inventory–II

Lauren Leslie
Marquette University

JoAnne Caldwell
Cardinal Stritch College

An imprint of Addison Wesley Longman, Inc.
New York • Reading, Massachusetts • Menlo Park, California • Harlow, England
Don Mills, Ontario • Sydney • Mexico City • Madrid • Amsterdam

Executive Editor: Christopher Jennison
Project Coordination: Ruttle, Shaw & Wetherill, Inc.
Design Manager: Nancy Sabato
Text Design and Electronic Page Makeup: Kris Tobiassen
Illustrations: Stephen Marchesi
Electronic Production Manager: Valarie A. Sawyer
Manufacturing Manager: Helene G. Landers
Printer and Binder: Malloy Lithographing, Inc.
Cover Printer: The Lehigh Press, Inc.

QUALITATIVE READING INVENTORY–II

Library of Congress Cataloging-in-Publication Data
Leslie, Lauren.
    Qualitative reading inventory, II/Lauren Leslie, JoAnne Caldwell.
      p.   cm.
    Rev. ed. of: Qualitative reading inventory.
    Includes bibliographical references.
    ISBN 0-673-99086-9
    1. Qualitative Reading Inventory.   2. Reading comprehension—Ability testing.   I. Caldwell, JoAnne.   II. Leslie, Lauren, Qualitative reading inventory.   III. Title.   IV. Title: Qualitative reading inventory, 2.   V. Title: Qualitative reading inventory, two.
LB1050.75.Q34L47 1995
372.4'1—dc20   94-18636
                                                                                                                            CIP

12 13 14-WC-01 00 99

Contents

Preface

Changes in reading-assessment techniques continue to emerge. New research continues to be published. These factors have led to this revision of the *Qualitative Reading Inventory*. Of particular importance has been the current emphasis on authentic assessment of children's reading abilities, from the most emergent readers to advanced readers. While informal reading inventories traditionally have been used by assessment specialists, there is now a place for them in ongoing classroom assessment of children's growth in reading. The *Qualitative Reading Inventory*–II (*QRI*–II) addresses these current trends in reading assessment. Also new to this edition are the inclusion of pre-primer text, pictures accompanying pre-primer through second grade text, suggestions for classroom reading portfolios, a revised method for prior knowledge assessment, and expanded suggestions for the assessment of reading strategies and reading fluency.

The *Qualitative Reading Inventory*–II continues the long history of informal reading inventories. Like other informal reading inventories, it provides graded word lists and numerous passages designed to assess the oral reading, silent reading, or listening comprehension of a student. However, the *QRI*–II differs in several ways. The *QRI*–II contains narrative and expository passages at each pre-primer through junior-high level. All are self-contained selections highly representative of the structure and topic of materials found in basal readers and content-area textbooks. Passages at pre-primer through second-grade level are presented with and without pictures. Prior to reading, the knowledge of concepts important to an understanding of the passage is assessed, which allows the examiner to label a passage as familiar or unfamiliar to each student. The *QRI*–II measures comprehension in two ways: through an analysis of the student's retelling and through the answers to explicit and implicit comprehension questions.

This test allows the user to evaluate a reader's comprehension abilities in light of his or her background knowledge about a subject and whether the text was narrative or expository. The reader's answers to explicit and implicit comprehension questions allow the examiner to assess the reader's understanding of the text. The examiner can also assess the reader's understanding of the structure of the text through a qualitative analysis of his or her retelling. The *QRI*–II can also be used to assess a reader's awareness and use of various metacognitive strategies for comprehending text.

The *QRI*–II provides a number of diagnostic options that serve a variety of purposes. It can be used to estimate reading levels, suggest directions for instructional intervention, or to compile a profile of a student's reading ability. Each examiner is encouraged to decide which of the *QRI*–II's components meet his or her diagnostic purposes.

We designed the *QRI*–II for students in graduate education courses, reading-assessment specialists, and school district personnel who offer inservice work in reading assessment. If the *QRI*–II is used with preservice education students, an instructor will need to acquaint the student with recent research on factors affecting the reading process. In addition, the *QRI*–II presumes a basic knowledge of informal reading inventories.

Finally, although the *QRI*–II is an informal assessment instrument, we conducted an extensive piloting of the test. We have included a technical manual with reliability and validity data in Section 16.

Acknowledgments

We would like to extend our appreciation to the following persons who aided in testing, scoring, and interpreting the *Qualitative Reading Inventory*-II:

Linda Allen, Marquette University
Joyce Boettcher, University of Wisconsin-Oshkosh
Anne Calhoon, Marquette University
Joanne Chimelewski, New Berlin Schools
Sr. Candy Chrystal, Mt. Marty College
Paula Cooper, Marquette University
Kiki Damrow, Cardinal Stritch College
Sue Glass, Brown Deer Schools
Mary Jett-Simpson, University of Wisconsin-Milwaukee
Lori Kiewig, Cardinal Stritch College
Chris McGill, Cardinal Stritch College
Anne Nordholm, Marquette University
Denise Peppin, freelance artist
Mary Petsch-Horvath, Cardinal Stritch College
Pat McCarthy Plotkin, Wauwatosa Public Schools
Barbara Rankin, Cardinal Stritch College
Meg Regner, Marquette University
Linda Schulteis, Cardinal Stritch College
Donnell Scott, Cardinal Stritch College
Jeanne Steele, University of Northern Iowa
Mary Lynn Thomas, Waukesha Public Schools
John Thompson, New Berlin Schools
Gloria Weiner, Milwaukee Public Schools

We would like to thank the Graduate School and School of Education of Marquette University for financial support and research assistant support for Lauren Leslie, and the Teacher Education Division of Cardinal Stritch College for their support for JoAnne Caldwell during this project.

We wish to thank our reviewers, Michael McKenna, Georgia Southern University, Steven Stahl, University of Georgia, and Kathy Jongsma, Northside Schools, San Antonio, Texas, for their constructive criticism and support for our efforts. Also, thanks to the many users of the first edition of the *QRI* for calling and writing with compliments and suggestions for this edition.

And finally our thanks to the staff at Longman, Chris Jennison and Shadla Grooms.

Lauren Leslie
JoAnne Caldwell

1 Introduction to the *Qualitative Reading Inventory-II*

The *Qualitative Reading Inventory*-II (*QRI*–II) is an individually administered informal reading inventory (IRI) designed to provide diagnostic information about (1) conditions under which students can identify words and comprehend text successfully, and (2) conditions that appear to result in unsuccessful word identification, decoding, and/or comprehension. The *QRI*–II was designed to provide a variety of different opportunities to observe a student's reading behavior. For example, because the *QRI*–II contains narrative and expository passages at each readability level, the examiner can determine the student's relative strengths and weakensses in these two types of text. Additional features that promote assessment with the *QRI*–II are presented more fully below.

The *QRI*–II provides a number of assessment options that serve a variety of purposes. The classroom teacher can use the *QRI*–II to estimate student reading level, group students effectively, and appropriately choose textbooks. Student performances on the *QRI*–II can be included in reading portfolios. Reading and assessment specialists can use the *QRI*–II to plan intervention instruction. Each user will choose different components of the *QRI*–II to administer. Later sections of this manual contain more complete guidelines for assessment alternatives.

The *QRI*–II is not a norm-referenced or standardized instrument. Norm-referenced tests provide comparative data; that is, an individual's score is evaluated in terms of the established norm. Although we conducted extensive piloting on the *QRI*–II, individual subject scores should not be interpreted in comparison to these data. Administration of standardized instruments remains identical across all subjects. However, users of the *QRI*–II should make their own decisions regarding the number and type of passages to administer. The *QRI*–II provides several assessment options and it is the role of individual examiners to decide which, if any, to use.

The *QRI*–II continues a long history of informal reading inventories. For forty years, informal reading inventories have been used to identify subjects' reading levels—independent, instructional, and frustration—as well as to provide valuable diagnostic information (Bader & Wiesendanger, 1989). Like other informal reading inventories, the *QRI*–II provides graded word lists and numerous passages designed to assess the oral reading, and/or listening of students from the pre-primer through the junior-high level. However, the *QRI*–II differs from other informal reading inventories in several ways.

First, the *QRI*–II provides both narrative and expository text at each level. At the pre-primer through second-grade levels, the passages are divided into those with pictures and those without pictures. Passages with pictures are more representative of what beginning readers typically encounter. Comparing performance on a passage with and without pictures can suggest the extent to which the student relies on external clues for word identification and comprehension.

Another difference involves assessment of the student's prior knowledge of passage content. Each passage includes at least three questions designed to ascertain student familiarity or unfamiliarity with the topic of the selection. In addition a prediction task is presented as an option to the examiner. These tasks allow the examiner to label a passage as familiar or unfamiliar to each individual student.

The topics of the pre-primer through second-grade passages are generally familiar. At levels three through junior high, the topics of the selections vary in their familiarity to the reader. When a reader possesses background knowledge about a topic, he or she will find it easier to comprehend and retain information. Conversely, readers have more difficulty understanding text about an unfamiliar topic. Readers may have different instructional levels for familiar and unfamiliar text. By using passages that vary in familiarity, the *QRI*–II allows the examiner to arrive at a more precise description of a student's reading ability.

The *QRI*–II provides two ways of assessing comprehension: student unaided recall and questions. Each passage has an accompanying map for recording and evaluating the retelling. The questions are of two kinds: explicit and implicit. Answers to explicit questions can be found in the text; answers to implicit questions require the reader to make an inference based on a textual clue.

In summary, the *Qualitative Reading Inventory*–II is an informal reading inventory that contains word lists and passages at pre-primer through junior-high levels. It includes both narrative and expository passages. For each one, we have provided a task to assess the student's prior knowledge for the content of the selection. The *QRI*–II evaluates comprehension by an analysis of retelling and questions.

The *QRI*–II provides quantitative scores; however, for many students these scores will depend on the type of text read, their background knowledge, and the manner in which comprehension is assessed. Interpretation of their scores must therefore be qualified by the above factors. For this reason, this inventory has been titled the *Qualitative Reading Inventory*–II.

Section 2 provides the research rationale for the development of the *QRI*–II.

2 Why Another Informal Reading Inventory?

A Research Perspective

Early Reading Assessment: A Developmental Perspective

Factors Related to Comprehension

Text Structure
Prior Knowledge
Oral and Silent Reading
Strategies

Factors Related to Word Identification

Speed and Automaticity
Oral Reading Miscue Analysis

There are over a dozen informal reading inventories on the market. Why would we want to design another one? The reason is because current research suggests that there are factors that affect word identification and comprehension that are not considered together in any other informal reading inventory currently published (Caldwell, 1985). In addition, since the first edition of the *QRI* was published, we have continued to read and conduct research on factors affecting word identification and comprehension. As indicated in Section 1, the *Qualitative Reading Inventory*–II *(QRI–II)* reflects several advances based on research.

Early Reading Assessment: A Developmental Perspective

Developmental descriptions of the reading process have been provided by Chall (1983), Hood (1984) and Ehri (1991), and serve to organize Wisconsin's *Guide to Curriculum Planning in Reading,* (Wisconsin Department of Public Instruction, 1986). These descriptions suggest that the knowledge sources that children use to construct meaning from text and the aspects of constructing meaning that give them trouble vary depending upon their stage/level of reading acquisition. For example, children who are beginning to learn to read are trying to make sense of print. They are using their oral language skills, pictures, knowledge of the purposes of reading, and knowledge of letter–sound relationships to make sense out of the squiggles on the page (Leslie, 1993). In general, they would understand the text if it were read to them, but they have difficulty making meaning directly from print, without the aid of pictures. Thus, when assessing these very beginning readers, who can be termed *transitional* (Jett-Simpson & Leslie, 1994), you may observe that they use context to predict text, and frequently look at the pictures to initiate or confirm their predictions. They also use pictures to facilitate word identification. The very beginning reader shows a focus on meaning by making meaningful predictions from oral language and pictures, but the words bear little resemblance to the word in print (Jett-Simpson & Leslie, 1994; Sulzby & Teale, 1991).

In contrast, a student who has a large base of words that can be recognized automatically may be focused on other aspects of the reading process. This student looks at pictures in a cursory manner prior to or during reading, but in general uses print for word identification. The student shows a focus on meaning by self-correcting any oral reading miscues that significantly change the meaning of the text. Unlike the very beginning reader, the advanced beginner illustrates a balanced use of cue sources (Clay, 1985; Jett-Simpson & Leslie, 1994).

Still another student may have mastered basic word-recognition skills, and can read narrative text with fluency, comprehend it, and retell all major components of the narrative with a single reading, and now focuses on learning how to apply those same strategies to expository text (Chall, 1983).

This review of the developmental perspective highlights that what we observe depends on the student's development in learning to read. It should be noted that a developmental perspective does not imply rigid stages through which children pass at prescribed rates. Nor should it be inferred that at any point in learning to read, children are focused only on one aspect of reading. On the contrary, the interactive model of reading (Rumelhart, 1977; Stanovich, 1980) describes the interaction of many sources of information that students have available to them as they read. The more information they have in one area, the less they need in another (Stanovich, 1980). In the examples cited above, children are all attempting to construct meaning from text, but the beginning reader, having less knowledge of the phoneme–grapheme relationships, is using picture clues to aid the process. The most advanced reader described above has developed automatic word identification and can free her limited attentional resources to learning different strategies for remembering information from expository text. All students are focused on meaning, but the balance of cue systems used varies with their development. We believe that assessment should observe developmental differences in learning to read. Thus, we have modified certain aspects of the original *QRI* in order to support such observations.

The *QRI*–II includes passages for assessment of earlier stages of beginning reading. Users of the original *QRI* will remember that the readability of the lowest level passages was *primer*, and the text was laid out on a single page or two without pictures. Examiners who were assessing very beginning readers found the layout intimidating to children. Although children might have been able to read the words, their response to looking at the page was, "Do I have to read all that?" Also, because most literature for beginning readers includes pictures, we wanted to make our passages more representative of what children encounter regularly. In addition, many users asked for easier passages in order to assess earlier stages of beginning reading.

The *QRI*–II contains three *pre-primer* passages, two of which are narrative and one expository. One narrative has pictures and one does not. The expository text has pictures. All the texts are written to be predictable. That is, they contain repetitive language patterns. In addition, one narrative passage at primer, and levels one and two now includes pictures and each is laid out over three pages. We included pictures to allow examiners to compare how students' performance differed when pictures were available to them versus when they were not.

Our research with the pre-primer passages found that the relationship between pictures and word recognition and comprehension varied. That is, when pictures were present, very beginning readers were able to "recognize" words that they could not recognize without the picture, in other words, children could read words in the stories that they couldn't read on the word lists. When pictures were present in the passages, word-recognition accuracy and comprehension were not significantly correlated. However, on the pre-primer passage without pictures, word-recognition accuracy and comprehension were correlated at .94! See Section 16 for details.

We also compared passages on the first edition of the *QRI* with the same passages on the *QRI*–II, which now contain pictures. At the primer level, no differences were found on any measure on "The Pig who Learned to Read." At first-grade level, although no differences were seen on word-recognition accuracy or retelling, comprehension of "Bear and Rabbit" with pictures was significantly higher than without pictures. At the second-grade level, although no differences were seen on word-recognition accuracy or comprehension, retelling of "Father's New Game" was significantly higher with pictures than without. Thus, it seems that the role of pictures depends upon several factors. At the pre-primer level, pictures help children "read" words that they do not recognize automatically. Above that level, the pictures did not provide as much word recognition support, but rather assisted comprehension and retelling. See Section 16 for details.

Factors Related to Comprehension

Text Structure

Research in the last decade has described the structures of narrative (Graesser, Golding, & Long, 1991; Johnson & Mandler, 1980; Stein & Glenn, 1979) and expository text (Meyer & Rice, 1984; Weaver & Kintsch, 1991). Narratives, which follow the structure of fables (setting-character-goal/problem-events-resolution) have been found to be easier for children to recall than narratives without the major story components (Stein, 1979; Brennan, Bridge & Winograd, 1986), or with structure disrupted (Mandler & DeForest, 1979). Research with children finds that throughout the elementary school years narrative is easier for children to recall and comprehend than expository texts (Berkowitz & Taylor, 1981; Leslie & Caldwell, 1989; Leslie & Cooper, 1993; Leslie, unpublished).

There are many reasons why narrative text holds this privileged status (Graesser & Goodman, 1985; Graesser, Golding & Long, 1991). One reason is structural familiarity: it is highly likely that readers' familiarity with the structure of narratives is greater than their familiarity with the structures of expository text. In the most general sense, narratives are written about people engaging in goal-directed action, that is, the sort of events that are proposed to be the building blocks of cognition (Mandler, 1984; Nelson, 1986). Children are more likely to have been read narrative than expository texts, primary-grade instructional materials are predominantly narrative texts (Durkin, 1981), and the type of narrative most frequently read is the fable. Thus, the narrative texts with which children have the most experience have a single, common structure (Mulcahy & Samuels, 1987). In contrast to children's rather stable knowledge of narrative structure, their knowledge of expository structures is variable (Englert & Hiebert, 1984). Children may also be less familiar with any single structure of expository text because of the variety of expository structures, such as compare–contrast, problem–solution, and description, which rarely occur in pure form in student textbooks (Taylor, 1982).

Other reasons why narratives are easier to recall or comprehend may be readers' knowledge of content, or the strategic approaches they employ in reading texts. Although the effects of content knowledge and strategic approaches to reading on comprehension will be discussed separately in detail in this section, it is important to remember that differences between the recall and comprehension of narrative and expository texts may be related to these factors. If students know more about the topics discussed in narrative writings (as compared to those more usually presented in expository texts), then it is likely that they will recall and comprehend more of the narrative text. Only by assessing prior knowledge of concepts will we be able to separate this effect. Similarly, differences between recall and comprehension of narrative and expository text may be traced to strategic differences. A student reading a narrative for entertainment might read quickly to find out what happened, and recall only the action line of the story. However, when reading to remember information for a test, the student might read more slowly, self-test on important main ideas, and so forth.

If structural differences are one of the reasons for the superiority of narrative text, then differences between a student's recall of narrative and expository texts should be evident even when comprehension differences are not significant—if structural knowledge is more important for recall than comprehension (Kintsch, 1990).

The *QRI*–II contains narrative and expository passages at pre-primer through junior-high levels. There are two narrative and one expository passage at the pre-primer level. There are two narrative and two expository passages at the primer, first-, and second-grade levels, and three narrative and three expository passages at the third- through junior-high levels. Our pilot data for the *QRI*–II confirmed the differences between narrative and expository text that we found with the original *QRI*. See Section 16 for details.

Prior Knowledge

Within the last fifteen years, it has been shown repeatedly that readers with higher prior knowledge, *consistent with the content in the text,* recall and comprehend better than those with less consistent knowledge (Alvermann, Smith & Readance, 1985; Lipson, 1983). This finding is true for adults (Anderson, Reynolds, Schallert & Goetz, 1977) and children (Pearson, Hansen & Gordon, 1979; Taft & Leslie, 1985). Furthermore, the results can be generalized to poor readers as well as good readers (Taylor, 1979; Stevens, 1980). In fact, recent research has found that good and poor readers' ability to recall and summarize did not differ significantly if the groups were similar in their levels of knowledge (Recht & Leslie, 1988). The implications of these findings for assessment seem obvious (Johnston, 1984). A student with high knowledge of a particular content that is consistent with the information presented in text will be able to recall more and answer more questions correctly about that content than would be possible on material of the same readability about which the student had less or inconsistent knowledge.

These variations in comprehension as a function of prior knowledge prod us to design new reading-assessment devices. There are many ways in which to measure prior knowledge (Holmes & Roser, 1987): multiple-choice test, interview, oral free association, written free association, open-ended questions, and oral or written prediction. Researchers have found varying correlations among prior-knowledge measures. Recht (1986) found the correlation between multiple-choice tests and free association measures of prior knowledge to be .92. More recently, however, Valencia, Stallman, Commeyras, Pearson, and Hartman (1991) concluded that interviews, judgements of the likelihood that statements would be included in a passage on a certain topic, and written predictions of content given topical prompts, all measure different aspects of prior knowledge. Because they did not measure comprehension, no conclusion can be made about the ability of these measures to predict comprehension, which is termed predictive validity.

Other studies have examined the predictive validity of prior-knowledge measures. Free-association tasks have been shown to be significantly correlated with comprehension of narrative (Langer, 1984; Leslie & Caldwell, 1989; 1990; Leslie & Cooper, 1993) and expository text (Hare, 1982; Langer, 1984; Leslie & Caldwell, 1989; 1990; Taft & Leslie, 1985). Recent research (Leslie & Cooper, 1993) suggests that instructions for the free-association task, which ask for more precise responses, rather than general associations, were more predictive of sixth graders' comprehension and retelling of narrative text.

Also, prediction tasks have been shown to correlate somewhat with comprehension, although the findings are less consistent than those using free-association concepts. Valencia and Stallman (1989) found written prediction tasks to be minimally (.23), but statistically significantly, correlated with comprehension of expository text. Leslie and Cooper (1993) gave sixth-grade average readers the title of the selection and the concepts to which they had just responded and asked them to make a prediction of what the selection would be about. The prediction score correlated with students' retelling and comprehension of expository text. Our pilot data found that the same prediction task correlated with third-graders' retelling of narrative text. We have found that children vary tremendously in their familiarity with prediction tasks. In classrooms in which prediction based on pictures, or titles and pictures, is a common occurrence, we found that children were much more able to make predictions in our task, than children in classrooms in which predictions were never taught or modeled. In general, we found that early primary grade children (K and first grade) only used the title to make predictions. As children increased in age, their ability to integrate the concepts with the title increased. See Section 16 for a more detailed description of our findings on the prediction task.

The *QRI*–II measures prior knowledge by asking children to answer questions that were written to tap their understanding of key concepts (Langer, 1984). In addition, a prediction task based on the concepts and the title of the selection is provided. Based on the results of Leslie and Cooper (1993) and our piloting for the *QRI*–II, we have changed the format for the prior-knowledge task to asking precise questions, rather than asking for free association (see Section 8 for details).

Oral and Silent Reading

Although overall differences in oral and silent reading comprehension may be minimal, some children may comprehend better in one mode than in the other. Results of research examining differences between oral and silent reading comprehension are mixed; some studies find no differences (Pinter & Gilliland, 1916; Swalm, 1972) and others find oral superior to silent (Rowell, 1976) or silent superior to oral (Pinter, 1913). The most consistent findings appear to be that poor readers of fourth grade and below tend to comprehend better when reading orally (Swalm, 1972; Burge, 1983).

In addition to examining comprehension differences between oral and silent reading, rate differences may suggest the reader's level of reading development. Children for whom oral and silent rates are similar may not yet have developed fast and accurate word recognition, called *automaticity*. Generally authors say that more fluent reading is indicated when a child reads faster silently than orally

(Harris & Sipay, 1985). Huey (1908; 1968) states that good (fluent) readers read one-and-a-half to two times faster silently than orally. In order to allow comparison of a student's ability in both oral and silent reading, the *QRI*–II includes two narratives at pre-primer through second-grade levels, two expository passages at primer through second-grade levels, and three narrative and three expository passages at levels three through junior high.

Strategies

The effects of knowledge and application of metacognitive strategies on reading comprehension has been examined extensively during the past decade (for reviews see Baker & Brown, 1984; Paris, Wasik & Turner, 1991). Studies using interviews and observations of students' behavior have found that poor readers rated negative strategies as positive (and vice versa), and failed to ask questions, take notes, or use a dictionary as often as did good readers. Poor readers were also less accurate in applying the monitoring skills useful for resolving comprehension failures. Differences in skilled and less skilled readers' strategy use are particularly obvious when the readers are faced with difficult text (Kletzien, 1991; Zabrucky & Ratner, 1992). Specifically, research on "look-backs" in text containing inconsistencies designed to cause comprehension failure, indicated that students younger than eighth grade rarely used this strategy spontaneously (Garner & Reis, 1981). It is posited that students may not look back because they: (1) did not realize that they have not understood (Markman, 1977; 1979); (2) realized that the text did not make sense but made inferences to make sense of the text rather than look back (August, Flavell & Clift, 1984); (3) have expended so much attention on decoding and meaning construction that they do not have enough resources left to compare new information to prior knowledge and evaluate the consistency between them (Paris, Wasik & Turner, 1991); and (4) have been unable to form a coherent representation of the text from which to compare and evaluate (Vosniadou, Pearson & Rogers, 1988). However, direct instruction over five days to poor readers improved students' strategic look-backs in text (Garner, Hare, Alexander, Haynes & Winograd, 1984). Thus, through direct instruction with modeling and explanations of which strategies are important, as well as when and why to use them, young readers can become more strategic.

The *QRI*–II includes the option of asking students to engage in look-backs to resolve comprehension failures. Section 12 provides a variety of options for engaging students in look-backs. We chose to measure students' ability to perform look-backs rather than include a self-report instrument (Meyers & Paris, 1978; Schmidt, 1990) because we believe that students' abilities to *use* strategies are more important to reading comprehension than their self-report of useful strategies. We recognize that asking students to look back is not the same as spontaneous look-backs, which is the topic of much of the research. We expected students to be able to *use* information from directed look-backs at an earlier age or reading ability level than the research on spontaneous look-backs suggests. We believe that examining whether students can look back when prompted will give valuable information for instruction.

Our pilot research indicates that students as young as those at the end of second grade, with second or third-grade reading instructional levels were able to increase their explicit and implicit comprehension scores by looking back in the text. Prior to this level, students' focus was on word identification and look-backs frequently resulted in the student rereading the entire text rather than being able to quickly look back to the section in text containing the relevant information. See Section 16 for details.

Factors Related to Word Identification

Speed and Automaticity

The ability to recognize words is characterized by accuracy, automaticity, and speed (Ehri & Wilce, 1979). As readers practice accurate identification of words, they begin to read these words with less conscious attention to letter–sound matching and, therefore, more rapidly. While word identification automaticity, and word-identification speed are different constructs (Stanovich, Cunningham & West, 1981), reading rate can suggest the presence of automaticity.

Perfetti's (1985, 1988) verbal efficiency theory hypothesizes that children who do not develop the ability to read words accurately and quickly will encounter difficulty in comprehension. Because most of their attention is directed toward identifying individual words, they are unable to efficiently access word meanings and integrate sentence meanings across an entire passage. LaBerge and Samuels (1985) also stress the importance of fast and accurate automatic word identification. Both word identification and comprehension require attention on the part of the reader. Attentional resources are limited. The more attention that is directed to word identification, the less is available for comprehension.

The *QRI*–II measures word-identification speed (and automaticity) in two ways. The timed portion of the word lists provides one measure. Our pilot data illustrates that words read within one second predict reading rate in context better than the total number of words read correctly.

Some may argue that use of word lists for assessment is not an authentic task. We agree. Readers do not curl up with a good list of words. However, the ability to identify words accurately and quickly *out of context* is a characteristic of the skilled reader (Perfetti, 1983; 1988 Stanovich, 1980). Therefore, use of the word lists may provide an important piece of assessment information. Readers who take more than one second to accurately identify a word may not have achieved automaticity for that word.

The *QRI*–II provides another measure of word-identification speed, rate of reading as measured in words per minute on the passages. Definitive research in this area has been elegantly reviewed by Carver (1990). Carver describes five different reading processes: memorizing, learning, rauding, skimming, and scanning. Memorizing involves the slowest reading rate and scanning is the fastest. Rauding is the process normally used by readers for relatively easy material. Rauding occurs at a generally constant rate for individuals with speed of word identification being the most important factor affecting that rate.

Reading rate is affected by a variety of factors (Carver, 1990). Rate varies according to the purpose of the reader and the process chosen. For example, a reader engaged in the rauding process might well shift to the learning process if the material becomes relatively difficult. This shift would result in a slower reading rate. In this example, we can note that text difficulty as determined by the structure of the text, the familiarity of the content, and the difficulty level of the author's vocabulary, can be an important determiner of reading rate. Reading rate can vary according to the mode of reading (oral versus silent), the age of the reader, and reading skill. Finally, reading rate is also determined by individual cognitive processing speeds. The complexity of variables affecting rate suggest that hard-and-fast norms may be impossible to formulate. In Section 10, we offer some general suggestions for evaluating reading rate, based upon our pilot data.

Oral Reading Miscue Analysis

Since the late 1960s, Goodman (1969) has drawn attention to the rich information that an assessment specialist can gain from examining how a student's oral reading deviates from the written text. Prior to Goodman, assessment specialists only analyzed how deviations from print (then called errors) reflected what the reader did not know about sound–symbol correspondences. Goodman's research encouraged others to go beyond what appeared to be wrong with the reader and attend to the cue systems that the reader was using when his/her reading deviated from the print. Goodman calls these deviations *miscues* because he believes that they indicate how the reading process was miscued by characteristics of the text and by prior knowledge of the reader. Goodman's work has led assessment specialists to examine what miscues tell us about how readers are using the cue systems. Two of the cue systems discussed by Goodman that are of pertinence to the *QRI*–II are the graphophonic cue system and the semantic cue system.

Graphophonic cues refer to the relationships between graphemes (letters) and phonemes (smallest units of sound). If a reader says the word "was" for "saw," one can infer that the reader is utilizing graphic clues because the letters are the same in both words. However, the phonemic similarity is low; these words don't sound alike at all. On the other hand, a reader who identifies "horse" as "house" is using both graphic and sound cues.

Semantic clues are meaning clues. They are obtained from the semantic content of what is being read. For example, if a reader reads the sentence, "I received six presents for my birthday" as "I received six gifts for my birthday," we can infer that the reader is using semantic information in saying "gifts" for "presents". The reader is not using graphophonic clues because these words do not share similar letters or sounds.

Leslie and Osol (1978) and Leslie (1980) examined how the quantity of miscues related to the quality of miscues. They asked whether the acceptability of miscues decreases as the reader makes more and more miscues. The results showed that as the percentage of miscues increased, the proportion which changed the author's meaning and which was left uncorrected also increased. As the reader makes more and more deviations from text, s/he begins to lose meaning, which is reflected in miscues of less quality.

These findings support the 90% oral reading accuracy recommended by Betts (1946) and retained by Harris and Sipay (1985) as the cutoff for frustration-level reading. The oral reading research suggests that reading with less than 90% accuracy may result in an inability to obtain meaning. The research points to an implication, which hasn't been tested, that students reading materials with which they frequently make more than 10% errors will not learn to correct errors that change meaning. Furthermore, they may learn to expect that reading doesn't make sense (Bristow, 1985).

Another factor that has been shown to affect the quality of miscues is prior knowledge. Taft and Leslie (1985) found that students with prior knowledge about content made fewer miscues that changed the author's meaning than students who had little knowledge about the content area. Those with little knowledge made a higher proportion of miscues that were graphically similar to the word in print. The results suggested a trade-off between the use of semantic and graphic cues. If more semantic cues are available, readers may need to pay less attention to graphic cues. Conversely, when a reader does not have enough semantic information, s/he will rely on graphic cues (Stanovich, 1980).

Users of the *QRI*–II can examine oral reading behavior quantitatively and qualitatively. The quantitative criteria used to determine independent, instructional and frustration levels follows the recommendations of Harris and Sipay (1985). Our pilot data suggests that the best predictor of instructional level comprehension is 95% for Acceptable Accuracy. Acceptable Accuracy is the measure of accuracy attained when only uncorrected, meaning-change miscues are counted.

We encourage qualitative analysis of the reader's use of semantic and graphic cues to ascertain how much attention the reader is paying to meaning and how much attention is paid to the graphic elements of the text. In addition, because prior knowledge has been found to influence miscue patterns (Taft & Leslie, 1985), the assessment specialist can examine whether the use of the semantic and graphic cues changes as a function of text familiarity or unfamiliarity.

3 A General Description of the *Qualitative Reading Inventory–II*

The Word Lists

The Passages

Pre-primer, Primer, First-, and Second-Grade Passages
Third- Through Junior-High Passages
Measures of Comprehension

The Word Lists

Each of the *QRI*–II's nine word lists contains twenty words which we have selected from passages at the same level of readability. For example, the primer word list contains words from the primer passages.

The word lists are designed:

1. To assess accuracy of word identification
2. To assess speed and automaticity of word identification
3. To determine the starting point for reading the initial passage

The Passages

The passages to be read orally or silently assess the subject's ability to read and comprehend different types of text. Table 3.1 presents the *QRI*–II passages grouped according to readability level and text type. Because the types of text vary with the level of readability, we will discuss the pre-primer through Second-Grade passages separately from the Third-through Junior-High passages.

Pre-primer, Primer, First-, and Second-Grade Passages

At the pre-primer readability level, there are three passages. Two are narratives and one is expository. One of the narratives and the expository passage are

TABLE 3.1
Passages on the *Qualitative Reading Inventory*–II

Readability Level	Narrative	Expository
Pre-primer	Lost and Found Just Like Mom (Pictures)	People at Work (Pictures)
Primer	A Trip The Pig Who Learned to Read (Pictures)	Who Lives near Lakes Living and Not Living
1st	Mouse in a House The Bear and Rabbit (Pictures)	Air What You Eat

2nd	What Can I Get for
	  My Toy
	Father's New Game
	  (Pictures)
		Seasons
		Whales and Fish

3rd	The Trip to the Zoo The Surprise The Friend	Cats Where People Live Wool
4th	Johnny Appleseed Amelia Earhart Sequoyah	Busy Beaver Saudi Arabia Cahokia
5th	Martin Luther King Christopher Columbus Margaret Mead	Octopus Getting Rid of Trash Laser Light
6th	Pele Abraham Lincoln Andrew Carnegie	Computers Predicting Earthquakes Ultrasound
Junior High	Lewis & Clark Ferdinand Magellan Peter the Great	Fireworks Diamonds The City of Constantine

presented with pictures. The primer, first-, and second-grade readability levels have four passages—two narrative and two expository. At each level, one of the narrative passages is presented with pictures. Research suggests that emergent readers depend upon picture context for both word identification and passage comprehension. In addition, text with pictures more closely approximates the type of selections presented to beginning readers. The diagnostician can assess the effect of pictures upon a subject's word identification and/or comprehension by contrasting performance on passages with and without pictures.

In addition to the narrative selections there are one or two expository passages at each level. Because the amount of expository material is increasing in basal readers and because children have had difficulty making the transition from narration to exposition, we felt that it was important to include expository material at all levels. The inclusion of expository material also makes the *QRI*–II more usable by teachers working with adult beginning readers who might be put off by children's narratives. Examiners who give passages from pre-primer through second grade will be able to ascertain the subject's relative strengths in recalling and comprehending narrative versus expository material. In addition, we have included enough passages to assess differences between oral and silent reading, which, if they are likely to occur, should be more predominant at these early reading levels.

All passages contain concept questions that are designed to measure prior knowledge of the major concepts within each passage. Each passage assesses knowledge of three to four concepts. Scores on the concept task should help the examiner to determine whether the subject possesses knowledge of basic concepts necessary to comprehend the selection.

Third- Through Junior-High Passages

The passages for use from third grade through junior high include three narrative and three expository passages at each level. The narratives above the third-grade level are biographies of famous people who had a goal or dream. Two of the people are relatively well known (such as Martin Luther King) and/or contain concepts that should be familiar to the readers because similar concepts were included in several content area texts at that level (such as Lewis and Clark). We chose biographies in order to provide a more controlled assessment of prior knowledge. For example, it is easier to assess prior knowledge of Abraham Lincoln than to evaluate a student's knowledge of the content of a fictional narrative. In addition, the purpose of biographies is to inform (Brewer, 1980). Thus, the purpose for reading these narratives is the same as for our expository passages. This control allows us to examine the effect of text structure without the confounding of purpose. The other passage in each level is about a person likely to be unknown to the readers (like Peter the Great). By including familiar and unfamiliar topics as indicated by our pilot data, *QRI*–II results can be useful in suggesting why subjects are having trouble in comprehension.

The expository passages are descriptive science and social studies materials written about various topics. As in the narratives, two of the passages are about relatively familiar topics (such as fireworks) and one is on a less familiar topic (like ultrasound). We included passages which, according to our pilot data, ranged in familiarity. Again, we did so because of research findings suggesting that the level of prior knowledge is an important determinant of reading comprehension.

All the passages on levels four through junior high were taken from published science and social studies texts, so they are representative of the material that readers at these grade levels are exposed to in class. Prior knowledge tasks were designed for each passage to assess reader familiarity or prior knowledge of the important concepts included within the selection. This should aid the examiner in determining whether high or low comprehension scores on a passage were due, in part, to the level of prior knowledge a subject had about the topic. Because of the variety and number of the passages we have provided, test administrators can examine differences in comprehension of familiar versus unfamiliar material, narrative versus expository material, and oral versus silent reading.

The passages are designed:

1. To determine a student's independent, instructional, and/or frustration levels for word identification in context
2. To determine a student's independent, instructional, and/or frustration levels for comprehension

3. To assess a student's ability to read different types of text: narrative and expository text; text with and without pictures; (pre-primer through grade two); and text of varying familiarity
4. To assess a student's ability to comprehend in different modes: oral and silent

Measures of Comprehension

QRI–II assesses comprehension of all passages in two ways: retelling and questions.

Retelling. After reading the selection, the student is asked to retell the passage as if s/he were telling it to someone who never heard it before. The student's retelling is scored from a map of important idea units or propositions contained in the passage. For example, "John Chapman was born in Massachusetts," contains two propositions: John Chapman was born and he was born in Massachusetts.

What the student is able to retell can provide information about the reader's ability to recall important ideas which are structured in some logical way. For example, in recalling goal-based stories, a student who knows the structure of stories may retell the passage in the order of a well-structured narrative: setting-character-goal/problem-events-resolution. In exposition, examiners should note if a student recalls main ideas first followed by supporting details.

Questions. Next the examiner asks the student two types of questions. Questions with answers stated explicitly in the text are called *text explicit questions*. Questions with answers that the subject must infer from information in the text are called *text implicit questions*. Answers to the text implicit questions are based on the interaction of text information and prior knowledge. However, correct answers to text implicit questions must be tied to information in the story and not simply derived from prior knowledge. Independent, instructional, and frustration levels for comprehension are derived from scores on the question measure.

The comprehension measures are designed:

1. To assess the quality of the reader's unaided recall
2. To arrive at independent, instructional, and frustration levels for text comprehension

In summary, the *QRI*–II consists of graded word lists and narrative and expository passages. The word lists and passages, which range from pre-primer to junior high level, vary in familiarity, and prior knowledge is assessed before reading each passage. Comprehension is assessed through retelling and questions.

Section 4 describes the assessment information provided by the *QRI*–II.

4 Information Provided by the *Qualitative Reading Inventory*–II

Finding Reading Levels

The Independent Level
The Instructional Level
The Frustration Level
Level Variety

Determining Reader Strengths and Needs

Finding Reading Levels

The *Qualitative Reading Inventory*–II can provide two kinds of information: the student's reading levels and his/her reading strengths and/or needs. When used to determine a student's reading levels, the *QRI*–II can help find the level at which a student can read independently, with instructional guidance, and with frustration.

The Independent Level

This is the level at which a student can read successfully without assistance. Oral reading should be fluent and free from behaviors such as finger pointing and overt signs of tension. The student's accuracy in word recognition while reading orally should be 98% or higher. Silent reading should also be free from finger pointing. For both oral and silent reading, comprehension should be excellent. The reader should be able to answer 90% or more of the questions correctly.

An examiner should choose materials written at this level for the student's free reading pleasure or for tasks which the reader is expected to perform independently. It is also wise to choose materials at an independent level for reading strategy instruction or fluency practice. This allows the reader to learn and practice a strategy on relatively easy text before transferring to more challenging material.

The Instructional Level

This is the level at which a student can read with assistance from a teacher. Both oral and silent reading should be free from behaviors that often indicate serious difficulty, such as finger pointing or tension. While oral reading may be less fluent at this level than at the independent level, it should retain some sense of rhythm and expression. The examiner should use a criterion of 95% accuracy whenever s/he is counting only those miscues which changed the meaning of the passage. Our pilot data found that 95% acceptable accuracy best predicts instructional level comprehension. If the examiner is counting all miscues, s/he should use a criterion of 90% accuracy, and the subject should correctly answer 70% of the questions asked.

Materials written at this level should be chosen for reading and content-area instruction. This placement assumes that the teacher will introduce words and concepts which are likely to be unfamiliar to the readers. S/he presents the identification and meaning of these concepts and provides appropriate background knowledge necessary for understanding the material. Obviously, when students are placed at the instructional level, the teacher should not say, "Read Chapter 5 and we'll have a test tomorrow."

The Frustration Level

At this level, the student is completely unable to read the material with adequate word identification or comprehension. Signs of difficulty and tension are evident. Oral reading lacks fluency and expression; a word-for-word, halting style is common. Word recognition accuracy is less than 90%, and less than 70% of the questions are answered correctly. Teachers should avoid materials at this level.

Level Variety

While it was once common, it is now simplistic to talk about a single independent, instructional, or frustration level for an individual. The act of reading is highly complex and contextual. When a student possesses extensive prior knowledge about a topic, s/he can read and comprehend at a higher level than in unfamiliar material. This is well illustrated by mature readers' difficulty with an income tax form or the language of an insurance policy. Text structure also affects a student's reading ability. The diverse structure and concept density of expository material makes it more difficult to comprehend than narrative text. Whether a student reads orally or silently can affect comprehension, depending on the age of the subject. Younger, less fluent readers generally do better in oral reading, while older readers are often constrained by the performance aspect of oral reading and their comprehension suffers accordingly. The variety of passages on the *Qualitative Reading Inventory*–II allows the examiner to evaluate the effects of background knowledge, text structure, and reading mode upon the independent, instructional, and frustration levels of the reader. It is not inconceivable that a single reader may have different levels for familiar and unfamiliar text, for narrative and expository material, and for oral and silent reading modes.

Which reading level is most important? Given the constraints of time few examiners would be able to determine all possible reading levels that a student might have. Based upon individual purpose and needs, each examiner will have to choose which reading level to isolate for a given student. Which level best estimates the overall reading ability of the student? Determination of the familiar narrative reading level seems most essential. Because reading familiar narrative text generally represents an easier task than dealing with expository and unfamiliar material, the familiar narrative level probably represents a reader's best effort.

Determining Reader Strengths and Needs

The major purpose of the *QRI*–II is to indicate the conditions under which a student would perform successfully or unsuccessfully in reading. Assessment specialists believe that a student has a reading disability if there is a substantial difference between his/her expectancy level or reading potential and his/her instructional level in familiar material. Expectancy level or reading potential is generally based upon IQ and therefore requires the administration of an individual intelligence test. However, many reading-assessment specialists either cannot administer such an instrument or do not have access to such scores. For this reason, it may be easier to talk of reading disability in terms of a discrepancy between the child's reading level and his/her chronological grade level.

For most readers with serious disabilities, strengths and needs in reading are evident. The *QRI*–II was designed to identify these strengths and needs by providing more information as to why a student is not reading well. Following are questions which the *QRI*–II was designed to answer.

Can the Student Identify:
words accurately?
words automatically?

When Reading Orally, Does the Student:
correct word identification errors that do not make sense?
make word identification errors that are contextually appropriate?
make word identification errors that suggest use of graphic or letter clues?

Can the Student Comprehend Successfully in:
narrative material?
expository material?
familiar material?
unfamiliar material?
material with pictures (Pre-primer through Second Grade)?
material without pictures?

What Is the Quality of the Student's Recall?
Does the student organize recall in stories according to elements of story
    structure?
Does the student organize recall in exposition according to main idea and
    details?

The sections that follow will illustrate how the *QRI*–II can answer the above questions. Table 4.1 provides a summary of the options offered by the *QRI*–II.

TABLE 4.1
Assessment Options of the *Qualitative Reading Inventory*-II

Determination of a Student's Reading Levels

Independent
Instructional
Frustration
In:
    Narrative text
    Expository text
    Text read orally
    Text read silently
    Familiar text
    Unfamiliar text
    Text with pictures (Preprimer–Second Grade)

Description of a Student's Strengths and Needs in Reading

Word Identification Ability

In isolation
    Accuracy
    Automaticity
In context
    Oral reading of passages
        Accuracy
        Automaticity/rate
    Miscue analysis
        Use of graphic/letter cues
        Use of semantic cues
        Use of self-corrections

Comprehension Ability

Ability to comprehend narrative text
Ability to comprehend expository text
Ability to comprehend familiar text
Ability to comprehend unfamiliar text
Ability to comprehend after oral reading
Ability to comprehend after silent reading
Ability to comprehend with pictures
Ability to comprehend without pictures
Ability to recall
    Completeness of recall
    Organization of recall
    Accuracy of recall

Prior Knowledge

Concept question task
Prediction task

5 Uses of the *Qualitative Reading Inventory*–II

The Examiner as a Reflective Decision Maker

The Classroom Teacher

Using the *QRI*–II to Estimate Reading Level
Using the *QRI*–II to Match Students to Appropriate Text
Using the *QRI*–II for Reading Portfolios
Using the *QRI*–II to Verify a Suspected problem

The Reading-Assessment Specialist

Determining Reading Level
Describing Specific Reading Behavior as a Guide for Intervention Instruction

In order to use the *QRI*–II to its best advantage without undue testing and interpretation time, the user must be a decision maker. The examiner must decide what information s/he wants to obtain about the student and how to use the *QRI*–II to obtain it. S/he need not determine a complete range of levels (independent, instructional, frustration) for each student. S/he need not administer both word lists and passages to each student. S/he need not determine familiar/unfamiliar, narrative/expository, and oral/silent levels for each student. And s/he does not have to use all options (recall, questions, miscue analysis). This would be extremely time-consuming and, in many cases, totally unnecessary. The examiner must decide beforehand what information will be most helpful and choose the passages and options accordingly. In some cases, s/he may administer only one or two passages to estimate a reading level or to confirm the existence of a problem in a specific area, such as expository text. In other cases, the examiner may choose to engage in a more complete assessment of a reader's strengths and needs.

The *QRI*–II can be utilized effectively by the classroom teacher or the reading-assessment specialist. Each can choose those components of the inventory that will best suit their needs.

The Classroom Teacher

Using the *QRI*–II to Estimate Reading Level

The *QRI*–II can be effectively used by the classroom teacher to estimate the reading level of individual children. This is important for a variety of reasons. First, reading instruction is characterized by different organizational formats. Some classrooms group children according to reading ability; others employ a less structured approach with groups of children and/or individuals reading selections that they have chosen. Some classrooms depend upon basal reading series for instructional materials; others follow a literature-based approach and use a variety of tradebooks. Whichever format is used, its success depends upon placing children in materials appropriate to their reading level.

The movement away from basal reading series to a literature-based approach has presented the classroom teacher with the problem of estimating an individual's reading level. Some school districts require that a child's reading level be placed on a report card or in a cumulative folder. Parents often ask for an estimation of reading level. Is their child performing at the level of his/her peers? Formerly, a classroom teacher could use a child's performance in a specific basal as an indication of individual level. If a child experienced success in a basal at grade level, the classroom teacher could assume that the child was on level. Similarly, performance in a higher or lower basal could suggest a reading level above or below grade placement. However, tradebooks do not always come marked with reading levels. While some suggest appropriate grade levels for use, this is sometimes based upon the topic and not the difficulty level of the text.

In estimating individual reading levels, the classroom teacher does not have the luxury of ample time for assessment activities. Administration of the *QRI*–II should involve only a few passages. The teacher should choose a narrative at the appropriate grade level, for example, a third-grade passage for use with third graders. The teacher should have the child read orally or silently, depending upon which mode is primarily utilized in the classroom. We recommend using oral administration for second grade and below and silent administration for third grade and above. If the teacher is listening to the child read orally, s/he should count all reading miscues and use a 90% cut-off score. It takes less time to count all miscues than to evaluate which ones represent meaning-change miscues and which do not. Again, because it is easier, the teacher should ask the comprehension questions as opposed to scoring recall.

If the student achieves at an instructional level, the teacher can estimate that the child is at least at grade level. The teacher has the option to move up to the next highest passage in order to determine if the child can read higher level passages. If the student is at a frustration level, the teacher should administer the next lowest passage in order to determine the instructional level. Usually the teacher only needs to administer two passages in order to determine reading level. It is not necessary to exercise the options of miscue analysis or unaided recall, nor is it necessary to contrast various types of text. It is important to remember that this offers only an estimation of reading level as many other variables affect whether or not a child can comprehend a specific selection. Section 14 contains examples using *QRI*–II passages to estimate reading level.

Using the *QRI*–II to Match Students to Appropriate Text

Once the teacher has an estimate of reading level, s/he can match this level to a specific reading-group placement or basal text. Of course if the school's basal reader has its own informal reading inventory (IRI), we suggest using this instead of the *QRI*–II for several reasons. First, the passages in the basal are often taken directly from the book that will be used for instruction; thus, one can tell how well the child will do on that material. Second, basal IRIs often utilize questions similar to those in the teacher's manual. For these reasons, a child's performance on the basal IRI should be most like his or her classroom performance.

The teacher can also use the *QRI*–II to place students in appropriate content textbooks. Some classrooms provide a range of such textbooks to use with the students. Matching an individual's reading level to a content text involves the same process as above. However, instead of using narrative passages from the *QRI*–II to estimate reading level, the teacher should use expository ones.

Matching an individual's reading level to tradebook selection represents a less exact process. Because few trade books are designated as written at specific reading levels, the teacher cannot expect to match a child who is at a third grade instructional level on the *QRI*–II with a tradebook leveled at grade three. Even if this were possible, it would not necessarily ensure success. Children can read more difficult books on very familiar topics or on topics of great interest to them.

Of course, the best way to estimate whether a child can handle a specific book is to listen to him/her read several pages from the book in question, note word-recognition skill and ask for a brief recall. However, this can represent a very time-consuming process for a classroom teacher. An individual child may need to try out several tradebooks before finding an appropriate one. In addition, a teacher rarely deals with only one child, but instead has an entire class to match to appropriate texts. Administration of the *QRI*–II can offer a viable alternative. If the teacher has an instructional level from the *QRI*–II, s/he can use this as a rough estimate of ability level. If a tradebook is marked as suitable for a specific grade and if the child's instructional level matches this grade, there is a strong probability that the child can handle the selection with relative success.

Many classrooms are compiling classroom libraries. It is important that these libraries represent a range of difficulty levels so that appropriate text is available to all students. If the *QRI*–II has been used as an estimate of individual levels, this can provide the teacher with a suggestion of the necessary span of materials to be included in the library.

Using the *QRI*–II for Reading Portfolios

The concern for authentic assessment has led many classroom teachers to employ reading portfolios as an integral part of their assessment. The *QRI*–II can become one component of a reading portfolio. Asking a student to read a passage and then recall it is an authentic task that parallels the actual reading process. While using actual tradebooks or textbooks can serve the same purpose, the *QRI*–II offers the convenience of scoring protocols and leveled passages with reliability and validity data on the questions and the difficulty of the passages.

There are several ways in which the *QRI*–II can be used in a reading portfolio. First, the classroom teacher can administer the *QRI*–II as an estimation of reading level and place the scored protocol in the child's portfolio. If this is done at the beginning of the year, the same passage or another of the same genre or level of difficulty can be administered at the end of the year or at the end of a grading period to evaluate growth. The two scored protocols can be clipped together with a brief teacher comment as to progress. The protocol can also be shared with the student and used as a vehicle for student self-assessment of progress.

The reading portfolio can contrast the student's performance on narrative and expository text. Both can be administered and then re-administered at a later date. Again, both the teacher and the student can offer comments on performance growth.

QRI–II passages can be used for student self-analysis, an important component of a portfolio. The teacher can choose a passage at an appropriate grade level and have the student engage in activities designed to foster self-awareness of strategic reading. Of course, this can be done with any tradebook or textbook. However, using *QRI*–II passages allows the teacher to assess a child's performance in leveled material. The teacher can conveniently choose different passages to correspond to the different ability levels in the classroom. The passages can be easily duplicated for students to write on without violating copyright. Several activities for student self-analysis follow. These activities can be done in the presence of the teacher as a form of conferencing, in cooperative groups, or individually.

Have the student read a passage orally or silently and underline all new or unknown words. Have the student suggest possible strategies for determining the pronunciation and/or meaning of the words. The student should then attempt to utilize the suggested strategies and comment on his/her success.

Have the student read a passage orally or silently and write down his/her recall without looking back at the passage. The recall could also be read into a tape recorder. The student should then return to the passage and evaluate the completeness of the recall.

Have the student read a passage into a tape recorder and listen to the tape. Using a teacher-provided checklist, the student can evaluate his/her accuracy, fluency, and expression.

Have the student read a passage and answer the accompanying questions. The student can then correct the questions, using the passage as a guide. The student should correct explicit questions by underlining the answer in the passage. The student should correct implicit questions by underlining the clue provided in the passage. After correction, the student can then evaluate his/her success.

Using the *QRI*–II to Verify a Suspected Problem

In some cases, the classroom teacher may suspect that poor performance in science, social studies, or other content classes may be due to a specific reading difficulty. The teacher can use appropriate passage/s from the *QRI*–II to verify the existence of such a problem.

To Verify a Possible Problem with Expository Text. The teacher should choose an expository passage that is probably familiar to the student and that corresponds to the reading level of the content textbook used in the class. Because most content reading is done silently, s/he should have the student read the passage in this mode and then ask the accompanying questions.

To Verify a Possible Problem with Unfamiliar Topics. The teacher should choose a narrative or expository passage that is probably unfamiliar to the student. S/he should choose this passage to correspond to the reading level of the textbook used. The student should read it orally or silently and answer the questions that follow. If time permits, it may be helpful to contrast this passage with a familiar one at the same level in order to note if comprehension differences are indeed present in familiar and unfamiliar text.

To Verify a Possible Problem with Silent Reading Comprehension. The teacher should choose a narrative passage that is likely to be familiar to the child. Many children who are effective oral readers and comprehenders often experience difficulty in making a transition to independent silent reading. S/he can ask the child to read the passage silently and ask the accompanying questions. If time permits, s/he can contrast this with a similar passage read orally, timing both. If the child's rate of silent reading is similar to his/her oral reading rate, this may indicate that the child is not engaging in effective silent reading strategies.

To Verify a Possible Problem with Ineffective Note-taking. The teacher should choose a familiar expository passage at a level that corresponds to the level of the content textbook. S/he should ask the student to read silently and take notes on the important parts of the passage. An alternative would be to have the student underline the important parts as s/he reads. The teacher can then examine these notes and/or underlining to ascertain if the reader has internalized effective note-taking strategies for finding important elements in the text.

To Verify a Possible Problem with Recall Following Reading. The teacher should choose a familiar passage at a level that corresponds to the textbook being used by the subject. S/he should ask the student to read silently and ask for unaided recall. The teacher can compare this recall to the retelling scoring sheet in order to evaluate the quality of the reader's memory for what was read. Then s/he can ask the accompanying questions and contrast the subject's ability to give correct answers with his/her ability to offer unaided recall of a selection.

The classroom teacher can utilize the *QRI*–II effectively to determine reading group and textbook placement and to verify the existence of a suspected problem. Due to time constraints, the teacher will rarely employ all the diagnostic options provided by the *QRI*–II, but s/he will instead choose one or two passages to serve a very specific purpose.

The Reading-Assessment Specialist

The reading-assessment specialist can be a school-based reading specialist or a reading clinician employed by a university reading clinic or a private educational institution. The role of the reading specialist often involves determining if a student qualifies for exceptional educational placement or for other forms of reading intervention. The reading specialist may assess individually those students suspected of having a reading problem and may act as part of a multidisciplinary team that evaluates a student in areas other than reading. Once a reading problem is verified, the reading specialist plays a key role in planning intervention instruction.

The function of the reading clinician is to provide a complete assessment of the reading behavior of disabled readers. Often these students have been referred for clinical diagnosis as a verification of district placement. Some are students in schools that do not provide extensive assessment or intervention services. Many are "grey-area" children, who have not met district criteria for special services, but are experiencing difficulties in the classroom.

In many school districts, criteria for reading intervention involves scores obtained on individualized, standardized, norm-referenced tests. These tests seldom present reading in a natural context. That is, they tend to include isolated word lists, multiple-choice vocabulary tests, and comprehension assessments based upon brief, decontextualized passages. In addition, while some may provide a valid estimate of a student's instructional reading level (Blanchard, Borthwick, & Hall, 1983; Smith & Beck, 1980), others may be of limited use in ascertaining the level of text that a student can read successfully.

The *QRI*–II provides both the reading specialist and the reading clinician with a tool for observing the reading behavior of a subject in a context that more closely approximates a classroom setting. It can be used to indicate the level at which a reader can succeed in different types of text. Neither the reading specialist or the reading clinician have unlimited time for assessment. Both must choose those parts of the *QRI*–II that will offer the most valuable diagnostic information for a given student. Two general diagnostic areas are important: determination of the student's reading level, and description of specific reading behaviors as a guide for intervention instruction.

Determining Reading Level

The reading-assessment specialist generally has several kinds of data to use in estimating which passages to administer in determining a student's instructional level. Because of time constraints, it is important to avoid administration of unnecessary selections. Classroom information may be a viable starting point. For example, if the student is not functioning successfully in the second-grade classroom, this suggests that first grade may represent an appropriate instructional level, and the level validation may begin with a selection at that level. The score on a standardized reading test may also provide a starting point. We suggest administering a passage that is one or two grade levels below the grade equivalent attained on a test. By careful use of existing data, the reading-assessment specialist can use a minimum amount of *QRI*–II passages to ascertain level placement for the student. Of course, if time permits, the word lists can also be used as a guide for passage administration.

While the familiar narrative level is most important, in that it probably represents the student's best effort, the reading-assessment specialist may choose to exercise one of the following options.

If the familiar instructional level was obtained through oral reading, the examiner may choose to verify this level in silent reading. A discrepancy between the student's oral and silent reading comprehension may suggest which mode to stress during instruction.

The examiner may choose to determine the student's instructional level for familiar expository text as a guide to the type of instructional materials to select. For example, a lower level for expository text may suggest that this type of material should receive primary emphasis.

Finally, the examiner may choose to ascertain a level for unfamiliar text. While most readers do score at a lower level for unfamiliar material, designation of a specific level for unfamiliar material can help the assessment specialist plan specific background enhancement activities for the student.

Describing Specific Reading Behaviors as a Guide for Intervention Instruction

The reading-assessment specialist may already know the student's reading level or may choose not to use the *QRI*–II to determine placement levels. However, selected passages and assessment options on the *QRI*–II can be used effectively to isolate areas for intervention emphasis. Again, it must be stressed that the assessment specialist is a decision maker. S/he should ask, "What do I want to know about this student?" and then s/he should choose *QRI*–II components accordingly. Some possible assessment questions are presented below and the *QRI*–II components that can be used to answer each one are listed. Guidelines for using these components are given in greater depth in the following sections of the manual.

How Accurate Is the Student in Identifying Words? The total score on the word lists and number of miscues made during oral reading of the passages can provide this information.

How Automatic Is the Student in Identifying Words? The timed administration of the word lists can suggest a level of automaticity. Automaticity can also be inferred from the student's oral and silent reading rate on the passages. Accuracy and automaticity can be contrasted.

What Strategies for Word Identification Are Used by the Student? The reading-assessment specialist can evaluate the nature of the miscues made on the word lists or when reading the passages by engaging in miscue analysis. Does the student use graphic or letter cues? Does the student self-correct miscues that do not make sense, suggesting that some self monitoring or comprehension is present? Does the student use semantic cues and produce miscues that do not distort text meaning? An examination of miscues can often suggest which phonics principles are known or unknown and/or which are consistently misapplied.

Is There a Difference Between a Student's Ability to Identify Words in Isolation and Words in Context? If the student has a higher level of word-identification skill when reading passages as opposed to the word lists, this may suggest effective use of context. On the other hand, context-free word identification is characteristic of a skilled reader whose word-identification levels in isolation and context should then be similar (Perfetti, 1985, 1988; Stanovich, 1980). The assessment specialist can also note specific words on the word lists and contrast the student's ability to identify these with the same words in the passages. All list words are underlined in the passages wherever they occur at that level. For example, the word "in" on the Pre-primer list is underlined wherever it occurs in the Pre-primer passages.

Which Types of Text Can the Student Handle Most Successfully? The examiner can compare narrative and expository text. This is probably more important for upper-level elementary level students. Our pilot data showed comprehension and/or retelling of narrative material to exceed that of exposition at up through Level Six. For younger children and those reading at Pre-primer through Second-Grade levels, the examiner can contrast reading when pictures are present and when they are absent.

Which Modes of Reading Represent a Strength for the Student? The examiner can compare oral and silent reading comprehension to determine which mode to emphasize during instruction. Then s/he can compare comprehension following listening and reading. Listening comprehension is often regarded as representative of a child's comprehension potential in the absence of decoding problems (Gough & Juel, 1991; Stanovich, 1991).

How Does the Student Perform in Familiar and Unfamiliar Text? The examiner can note any differences between performance on familiar and unfamiliar text. While students may not comprehend as well in unfamiliar text, the examiner can note if this difference represents a change in instructional level. Lower levels in word identification in unfamiliar text may suggest that the student is overly dependent upon familiar context for word identification.

The reading-assessment specialist will have to decide which of the above will be most helpful on describing the reading behavior of an individual and in planning suitable intervention instruction. No two students are the same and it is likely that the assessment specialist will use different components for different students. Because the *QRI*–II is not a standardized instrument, the assessment specialist can decide which options to choose, given the constraints of time and the needs of each individual student. Table 5.1 summarizes the various uses of the *QRI*–II.

TABLE 5.1
Uses of the *Qualitative Reading Inventory*–II

Use the *QRI*–II to Determine Reading Level

Find the instructional level for familiar text
    Choose passage based upon word lists and/or classroom performance.
    Find the instructional level for narrative text.
    Use oral or silent reading depending upon passage level: oral reading for pre-primer through grade 5; silent reading for grades 6 through junior high.
    Count miscues according to Total Accuracy or Total Acceptability.
    Ask comprehension questions.
Find the instructional level for expository text.
Find the instructional level for unfamiliar text.

Use the *QRI*–II to Plan Supportive or Remedial Instruction: Diagnostic Options

Find the word identification accuracy level.
    Administer the word lists.
    Find instructional level for Total Number Correct.
    Administer the passages
    Find the word identification accuracy level in familiar text.
Find the word identification automaticity level.
    Administer the word lists.
    Find instructional level for Total Correct Automatic.
Contrast accuracy and automaticity.
    Contrast the word-list levels for Total Correct Automatic with the Total Number Correct.
    Evaluate word identification accuracy on oral passage reading in relation to rate of reading.
Describe word identification strategies.
    Do miscue analysis on passage miscues.
        Use of self-correction
        Use of graphic or letter cues
        Use of meaning cues
Compare word identification in isolation and in context.
    Contrast instructional level of Total Number Correct on the word lists with instructional level in passage reading.
Contrast narrative and expository text.
Contrast text with pictures and without pictures (Pre-primer–Grade two).
Contrast oral and silent reading comprehension.
Contrast reading comprehension and listening comprehension.
Contrast familiar and unfamiliar text.
Utilize alternative administration procedures for assessing strategic reading.

---

6 Administration and Scoring of the *Qualitative Reading Inventory–II*

Preparation for Testing

To ensure the best possible testing environment, the examiner should administer the *QRI*–II in a quiet place that is free from distractions. Before meeting the student, the examiner should gather all materials and place them in the testing room: the word lists, passages to be read, accompanying sheets for examiner recording, tape recorder, stopwatch or timer, clipboard, paper, and pencils.

It is often difficult to determine how many scoring sheets to prepare, especially if the examiner has never met the student. It is better to prepare too many; otherwise, the examiner may have to leave the room to obtain more. We recommend that the examiner prepare a kit of scoring sheets for all the passages and organize them according to grade level. The examiner can then be assured of having the correct passages on hand. The examiner may wish to laminate the student's copy of each passage or to encase it in a plastic cover for protection.

Before beginning the testing, the examiner should strive to put the student at ease. Engaging in conversation about the student's interests, feelings toward school and other subjects, or favored activities can act as an effective icebreaker as well as provide valuable information. Some students are concerned with the use of a stopwatch or with the examiner writing. Sitting across from the student can make the act of writing somewhat less noticeable. Using a clipboard that rests on the examiner's lap and a stopwatch that rests on a chair placed to one side can also make these items less obtrusive.

We highly recommend that the entire testing session be taped, especially in the early stages of learning how to administer the *QRI*–II. Even experienced examiners often find a tape helpful in scoring. Some students are upset by the use of a tape recorder. Explaining the need for this and allowing the student to experiment with it may help to alleviate anxiety.

If the examiner is using the word identification lists to estimate a starting point for passage administration, s/he gives those to the student first and scores them immediately in order to estimate which passages to administer. Next, the examiner administers the prior knowledge task for a passage prior to the student reading the passage. This allows the examiner to determine if the content of the passage is familiar to the reader. It need not be scored before proceeding; however, the examiner should estimate familiarity with the text topic. Third, the examiner gives the student the passages. If the passages are being used to determine an instructional level, the examiner must score oral reading accuracy and responses to comprehension questions in order to know what additional passages to administer. We recommend that during the actual administration the examiner should determine oral reading accuracy by counting all errors or miscues. This allows for a quick estimation of the word identification level so the examiner can ascertain which passage to administer next. After the administration, if desired, the examiner can then determine passage level by counting only those miscues which change meaning.

Lastly, the amount of time spent in administering the *QRI*–II will vary depending on the assessment questions posed by the examiner. It is important that the examiner be sensitive to the student's energy level and attention span. Frequent short breaks are often helpful. If somewhat lengthy testing is required, there is no reason why testing cannot be scheduled across several days, if this can be arranged.

7 Administration and Scoring of the *Qualitative Reading Inventory–II*

The Word Lists

Purposes for Administering the Word Lists

Estimating the Starting Point for Passage Administration
Estimating Automatic Word Identification
Estimating Knowledge of Letter–Sound Matches
Analyzing the Differences Between Word Identification in Isolation and in Context

Procedures for Administering the Word Lists

General Procedures
Instructions to the Student
The Beginning Point
Recording Subject Responses: Accuracy and Automaticity

Procedures for Scoring the Word Lists

Criteria for Determining Reading Levels from Word Recognition Scores in Isolation
Estimating the Starting Point for Passage Administration
Estimating Automatic Word Identification
Additional Diagnostic Uses of the Word Lists

Purposes for Administering the Word Lists

Estimating the Starting Point for Passage Administration

The word lists can aid the examiner in deciding which level of passage to administer to the student first. The word lists provide a quick estimate of the student's word-identification ability. If the examiner has little information about a student's performance, the lists may help the examiner estimate the level on which to begin testing. If the student has word identification problems, his/her performance on the word lists will be a realistic assessment of a beginning point for passage administration. If, however, the student can identify words well, but has problems in comprehension, the word lists may suggest a starting point which will be too difficult for the reader to comprehend.

Estimating Automatic Word Identification

The examiner can estimate automaticity of word identification by counting the number of seconds that it takes the student to read each word on the word lists. If a student reads a word within one second, we can assume that the word has been identified automatically without needing to sound it out through applying decoding rules. The more words that a reader identifies automatically, the more likely that s/he will be a fluent reader in the corresponding level of passages.

Words that are automatically identified have often been termed *sight vocabulary*. It was thought that a direct link occurred between the visual aspects of a word and word meaning. However, automatic word identification may involve a strong sound component (Ehri, 1992). Therefore, the term "sight vocabulary" may be a misnomer and we prefer to avoid its usage in favor of *automatic word identification*.

Estimating Knowledge of Letter–Sound Matches

All other words that the student reads correctly beyond a one-second limit are probably due to decoding ability, that is, the student is matching letters and sounds in order to identify the word. The examiner can examine correct and incorrect pronunciations in order to assess the letter–sound matches that are known by the student and which might need emphasis in an intervention program.

Analyzing the Differences Between Word Identification in Isolation and in Context

Many words on the word lists were taken from the passages. Thus, the examiner can determine how well the reader is able to use context to identify words by examining whether the student can identify words in a passage that s/he could not identify in isolation. If the reader cannot identify more words in context than in isolation and the words are within a frequency range appropriate for his/her instructional reading level, then instruction on context utilization may be in order. The words underlined in the passages are those which appear on the word list of the same readability level.

Procedures for Administering the Word Lists

General Procedures

The student is given the list of words and is asked to pronounce them. As this is done, the examiner records the answers on the accompanying scoring sheet, carefully differentiating between words identified automatically and those identified after some delay. Those identified automatically are marked in the Identified Automatically column; those identified after some delay are recorded in the Identified column. There are several ways to administer the lists. While each may seem awkward at first, with practice, the examiner will soon choose the one with which s/he is most comfortable.

The examiner can sit next to or across from the student and cover each word with an index card, which is then moved down to reveal the word. Immediately after the word is completely exposed, the examiner says mentally "one thousand and one." This acts as the equivalent of one-second timing. If the student has not pronounced the word within that time frame, any attempt, correct or otherwise, is marked in the Identified column. Older students may choose to move the card themselves, and the examiner must watch when the word is uncovered and say mentally "one thousand and one" in order to estimate their ability to pronounce words automatically.

The examiner may also choose to place individual words on index cards. Each word should be printed on both sides of the card. The student reads one side and the other side provides a way for the examiner to keep track of which word is being read. The words are presented by the examiner one at a time. The words known automatically are placed in one pile, those identified after some delay in another, and a third pile is for those not known. The first pile is recorded in the Identified Automatically column and the last two in the Identified column.

The examiner may find it more comfortable to dispense with cards and simply hand the list to the student to read at his/her own pace. The important thing is to keep track of automatic pronunciation by saying mentally "one thousand and one."

Another alternative is to utilize a window card, which is pictured in Figure 7.1. Using a piece of cardboard, the examiner cuts a rectangular slit that corresponds in length to the longest word in a list. (We have provided a pattern for this card in Figure 7.1.) When the examiner places the card over each word, the student sees only one word at a time, preventing him/her from becoming distracted by previous words or those that s/he will have to identify next.

FIGURE 7.1
Pattern for a Word List Window Card

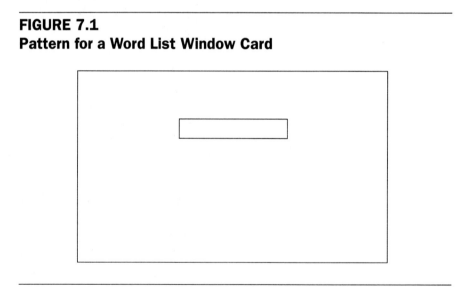

As the examiner juggles the word lists and the timing, recording the student's answers may seem difficult at first. Until s/he becomes more accustomed to timing, listening, and recording all at once, the examiner should tape the entire session.

Instructions to the Student

The examiner should introduce the word lists to the student by saying: "I have some lists of words that I want you to read one at a time. Some of the words will be easy for you and some I expect to be very hard. Don't worry.

Administration and Scoring of the *Qualitative Reading Inventory*–II

You are not expected to know all of them. If you don't know a word right away, try your best to figure it out. I cannot help you in any way and I cannot tell you if you are right or wrong. Just do your very best. Are you ready?"

The Beginning Point

Whether the examiner is using the word lists to estimate automatic word identification or to suggest a level for passage administration, s/he must determine a realistic beginning point. In order to avoid initial frustration, the examiner should begin with a word list two or more years below the student's chronological grade placement. This is especially important if the examiner suspects a serious reading problem. For example, the pre-primer or primer list is a good starting point for children in first through third grades. S/he should begin with the second- or third-grade list for students in grades four through six. The fourth- and fifth-grade list can be beginning points for those in sixth grade and above. It is better to begin too low than to place the subject in a frustrating situation immediately. If the list is too easy, little time will be lost and the initial experience of success may place the student more at ease.

Recording Subject Responses: Accuracy and Automaticity

There are two things for the examiner to keep track of while administering these lists: accuracy of identification and automaticity of response. *Accuracy* simply refers to whether or not the student reads the word correctly. If the student makes an error, the examiner should write down the phonetic equivalent of the mispronunciation. For example, if the student reads "live" with a long "i" sound, the examiner should use the—mark above the "i." If the student changes the word quite a bit, the examiner should write the best phonetic equivalent. This information provides an indication of how the student approaches word identification. If a student self-corrects an error, the examiner should write "C" and count it as correct. If the student skips a word, the examiner should write "d.k." (don't know).

Automaticity of response refers to whether or not the student gives a response (correct or not) within one second. To provide a realistic estimate of one second, the examiner can say mentally, "one thousand and one." Any response begun within one second is recorded in the Identified Automatically column. If the response is correct, the examiner should simply put a "C" in the column. If it is incorrect, s/he should write the phonetic equivalent.

If the student takes more than one second to begin a response, the examiner should record the response in the Identified column. If it is a correct response, the examiner should put a "C" in the Identified column. If it is incorrect, s/he should write the phonetic equivalent. It is possible that a student could give an incorrect response within one second but then correct it. In this case the word is a correct decoded word. Figure 7.2 contains an example of recorded and scored word lists.

Procedures for Scoring the Word Lists

Scoring procedures vary depending upon the purpose for word list administration. Finding a beginning point for passage administration simply involves counting the number of correct responses in both the Identified Automatically and Identified columns. Independent, instructional, and frustration levels are determined from this total. If the purpose of word list administration is to estimate automatic word identification, then the examiner must count the Identified Automatically column separately from the total correct in both columns. The following sections explain these two scoring procedures in more depth.

FIGURE 7.2

Examiner Word Lists

Third	Identified Automatically	Identified
1. lunch	c	
2. special	c	
3. believe	belief	
4. claws		c
5. lion		c
6. rough	rug	sc
7. wear	c	
8. tongue		c
9. crowded	c	
10. wool	c	
11. removed	removed	sc
12. curious		kircus
13. sheep		c
14. electric		c
15. worried	c	
16. enemies	enemy	
17. hid		c
18. clothing		c
19. swim		c
20. entrance	entray	sc

Fourth	Identified Automatically	Identified
1. escape	escarp	sc
2. desert		c
3. crop	c	
4. islands		c
5. chief		chif
6. mounds		munds
7. busy	c	
8. pond		c
9. signs		c
10. ocean	c	
11. pilot		plot
12. fame		fim
13. precious		DK
14. settlers		settle
15. guarded		guard
16. passenger		passed
17. boundaries		DK
18. communicate		DK
19. adventurer		aventrer
20. invented		c

Total Correct Automatic   6 /20 = 30 %
Total Correct Identified   11 /20 = 55 %
Total Number Correct   17 /20 = 85 %

Total Correct Automatic   3 /20 = 15 %
Total Correct Identified   6 /20 = 30 %
Total Number Correct   9 /20 = 45 %

LEVELS		
Independent	Instructional	Frustration
18–20	14–17	below 14
90–100%	70–85%	below 70%

Criteria for Determining Reading Levels from Word Recognition Scores in Isolation

The following criteria (McCracken, 1966) help determine levels for word identification on the word lists.

Independent:	Total correct:	90% and above	18–20 words
Instructional:	Total correct:	70%–89%	14–17 words
Frustration:	Total correct:	Less than 70%	13 words or less

The above guidelines are included on each word list to ease scoring.

Estimating the Starting Point for Passage Administration

The examiner should administer the first list and score it immediately to determine which level it represents. If the student scores at an instructional or frustration level, the examiner should move down until the student reaches an independent level. Then the examiner should continue upward until the student attains a frustration level. The examiner may also stop before the frustration level if the student reaches a word list that corresponds to his/her chronological grade placement. These levels suggest what passages may represent a realistic starting point. Word identification in isolation is a rough predictor of the level of passage that a student can decode reasonably well. If a student scores at an independent or instructional level on a word list, s/he will probably decode a passage of similar readability level with some measure of success.

Students often score at an independent or instructional level across several lists. For example, a student may score at an independent level for the primer and first-grade lists and at an instructional level for lists two through four. If the examiner wants to be safe and present an initial passage that will ensure success, s/he should choose one that corresponds to the highest independent level attained on the lists. If the examiner is operating under narrow time constraints, s/he can estimate the beginning passage level from the lowest instructional level attained on the word lists.

Word-list scores for Chris, a third-grader, provide an example of how to estimate a starting point for passage administration. Initially, Chris was asked to read the first-grade list. He scored at an independent level. The second-grade list was administered and again, he attained an independent level. Chris scored at an instructional level for the third- and fourth-grade lists and reached frustration at the fifth-grade level. The examiner chose to administer a second-grade passage first in order to ensure that Chris met success with his initial attempt at oral reading. (However, a third-grade passage could also have been a viable starting point.) Chris scored at an independent level in second-grade text and attained an instructional level in third-grade text.

When Joe, a fifth-grader, read a third-grade list, he scored at frustration level. The examiner moved to lower levels, and Joe scored at an instructional level for second grade and an independent level for first grade. The first passage chosen for Joe to read was at a second-grade level, which was his anticipated instructional level.

There are two types of readers whose levels will not be predicted accurately by the word-list scores. One is a reader who makes exceptionally good use of context and, thus, whose capabilities in context far exceed his/her word-identification in isolation. The word list scores will underestimate this reader's capabilities. The other type of reader has comprehension problems but s/he also has excellent word-identification capabilities. This subject's abilities will be overestimated by the word-list scores.

Estimating Automatic Word Identification

Estimating a student's ability to automatically identify words involves the number correct that the student attained on the Identified Automatically list. The examiner should count the number correct on this list to arrive at an independent, instructional, or frustration level for automatic word identification. Then s/he should count the total number correct on both the Identified Automatically list and the Identified list and use this to arrive at a level for total word identification. S/he should compare the two in order to estimate if automatic word identification represents a weakness for the student.

One example is Chris, a third-grader. His scores on the word lists were as follows:

First:	*Total Score:*	Independent level
	Identified Automatically Score:	Independent level
Second:	*Total Score:*	Independent level
	Identified Automatically Score:	Instructional level
Third:	*Total Score:*	Instructional level
	Identified Automatically Score:	Frustration level
Fourth:	*Total Score:*	Frustration level
	Identified Automatically Score:	Frustration level

Obviously, for second through third grade, Chris' levels for automatic word identification fall below his level for total word identification. This may suggest a possible weakness. It needs to be supported by assessment of Chris' word-identification ability in context, specifically by assessment of his ability to read selected passages at the same grade levels.

Caution: The graded word lists do not represent a natural reading situation and do not assess a student's comprehension ability. Also, some students identify words more effectively in context than in a list format. Therefore, a student's scores on an isolated list should never be used to estimate his/her overall reading ability.

Additional Diagnostic Uses of the Word Lists

Because many of the words on the lists are contained in the passage of accompanying readability, the examiner can choose to note whether a word missed on the list was identified correctly in context. While this may only involve a small number of words, it can suggest a reader who is not utilizing context effectively.

The examiner can also note the accuracy of the student's decoding attempts within the untimed format. For example, are there any consonant or vowel sounds that are missed consistently? Does the student attempt to apply phonetic strategies to irregular words? Which phonetic principles are applied erroneously? Word list administration can provide the examiner with a tool for probing into the student's strategies for pronouncing words. For example, the examiner can direct the student to various parts of unknown words and model word-analysis strategies to see if s/he can take advantage of them. The examiner can cover up parts of words and uncover them sequentially for subject pronunciation. The examiner can contrast an unknown word with one of similiar spelling and/or pronunciation to see if the student can transfer knowledge of that word to the unknown one. Of course, any success achieved through examiner aid should be noted on the scoring sheet, but a student should not receive credit for it when determining independent, instructional, and frustration levels for word identification in isolation.

Caution: A student's ability to decode words in isolation may be very different from his/her ability to identify words in context (Nicholson, Lillas, & Rzoska, 1988). Therefore, any diagnostic decisions made on the basis of word-list information should be corroborated by the student's performance while identifying words in the context of *QRI*–II passages.

8 Administration and Scoring of the *Qualitative Reading Inventory–II*

Assessment of Prior Knowledge

Assessing Prior Knowledge

Conceptual-Questions Task
Prediction Task

Assessing Prior Knowledge

Because students' knowledge has such a powerful effect upon comprehension, it is important to determine if the selection read by the student contains familiar or unfamiliar concepts. Understanding what students know and do not know about important concepts or ideas in the selection allows the examiner to evaluate comprehension difficulties in relation to students' knowledge base. The *QRI*–II provides two methods for assessing prior knowledge: conceptual questions and predictions. Before reading a passage, a student should be asked to participate in one or both activities in order to assess his/her familiarity with the topic of the selection. A student's lack of knowledge of the concepts, or a knowledge of the concepts that differs from that of the text may explain difficulty in comprehension. Engaging in the conceptual questions and/or prediction tasks prior to reading can also serve to activate any background knowledge that the student has for the information contained in the selection. If this knowledge is consistent with text information, facilitation of comprehension will occur.

Conceptual-Questions Task

General Procedures. For each passage there are three or four questions judged to be important to the comprehension of the passage. The content of the questions were chosen because they represented the topic of the selection (e.g., a class trip, uses of computers, soccer), or because they represented who the selection was about (e.g., Martin Luther King or Amelia Earhart). Other questions were designed because we believed that if students understood them, they would be more likely to answer the implicit comprehension questions correctly (e.g., animal defenses in the fifth-grade "Octopus" passage, and changing seasons in the second-grade "Seasons" passage).

The questions are on the examiner's copy of the passage, directly under the title of the passage. Before the student reads the passage, the examiner should ask all questions. The examiner should ask all questions for each passage that the student reads.

Instructions for the concept-question task are, "Before you read, I want to know what you already know about some ideas in the text. I will ask you a few questions to find out."

Scoring the Concept-Questions Task.   Each question is scored according to a 3–2–1–0 system, where 3 is the best score. The examiner can use the following guidelines for assigning scores.

3 Points:

A precise definition, or a definitional response to a phrase, or an answer to a question specifically related to passage content.

Examples:

What does "learning to read" mean to you?: pronouncing and understanding words

Why do people work?: to get money for their families

When do you see turtles outside?: in summer when it's hot, because turtles like the sun.

What do flowers need to grow?: sunlight, water, and food

What are the problems with living in the desert?: it's very hot and there's little water.

Who was Christopher Columbus?: a man who sailed the ocean and found America

What is Washington, D.C.?: where our nation's capital is and national laws are made there.

How do companies make a profit?: they make more money than they spend.

What happens to products after recycling?: they get made into other things.

What is circumnavigation?: to sail around the world

A Synonym

Examples:

What does "trade" mean to you?: to bargain

What are claws?: nails

What is fall?: autumn

2 Points: An Example of the Concept

Examples:

What does "doing something new" mean to you?: getting a new toy and playing with it

Where do people work?: at hospitals

What is working at home?: cleaning house, washing dishes

What does "being afraid of animals" mean to you?: grizzly bear

What is "racism"?: people who don't like black people because they are black

"What are changes in computers?": they can do things faster

What are animal defenses?: bite; spit; hunch their backs

What are evils of slavery?: people telling others what to do and whipping them

A Specific Attribute or Defining Characteristics

Examples:

What is a Mom?: a human being, someone who takes care of you

What is a bear?: furry with a black nose

What is an octopus?: thing with eight legs with suction cups

How is steel made?: from iron

What is an earthquake?: when the earth shakes

What is circumnavigation?: to circle around something

What is a saint?: someone recognized for being very good

A Function

Examples:

What is a class trip?: learn something new

What is taking notes?: so you remember something

Why do people use maps?: to find their way

What is Washington, D.C.?: city where Martin Luther King, Jr. did his "I have a Dream" speech

What are diamonds?: people put them in rings

What is the purpose of recycling?: to use something again

1 Point: A General Association

Examples:

What does "going to work" mean to you?: leaving the house

What does "trade" mean to you?: you trade something

Who was Constantine?: a man who lived long ago

Who was Sacajawea?: an Indian name

What is laser light?: beams of light flying all over

What does "size of earthquakes" mean to you?: big

Who were Lewis and Clark?: men

Isolation of Prefix, Suffix, or Root Word

Examples:

What is circumnavigation?: circumference

What is archaeology?: archaeologist

What is an octopus?: eight

What is ultrasound?: a noise

Firsthand, Personal Associations

Examples:

What does "people reading stories" mean to you?: baby sister picks them

What does "learning to read" mean to you? I learned to read in first grade.

What is a school trip?: my mother came on our field trip.

What does "an old house for sale" mean to you?: we just sold our house.

What are new toys?: I get new toys for Christmas.

What are fireworks?: I get bottle rockets.

0 Points: Sound-Alikes

Examples:

What is a bear?: wear

What is fall?: wall

Unconnected Responses

Examples:

What does "looking for something" mean to you?: Batman

Who was Martin Luther King?: wears a crown

No Response or I Don't Know

Interpreting the Concept-Question Scores. Generally we have found that students who score at least 55% of the points possible on the concept task score above 70% on comprehension questions on the related passage. See Section 16 for details.

Prediction Task

General Procedures. After administration of the concept-question task, the examiner may choose to administer the prediction task. If so, the examiner should say, "Given that the title of the passage is _____, and it includes the ideas _____, _____, _____, and _____ (naming all the concepts within the questions), what do you think the passage will be about? I want you to take a guess or make a prediction about what you think the passage will be about." For example, on the third grade selection, "A Trip to the Zoo," the instructions would be phrased, "Given that the title of the passage is, 'A Trip to the Zoo,' and it has the ideas 'class trip,' 'taking notes,' 'being by yourself,' and 'why people use maps,' what do you think the story will be about?" If the student simply restates the title of the passage, the examiner should provide a *general* probe for more information. For example, if the student says "Amelia Earhart," say "What about 'Amelia Earhart?'"

Scoring the Prediction Task. Leslie and Cooper (1993) examined three ways of scoring the prediction task and found that one of them significantly correlated with retelling and comprehension among sixth-graders. Further piloting of the task at other reading levels and ages found that the same method of scoring was related to retelling and/or comprehension at second- and third- grade reading levels. Thus, we have chosen to score the prediction task by counting the number of idea statements the student predicts that are contained in the passage either explicitly or implicitly. By idea statements we mean any proposition (verb and accompanying nouns) contained in the selection or implied by the selection. The following list provides students' predictions and our scoring from passages at diverse levels. The idea statements are in italics.

Pre-primer Story: "Just Like Mom"
2 Ideas:
—*Mom is going to work*, and having a good day. Dad is doing something at the end. *The girl does everything the Mom does.*
—*Mom is working at home* and *going to work.*
1 Idea:
—*Mom is working.*
—What a mom is and *mom going to work.*
—*Working with Mom*
0 Ideas:
—Mom

Primer Story: "The Pig Who Learned to Read"
2 Ideas:
—*The pig that just learned to read* and *he liked it.*
—*A pig that heard people read;* and *learned to read.*
1 Idea:
—*a pig learning how to read*
—*a pig that learns to read*
0 Ideas:
—the pig who told the boy how to read

Primer Story: **"Who Lives Near Lakes?"**
1 Idea:
—*People who live near lakes*
0 Ideas:
—fish

First-Level Story: **"The Bear and the Rabbit"**
3 Ideas:
—*Having no one to play with; the bunny would be afraid of the bear; and will make friends.*
2 Ideas:
—*It's about a bear and a rabbit; the rabbit is scared of the bear.*
1 Idea:
—*it's about friendship.*
—*about a rabbit that's scared of animals*

First-Level Passage: **"What You Eat"**
1 Idea:
—*different kinds of foods*
—*trying to keep healthy*

Second-Level Passage: **"What Can I Get for my Toy?"**
1 Idea:
—*person getting toys*
—*a kid who wants to trade for toys*

Second-Level Passage: **"Whales and Fish"**
2 Ideas:
—*how fish get born; how animals live in the sea*
1 Idea:
—*animals in the sea*

Third-Level Passage: **"A Trip to the Zoo"**
5 Ideas:
—*Somebody is going to a zoo on a field trip gets lost; looks at a map; and finds his way back*
3 Ideas:
—*taking a trip; and taking notes; and having a map for directions*
1 Idea:
—*about going to the zoo*
0 Ideas:
—things you can see, touch, or use

Third-Level Passage: **"Cats: Lions and Tigers in Your House"**
1 Idea:
—*cats protecting themselves lions, tigers, and cat families*
0 Ideas:
—cats

Fifth-Level Passage: **"Martin Luther King, Jr."**
3 Ideas:
—*Washington, D.C., where the marches are; segregation; and what Martin Luther King did for black people*
2 Ideas:
—*why blacks and whites didn't like each other back then and what Martin Luther King did about it*

1 Idea:
—his life and what he wanted to do

Fifth-Level Passage: "Getting Rid of Trash"
3 Ideas:
—about taking trash; recycling it; and *made it into other things*
1 Idea:
—trash and recycling it

Sixth-Level Passage: "Andrew Carnegie"
2 Ideas:
—a man who made steel; and *made a lot of money*
1 Idea:
—how steel is made and they raise money; *about a steel-making factory*

Sixth-Level Passage: "Earthquakes"
1 Idea:
—about earthquakes and how animals can tell if they're coming
—how animals sense earthquakes

Junior High Passage: "Lewis and Clark"
2 Ideas:
—two people exploring or *going a great distance; Lewis and Clark going North;* and an *expedition* mapping the U.S.

Interpretation of the Prediction Scores. As you can see from the predictions made by students, most students only gave one or two idea statements in their predictions. There seems to be three qualities of predictions. First, there are young readers, who only restate the title and do not integrate the concepts at all. Second, there are students who integrate some of the concepts and make a prediction using them. For example, on "A Trip to the Zoo," a student predicts, "taking a trip and taking notes and having a map for directions." Finally, there is the occasional student who is so knowledgeable about the concepts that a prediction is made that sums up many main ideas contained in the selection. For example, a sixth-grade student who read the junior high passage, "Diamonds," and predicted, "It's about how diamonds are mined deep in the earth, and how they are formed by great pressure. It probably describes what diamonds come from; I think it's carbon. Then it probably describes what diamonds are used for, like in jewelry."

In summary, predictions should be evaluated in light of the above examples, which are from our pilot data of average readers. Qualitative judgements can be made by examining whether or not students have integrated any of the concepts with the title in order to make predictions. Recognize that this skill, like all other skills, is learned, and is subject to instruction. If we want children to make good predictions, we have to teach them how by modeling.

9 Administration and Scoring of the *Qualitative Reading Inventory–II*

The Passages

Purposes for Administering the Passages

There are four main purposes for administering the passages.

1. Determination of a Student's Independent, Instructional, and/or Frustration Levels for Word Identification in Context.   The examiner determines these levels for word identification in context by asking the student to read graded passages orally. The examiner records the errors/miscues made by the student and then counts them to arrive at a level designation. The miscues can be counted in two ways, depending upon the preference or philosophy of the examiner. S/he can count all miscues regardless of quality and use this total to determine the level. We call this *Total Accuracy*. The examiner can choose to count only those miscues which change or distort passage meaning. This is referred to as *Total Acceptability*. Section 10 explains how to identify, count, and score miscues.

2. Determination of a Student's Independent, Instructional, and/or Frustration Levels for Comprehension. The examiner determines a student's independent instructional, and frustration levels for comprehension by asking the student to read graded passages orally or silently and answer questions based upon passage content. The examiner counts the number of correct answers to determine level designation. Section 11 explains the scoring of comprehension questions.

3. Assessment of a Student's Ability to Read Different Types of Text. The examiner can ask the student to read narrative and expository text, familiar and unfamiliar text, text with and without pictures (pre-primer through grade two). S/he can determine independent, instructional, and frustration levels for each type of text depending upon his/her diagnostic purposes. Not all levels should be determined for all passage types. To do so would require an inordinate and unrealistic amount of time. Determination of a familiar level is most important. For most students, determination of this level in narrative text is the primary concern. Narrative text is generally easier than expository text, so assessment of familiar levels in this genre tends to represent a student's best effort.

4. Assessment of a Student's Ability to Comprehend in Different Modes. The examiner can ask the student to read orally or silently. Then s/he determines independent, instructional, and frustration levels in oral reading from two scores: the number of miscues made while reading orally and the number of questions answered correctly. Guidelines for determining a total passage level for oral reading are explained later in this section. The examiner determines silent reading levels on the basis of the number of comprehension questions answered correctly. Section 11 contains guidelines for determining silent reading comprehension.

Assessment Options

Administration of the passages can also involve several diagnostic options:

1. Assessment of Prior Knowledge. There are two options for determining a student's prior knowledge for the topic of a passage: the concept question task and the prediction task. See Section 8 for an explanation of the use of both.

2. Oral Reading Miscue Analysis. There are three types of miscues made while reading orally: whole word substitutions, such as "tried" for "trade"; nonword substitutions, such as "trad" for "trade"; and omissions and insertions of words.

The examiner asks two questions about each miscue: Was the miscue semantically acceptable in that passage meaning was not changed or distorted, and/or was it self-corrected by the student? Was the miscue graphically similar to the original word? See Section 10 for an explanation of analyzing and interpreting oral reading miscues.

3. Assessment of Comprehension Through Unaided Recall. The examiner can ask students to retell the passage as if they were telling it to someone who had never read it. S/he can then record the number of ideas recalled by the student and map them on a recall grid. This recall can be evaluated for completeness, accuracy, sequence, and use of narrative and expository structure. (See Section 11 for guidelines for recording and interpreting unaided recall.) The quality of unaided recall can be contrasted with the student's ability to answer explicit and implicit questions about passage content.

4. Alternative Assessment Procedures. Alternative diagnostic procedures can involve such things as note-taking skills and the ability to look back in the text to locate answers to questions. See Section 12 for an explanation of these procedures.

Examiners must choose purposes that are germane to their diagnostic needs. Seldom will an individual diagnostician utilize all the diagnostic options of the *QRI*–II. The examiner must ask him/herself, "What are my purposes in administering the passages?" and choose the level and types of passages accordingly.

General Procedures for Administering the Passages

General Administration Guidelines

First, the examiner must choose a passage for the student to read, using the concept question and/or prediction tasks to ascertain familiarity with the topic of the selection. S/he should then ask the student to read the passage orally or silently.

If the student reads the passage orally, the examiner should record the student's miscues (substitutions, omissions, insertions) on the examiner copy of the passage. The examiner should also time the student's rate of oral reading. Once the student completes the passage, the examiner removes it and assesses comprehension by asking the reader to retell what was remembered, to answer explicit and implicit questions, or to do both. If the student reads the passage silently, obviously the examiner cannot mark oral miscues. Instead, s/he can time the student's rate of reading and assess comprehension in the above manner.

The examiner should then determine if the total performance on the passage represents an independent, instructional, or frustration level for the student. These levels are obtained from two scores. The total number of oral reading miscues determines the level for word identification in context. The percent of questions answered correctly determines the level for comprehension. The examiner then compares these two scores to determine a general passage level.

Instructions to the Student

"I have some passages for you to read. Some you will read orally and some silently. I will be making some notes as you read, and because I cannot remember everything you say, I will also be taping you. I cannot help you in any way. If you come to a word you do not know, just do the best you can and continue on. Afterwards I will ask you to tell me what you can remember about the passage just as if you were telling it to someone who had never heard it before. I will also ask you some questions about what you have read. Ready? The first passage is called _____."

Passage Selection

As a decision maker, the examiner must choose the number and type of passages to administer based upon his/her purposes. However, examiners often ask several questions regarding passage administration.

Which Level of Passage Should I Begin With?   An examiner can use the word lists to estimate a beginning point. S/he does not want to start too low, nor does s/he want the passage to be too difficult. Meeting frustration at the beginning of a diagnostic session can prejudice the student against the entire process. S/he should choose a level where the student has attained the independent level on the accompanying word list. (See Section 7 for a fuller explanation of using the word lists to estimate a beginning point.) If the examiner has data to suggest a viable starting point, such as test scores or reading group placement, s/he does not have to use the word lists for this purpose.

Must I Find Independent, Instructional, and Frustration Levels for All Types of Text?   No. To do so would demand an unrealistic amount of time, and student fatigue would be a very real concern. Determination of an instructional level is of primary importance in most cases. Determination of an instructional level in familiar text is more important than level determination in unfamiliar text. Once the examiner obtains the instructional level, s/he can often estimate the independent and frustration levels.

Do I Have to Administer All Passages Within a Readability Level?   No. Examiner choice will depend upon the purpose for giving the QRI–II. Assessment specialists may well use more passages than a classroom teacher attempting to determine an instructional level for text placement.

What Types of Passages Should I Start With?   Determining the student's instructional level for familiar text is the first step. Within this parameter, an examiner can select either narrative or expository text. For students suspected of reading at levels six through junior high, choice of narrative or expository text depends on the instructional needs and known capabilities of the student. Very often, students are performing acceptably in reading or literature classes but experiencing difficulties in content area classes. For these students, beginning in expository text would be more crucial than in narrative. If the examiner has no clear direction as to the desired text type, familiar narrative assessment represents a good beginning point. Because it is generally easier than expository text, it tends to lead to initial experiences of success on the part of the student as well as represent his/her best effort.

Which Mode Should I Use, Oral or Silent?   We suggest that examiners use an oral reading format with younger children and with older students suspected of reading below the third-grade level. The examiner can estimate this by the word list scores. At this point, they are still learning how to read, and listening to oral reading performance can offer much valuable information. However, if time permits, asking younger children to read a familiar narrative silently can sometimes provide information as to how well they are making the transition to silent reading.

For students reading at levels three through five, the examiner should use a combination of oral and silent reading. At these levels, oral reading miscues can provide important information. Once an instructional level is established for narrative material, the examiner may wish to change to a silent reading mode. It is better to evaluate ability in expository text through silent reading, since most students are expected to read expository material silently in school. For students reading at levels six through junior high, silent reading is the best format because individuals do little oral reading at these levels.

How to Find an Instructional Level

Finding the Instructional Level in Familiar Text

The examiner can use the word lists or his/her knowledge of the student to choose a beginning passage that will probably offer an initial experience of success to the reader. The passage should be a familiar narrative. If s/he is using the word lists, s/he can choose a passage of the same readability level as the highest word list on which the student scored at an independent level (see Section 7). The examiner should ask the student to read the passage orally and answer the questions. Then the examiner can count the oral reading miscues to determine a level for word identification in context. (See Section 10 for guidelines for counting miscues and using this count to arrive at independent, instructional, and frustration levels.) The examiner then counts the number of questions answered correctly to determine the comprehension level. (See Section 11 for guidelines for scoring comprehension.) Once the examiner has the word identification and comprehension levels, s/he is ready to determine total passage level using the following guidelines:

WR: Independent	+ Comp: Independent =	Independent Level
	+ Comp: Instructional =	Instructional Level
	+ Comp: Frustration =	Frustration Level
WR: Instructional	+ Comp: Independent =	Instructional Level
	+ Comp: Instructional =	Instructional Level
	+ Comp: Frustration =	Frustration Level
WR: Frustration	+ Comp: Independent =	Instructional Level
	+ Comp: Instructional =	Frustration Level

If the student reads silently, the examiner can determine the total passage level by the comprehension score.

If the student scores within the independent or instructional range on the first passage, the examiner should choose another familiar narrative passage at the next highest level. S/he should continue moving upward until the student reaches a frustration level. If the student reaches a frustration level on the first passage, the examiner should move downward until the student reaches an instructional level. There may be times when the examiner will not choose to find the highest instructional level. The student may reach an instructional level at his/her chronological grade level. If that happens, determining that the student can read above chronological grade placement or ascertaining the exact frustration level may have little value.

Once the examiner has found the student's instructional level, s/he may choose to have the student read the other familiar narrative passage at that level. If the student reads the first passage orally, s/he should read the second one silently. This allows the examiner to contrast the student's ability in both oral and silent reading. If performance is different, the student may be experiencing discrepancies between the two modes. If the student read the first passage silently, the examiner may choose to verify the attained level by asking the student to read the second one silently also. Verification of levels and comparison of oral and silent reading provide for a more in-depth assessment; however, they are options that the examiner may choose to bypass in the interest of time.

Finding the Instructional Level in Other Types of Material

Once the examiner has determined the familiar narrative instructional level, s/he may wish to contrast this level with the level attained in other types of text: text with and without pictures (pre-primer through grade two); unfamiliar selections; and expository text. For expository text, the examiner should begin at the instructional level attained in familiar narratives and move up or down as indicated by the student's performance. For unfamiliar text, the examiner should begin one level lower than the level attained in familiar material. Table 9.1 provides instructions for finding an instructional level. Table 9.2 presents the criteria for establishing these levels.

TABLE 9.1 How to Find an Instructional Level

1. Use the *word* lists to choose a beginning level.
   Select a passage at the same readability level as the highest independent level attained by the student on the word lists.
   OR
   Use *other* data to choose a beginning level.
   Select a passage at a readability level that your data suggest will provide the student with a successful experience.
2. Select a familiar narrative passage at the appropriate beginning level as determined above.
3. Have the student *read the passage orally* (if using passages for primer through fifth grade) or *silently* (if using passages for grades six through junior high) and *answer the questions.*
4. Determine the *total passage level:* a combination of the level for word recognition and the level for comprehension.
5. *Move to the next highest level* if the student scores at an independent or instructional level
   Move to the next lowest level if the student scores at a frustration level.
6. *Stop* when the student reaches his/her highest instructional level.
   OR
   Stop when the student reaches an instructional level at his/her chronological grade level.
7. Options
   a. Once you have the highest instructional level, you may *verify this level* by having the student read another familiar passage at that level orally or silently.
   b. To determine a level for *familiar expository text* or text with and without pictures, begin with a passage at the familiar instructional level as determined in the above procedure.
   c. To determine a level for *unfamiliar text,* begin with a passage one level below the familiar instructional level.
   d. To determine a *listening* level, begin with a passage one level below the student's chronological grade placement.

TABLE 9.2 Criteria: Independent, Instructional, and Frustration Levels

Independent Level:
The level at which a student can read and comprehend without assistance.
Word Identification in Isolation: 90% or higher
    Obtained from word lists
Word Identification in Context: 98% or higher
    Obtained from oral reading of passages
Comprehension: 90% or higher

Instructional Level:
The level at which a student can be instructed profitably
Word Identification in Isolation: 70% to 89%
    Obtained from word lists
Word Identification in Context:
    Obtained from oral reading of passages
        90% to 97%: Total Accuracy
        95% to 97%: Total Acceptability
Comprehension: 70% to 89%

Frustration Level:
The level at which a student is completely unable to read with adequate word identification or comprehension.
Word Identification in Isolation: Less than 70%
    Obtained from word lists
Word Identification in Context:
    Obtained from oral reading of passages
        Less than 90%: Total Accuracy
        Less than 95%: Total Acceptability
Comprehension: Less than 70%

Formula for Determining Percentages:
Word Identification in Isolation (word lists):
    Number of words correctly identified ÷ total number of words on the list (20).
Word Identification in Context (oral reading of passages):
    Number of words in passage – number of miscues ÷ number of words in the passage
Comprehension (questions):
    Number of questions correctly answered ÷ total number of questions

Rate:
To obtain the reading rate in words per minute, use the following formula:
WPM = Number of words in the passage × 60 ÷ number of seconds it took to read the passage

10 Administration and Scoring of the *Qualitative Reading Inventory–II*

Word Identification in Context: Oral Reading

Recording Oral Reading Miscues

Counting Oral Reading Miscues

Counting Total Accuracy
Counting Total Acceptability

Analyzing Oral Reading Miscues: Miscue Analysis

Recording Miscues
Counting Miscues
Analyzing the Miscues

Evaluating Automaticity

Recording Oral Reading Miscues

When the student is reading orally, the examiner marks any miscues the student makes. It is helpful to tape the oral reading segment; then the examiner will be sure to catch the miscues. As one becomes more proficient in recording student miscues, the tape becomes less important. We suggest the following system for recording miscues:

> *Substitution:* Write what the student said over the word as it appears in print.

Omission: Circle the omitted word.

Insertion: Write in the insertion and mark it with a $\wedge$.

Self-correction: If a student corrects a miscue, write the miscue and mark it with *C.*

Reversal: If the student transposes two words or phrases, such as "Said John" for "John said," mark the reversal with a $\frown\!\!\!\smile$ symbol.

Punctuation ignored: Mark an *X* on any punctuation that the reader ignores.

Examples:

TEXT: Once there was a very (big) bear. X

loved [C]   dark
He lived in the $\wedge$ woods.

One day his father saw the big bear crying.

Why are you crying, his father said.

In this example, the student omitted "big" in the first sentence and ignored the period by continuing to read. In the second sentence, s/he said "loved" for "lived" and self-corrected. The student also inserted "dark." In the last sentence, s/he read, "said his father" instead of, "his father said."

Most IRIs allow the examiner to offer assistance to the student when s/he encounters an unfamiliar word. We do not recommend this. It is impossible to assess the effect of word identification upon comprehension if the student is given the correct pronunciation for key words in the passage. If a student is unable to identify a word, gently ask him/her to move on. Figure 10.1 offers additional examples of recorded miscues.

Counting Oral Reading Miscues

Examiners can count miscues in two ways. The examiner can determine independent, instructional, and frustration levels by counting all miscues. We call this *Total Accuracy.* Or the examiner may choose to count only those miscues which change or distort passage meaning. We call this *Total Acceptability.* It is not necessary to do both. The diagnostic philosophy of the examiner will determine which scoring system to use. Our pilot data found Total Acceptability to be the best predictor of instructional level comprehension. However, during the actual administration, the examiner may find it easier to count all miscues in order to determine whether to move up or down a level. S/he can then determine Total Acceptability after completing the test administration.

Counting Total Accuracy

Any deviation from the printed text is counted as a miscue. This includes:

- insertions
- omissions
- substitutions
- reversals
- self-corrections

We do not count repetitions, hesitations, and omission of punctuation because they tend to be scored unreliably (Hood, 1975–76). Also, repetitions and hesitations may indicate uncertainty on the part of the subject or a desire to clarify meaning that was missed. It can also be argued that they do not alter the text materially and therefore do not truly represent an error (McKenna, 1983).

Miscues made on proper names represent a special problem because of the extreme variability in pronunciation of some names. We recommend the following: If the student pronounces a proper name as a nonsense name—a name the examiner has never heard—and repeatedly calls the character by that name, the examiner should count it as one miscue. For example, if the student consistently refers to "Maria" as "Marin," these deviations count as one miscue. If, however, the student refers to "Maria" as "Marin," "Morin," and "Meres," each deviation is a separate miscue.

FIGURE 10.1 Example of Reading and Scoring Miscues

It was a warm spring day. The children were going on a trip. The trip *wet¹ mc* *went² mc*

was to a farm. The children wanted to see many animals. They wanted to write *aminals³ mc*

down all they saw. They were going to make a book for their class. On the way *4 mc* *gone⁵ mc* *the⁶*

to the farm the bus broke down. The children thought their trip was over. *pumpkin⁷ mc* *8*

Then a man stopped his car. He helped to fix the bus. The bus started again. *stepped⁹ mc* *10* *won't c 11*

The children said, "yea!" The children got to the farm. They saw a pig. They *was c 12*

saw a hen and cows. They liked petting the kittens. They learned about milking *13hens* *looked¹⁴ mc* *looked¹⁵ mc*

cows. They liked the trip to the farm. They wanted to go again. (119 words) *and¹⁶*

The following miscues were substitutions:
 # 1, 2, 3, 5, 6, 9, 12, 13, 14, 15, 16
The following miscues were insertions:
 # 7, 11
The following miscues were omissions:
 # 4, 8, 10

The following miscues were meaning change miscues. They changed the meaning of the text or they were not self-corrected.
#1, 2, 3, 4, 5, 7, 9, 14, 15

If a student makes the same miscue on the same word several times in the passage and it does not change the meaning of the passage, the examiner should count it as one miscue. For example, if a student consistently refers to "puppy" as "pup" or "planes" as "airplanes," the deviations count as one miscue. If, however, the consistent miscue changes meaning, such as "poppy" for "puppy" or "please" for "planes," each pronunciation counts as a separate miscue. When a single word is repeated numerous times throughout a passage, students often pronounce it identically several times and then change to another pronunciation. How should this be scored? We recommend that each mispronunciation of the word be scored as a separate miscue. Examiners should assign *one* point to several miscues only if the mispronunciation does not change meaning and is consistent across the entire passage.

If a student omits an entire line, it is counted as one miscue because the omission represents a loss of place, not a conscious omission because of inability to identify words. Obviously, in this case, the student is not monitoring comprehension. However, counting each omitted word as a separate miscue could distort the final level designation.

Variations in pronunciations due to articulation difficulties or regional dialects should not be counted as oral reading miscues unless the student has been observed to pronounce the word or word part correctly in other words. For example, if a student who speaks one of the black dialects omits the "s" or "ed" marker sometimes but reads it in other cases, it should be counted as an oral reading miscue. The examiner should not assume that a student of a specific race speaks or does not speak a particular dialect, but s/he should determine speaking patterns through casual conversation with the student before, during, and after testing.

The examiner should count the total number of miscues and use this to determine whether the students performance reflects an independent, instructional, and/or frustration level. For ease and accuracy in scoring, we recommend that s/he number the miscues. The following criteria determine level designations for word identification in context:

Total Accuracy

Independent Level:	98% accuracy
Instructional Level:	90% to 97% accuracy
Frustration Level:	less than 90% accuracy

The examiner can determine percentages by subtracting the number of miscues from the number of words in the passage (listed at the bottom of his/her copy of the passage). This yields the number of words read correctly. S/he then divides this by the number of words in the passage, rounding upwards to find the percent of Total Accuracy. S/he may also wish to use the guidelines given at the bottom of each passage which indicate how many miscues result in independent, instructional, and frustration level reading. If s/he uses these, s/he will not need to determine percentages.

Example: *The Trip* has 119 words. A student made 8 total miscues.

119
− 8
111 ÷ 119 = 93% Total Accuracy

For Total Accuracy, the student scored within the criteria for the instructional level for word identification in context.

Counting Total Acceptability

Acceptable miscues are those that do not change or distort passage meaning. What is counted as a miscue that changes meaning? A meaning change miscue is any deviation from the printed text which results in an ungrammatical sentence or which results in a grammatical sentence that differs from the author's intended meaning. This includes:

- insertions
- omissions
- substitutions

If the student self-corrects a miscue, it is not counted as changing meaning.

If a student mispronounces a proper name, it does not count as a meaning change miscue unless the sex of the character is changed. For example, if a student mispronounces "Lopez" as "Lopz," it is not counted as a meaning change miscue. If a student mispronounces "Maria" as "Mary," do not count it as a meaning change miscue. However, the substitution of "Mark" for "Mary" is counted as a miscue that changes meaning. A nonword substitution for a common proper name such as "Marin" for "Mary" is not counted as a meaning change miscue if the student *consistently* offers this pronunciation. If, however, the student pronounces the name differently or correctly in other parts of the text, it is counted as a meaning change miscue.

Nonword substitutions such as "piloneer" for "pioneer" are always counted as changing meaning. If the same nonword miscue is repeated several times, we advise counting it each time because it distorts meaning and adversely affects comprehension.

If a student consistently makes the same miscue on the same word and it changes meaning, the examiner should count each miscue separately. We believe it should be counted separately because each mispronunciation, however consistent, distorts the meaning of the text in some way.

In order to judge whether a miscue results in a meaning change, the examiner should read the miscue in the context of the sentence. If it is ungrammatical and is not corrected by the subject, it is scored automatically as a meaning change. If it is grammatical, the examiner will have to decide whether it is semantically synonymous with what the author meant.

Examples:

TEXT: Maria went with the group to the monkey house where she
Marin   *her*   *monkeys'* *when*

spent a long time watching the chimps groom each other.
watch   *others*

The substitutions of "Marin," "her," and "monkeys" do not change the meaning of the text. "Marin" was a consistent miscue for this subject throughout the passage. The substitutions of "when," "watch," and "others" are not acceptable. They do not make grammatical sense. Tables 14.2 and 14.3 contains additional examples of meaning-change miscues.

The examiner should count the number of miscues that change or distort text meaning. For ease in scoring, we recommend that s/he mark each meaning change miscue as "M. C." Highlighting or underlining meaning-change miscues are other ways of keeping track. The examiner can then use this number to determine the level designations for Total Acceptability. The following criteria determine level designations for word identification in context (see Section 16 for a further explanation of these criteria):

Total Acceptability

Independent Level:	98% word accuracy
Instructional Level:	95% to 97% word accuracy
Frustration Level:	less than 94% word accuracy

The examiner then counts the number of meaning-change miscues and subtracts that from the number of words in the passage. Then s/he divides this by the number of words in the passage, rounding upwards to find the percent of Total Acceptability. S/he may also use the guidelines given at the end of the passage which indicate how many meaning-change miscues result in an independent, instructional, or frustration reading level.

Example: *The Trip* has 119 words. A student made a total of 8 miscues. Four of these were meaning change miscues.

$$\frac{\begin{array}{r} 119 \\ -\ 4 \end{array}}{115} \div 119 = 96.6 = 97\% \text{ Total Acceptability}$$

For Total Acceptability, the student scored within an instructional level for word identification in context.

Analyzing Oral Reading Miscues: Miscue Analysis

Recording Miscues

Examiners can qualitatively analyze any miscues that the student makes while reading passages orally. This analysis provides a rich body of information about the student's reading strategies. The Miscue Analysis Worksheet in Table 10.1 provides a format for analyzing the student's miscues qualitatively. Generally, the examiner will analyze all miscues made during oral reading. If the student reads enough passages, the examiner can analyze any miscues made at independent and instructional levels (as determined by the total passage level) separately from those made at the frustration level. Generally, students employ different strategies as they move into frustration level text, where meaningful context is not generally available to the reader.

1. The examiner writes the miscue in the first column and the text word in the second column. S/he should write substitutions and insertions as said by the student. Omissions are indicated by a dash.
2. Columns three and four evaluate the graphic similarity of the miscue to the text word. If the miscue resembles the text word in the initial letter/s, the examiner places a check in column three. Examples of initial similarity are if the miscue and the text word begin with the same letter ("call" for "claw") or the miscue and the text word share a common letter pattern ("broke" for "bright"). If the miscue resembles the text word in the final letter/s, the examiner places a check in column four. Examples are a miscue and a text word that end with the same letter or letter pattern ("fits" for "fins" or "decks" for "ducks"). Another example is a shared common ending ("looked" for "watched" or "going" for "sailing"). Why not record miscue and text similarities in the middle position? It has been

TABLE 10.1 Miscue Analysis Worksheet

Subject _____   Level of Miscues: Independent/Instructional   Frustrational

MISCUE	TEXT	GRAPHICALLY SIMILAR Initial	Final	SEMANTICALLY ACCEPTABLE	SELF-CORRECTED
Column Total Total Miscues Column Total / Total Miscues = %		_____ _____ _____	_____ _____ _____	_____ _____ _____	_____ _____ _____

our experience that the majority of miscues do involve a medial error probably because vowel sounds are more variable than consonants and thus are more confused by readers particularly those experiencing difficulty. Recording initial and final similarity is sufficient to suggest that the student is attempting to pay attention to letter–sound matching.

3. Column five evaluates semantic or contextual acceptability. Did the miscue retain the author's meaning? If the miscue was acceptable, the examiner places a check in this column. Semantically acceptable miscues suggest that the student is paying attention to meaning during the reading process. An example would be the substitution of "takes" for "drink" in the sentence, "The baby drinks milk from its mother for about a year."

4. Column six evaluates the number of self-corrections made by the student. Self-corrections suggest that the reader is comprehending during the reading process and thus is able to note a miscue that distorts the author's meaning. Self-corrections can also indicate attention to graphic cues. An example would be the reader who self-corrects a semantically acceptable miscue such as "put" for "divided" in the sentence "When they got to the zoo, their teachers divided the children into four groups."

Once the examiner has recorded all miscues, s/he must total each column as indicated on the worksheet. Now s/he can analyze the word-identification strategies of the subject.

Counting Miscues

The examiner should first count the total number of miscues made by the student (column one). Then the number of checks in each of columns three through six should be counted. The examiner can determine the percent of miscues in each category by dividing the column total by the number of total miscues as recorded in column one. For example, if the subject made a total of twenty three miscues and fifteen of these were similar in the initial position, 15 / 23 = 65%.

Analyzing the Miscues

The Miscue Analysis Worksheet can indicate the strategies used by the student when reading orally. The percentages should not be interpreted rigidly; no percentage limits are given. Rather, they should be used as a means of noting general patterns of reader behavior. The following guidelines may be helpful.

1. If the worksheet shows a high percentage of semantically acceptable miscues and/or self-corrections, the reader is probably comprehending during the reading process. Of course, an observation like this needs to be made in relation to the student's comprehension score on the passages.

2. If the worksheet shows a high percentage of initial and final graphic similarity coupled with a low percentage of acceptable or self-corrected miscues, the reader may be paying more attention to decoding words than to the meaning of the text.

3. If the worksheet shows a high percentage of initial graphic similarity and a low percentage of final similarity, the reader may only be paying attention to the beginning of words. Some children use only the initial letter/s as a basis for guessing the rest of the word.

4. If the worksheet shows a low percentage of initial and final graphic similarity coupled with a low percentage of acceptability and/or self-corrections, the reader may be a "wild guesser," one who is unable to use either phonics or context effectively.

As we mentioned previously, the examiner may analyze all miscues or only those made at independent/instructional levels versus those made at a frustration level. Comparing the types of miscues made at the independent/instructional levels versus the frustration level will typically show that the reader makes many more miscues acceptable to the author's meaning when reading independent/instructional text. As the reader moves into frustration text, the number of acceptable miscues and self-corrections tends to drop.

Evaluating Automaticity

Rate of oral reading can suggest automaticity of word identification. If a reader reads relatively quickly, one can assume that the words are no longer being decoded. Instead, the reader is processing the words as whole units. Words recognized in this way are often termed *sight vocabulary*.

The *QRI*–II provides the examiner with the means of determining oral reading rate as measured in words per minute. The number of words in the passage multiplied by 60 and divided by the number of seconds it took to read the passage will yield a word-per-minute score.

Reading rate is quite variable. It varies across passages. More difficult and/or unfamiliar passages tend to be read more slowly. Reading rate also varies according to reader purpose. If the reader is reading in order to learn or remember text content, this is typically done at a slower rate than pleasure reading. Reading rate also varies across individuals. Some readers are naturally faster than other, a phenomenon that may be attributed to speed of cognitive processing (Carver, 1990). For these reasons, any guidelines for evaluating reading rate must be interpreted as general in nature.

Our pilot data for the *QRI*–II looked at normal readers reading at their instructional level. We found that there was wide variation in the rates despite a steady growth in rate as reading level increased. We offer these rates, based upon means and standard deviations, as suggestive of the rates of typical readers when processing text at their instructional level.

Silent reading rate can also suggest automatic word identification. It, too, is variable across passages, purposes, and individuals. Therefore, the following guidelines from our pilot data should only be used to suggest typical rates. Silent rates are not offered for pre-primer through first-grade levels. Readers who are instructional at these levels have seldom made a transition to silent reading.

TABLE 10.2

Level	Oral Words Per Minute
Pre-primer	13–35
Primer	28–68
First	31–87
Second	52–102
Third	85–139
Fourth	78–124
Sixth	113–165

TABLE 10.3

Level	Silent Words Per Minute
Second	58–122
Third	96–168
Fourth	107–175
Sixth	135 241

11 Administration and Scoring of the *Qualitative Reading Inventory–II*

Comprehension

Retelling

General Procedures
Scoring
Analysis of Retelling

Questions

General Procedures
Scoring the Questions

Criteria for Determining Reading Levels

An examiner can assess a student's comprehension of orally and silently read passages in two ways. S/he can ask the student to retell the selection and/or ask questions about the selection. The percent correct on questions is used for assigning independent, instructional, and frustration levels. The examiner can evaluate the retelling qualitatively against a map composed of the important ideas contained in the passage. Examiners will use the questions more often than retelling; however, if an examiner should elect to do both, s/he should ask for the retelling before asking the questions. For that reason, we will look at retelling first.

Retelling

General Procedures

After the student has finished reading the selection, the examiner should remove the passage and ask the student to retell it as if it were being told to someone who had never read or heard it before. After the student has retold as much as s/he can, the examiner should ask if there is anything else s/he would like to say. If the student says that s/he can remember nothing, the examiner can draw the student's attention to the title of the passage and ask if s/he can remember what the author wrote about it. The examiner should not offer more extensive hints or direct suggestions, such as "Can you remember what Johnny Appleseed's journey was like?" The examiner will find it helpful at first to tape the retelling and use the tape for scoring at a later time. As s/he becomes familiar with the individual passages, s/he can often score the retelling directly onto the Retelling Scoring Sheet as the student is talking.

Scoring

Scoring is determined by comparing the idea units recalled by the student with those on the Retelling Scoring Sheet. The scoring sheet was designed from an examination of the idea units most frequently recalled by students in our piloting sample as well as a theoretical analysis of the important units. The examiner should place a check next to each explicit idea listed on the scoring sheet that was recalled by the student. As an option, the examiner may wish to indicate the sequence of the recalled ideas by using a number instead of a check mark; however, this is not necessary. S/he can write in any additional recalled ideas, such as explicit ideas not listed on the scoring sheet or inferences made by the student. The following paragraph is Peter's retelling of Johnny Appleseed, followed by a scoring example in Figure 11.1.

"Johnny, all the men nicknamed him 'Johnny Appleseed' because he had planted a lot of apple trees, because he had lived in Massachusetts and he went down west to put in a lot of apple trees. While he was planting a lot of apple trees, miles and miles, he had crossed rivers and all that through the forest where Indians and that were there. His clothes were wet and torn in the knees and used his shirt for a pillow or something. He still didn't give up. And he didn't have any shoes or nothin'. He lived like raggy and then the apple trees that are here weren't really here before."

Obviously, a student will not recall in the exact words of the text, and synonyms and paraphrases are acceptable. The examiner will have to decide if the subject's recall matches the meaning of the text.

Analysis of Retelling

While the retelling is not used to determine independent, instructional, and frustration levels, it can provide valuable information with implications for instruction. For example, if the student does not retell the central parts of a narrative, it implies that the student may not have an understanding of story structure. Similarly, if the student does not organize an expository retelling around the main idea and supporting details, the student may not understand the structure of paragraphs in exposition.

The examiner should use the retellings to answer the following questions:

1. Do the retellings of narrative material retain the basic structure of the narratives? Is the most important information included?
2. Do the retellings of expository material retain the main idea and supporting detail structure of the selection? Is the most important information included?
3. Are the retellings sequential?
4. Is the recall accurate?

Peter's recall can be evaluated in the following way. Although his recall was not offered in a sequential manner, Peter included information related to all four categories of story structure, the setting/background, the goal, the events, and the resolution. This suggests that Peter has somewhat internalized the structure of the story and is using it to help his recall.

FIGURE 11.1 Retelling Scoring Sheet for Johnny Appleseed

Setting/Background

____ John Chapman was born
____ in 1774.
____ He became a farmer
____ and grew crops.
____ John liked
____ to grow
____ and eat apples.
____ People were moving west.
____ Apples were a good food
____ for settlers to have.

Goal

____ John decided
_5_ to go west.
____ He wanted
_3_ to plant apple trees.

Events

____ John got many seeds
____ from farmers
____ who squeezed apples
____ to make a drink
____ called cider.
____ He left
____ for the frontier.
____ He planted seeds
____ as he went along.
____ He gave them away.

____ John walked miles.
_6_ He crossed rivers
_7_ and went through forests.
____ He was hungry
____ and wet.
____ He had to hide
_8_ from Indians
____ unfriendly Indians.
_9_ His clothes were torn.
____ He used a sack
____ for a shirt
____ and he cut out holes
____ for the arms.
_11_ He wore no shoes.

Resolution

____ John's fame spread.
_1_ He was nicknamed
_2_ Johnny Appleseed.
____ Settlers accepted seeds
____ gratefully.
____ Thanks to Johnny Appleseed
_12_ trees grow
_13_ in many parts
____ of America.

Other ideas recalled including inferences

4 lived in Massachusetts
10 didn't give up

General Procedures

After the student has retold to the best of his or her ability, the examiner should ask the comprehension questions and score them according to the suggestions provided. There are two types of questions. Explicit questions have answers that are stated directly in the passage. These questions assess whether the student can understand and remember information stated directly by an author. For implicit questions, the reader must use clues in the passage to make inferences in order to answer correctly. These questions assess the reader's inferencing abilities.

Scoring the Questions

We suggest that answers be scored as either right or wrong with no half points given. This is because the awarding of half credit tends to be unreliable. In addition, our piloting was done on the basis of either right or wrong answers (see Section 16 for details). Of course, the examiner should give credit for any answer which includes the same information in different words.

If the question is an explicit question, the answer *must* come from the passage. You cannot count correct an answer which comes from prior knowledge (even if it is accurate). For example, on the third-grade passage, "Cats: Lions and Tigers in Your House," explicit questions ask the reader to name ways that lions, tigers, and cats are alike. If a student says that they all have sharp teeth or fur, this would be an incorrect answer. While such information is accurate, it is not stated explicitly in the passage.

Similarly, an implicit question cannot be considered correct if the answer does not relate to a clue in the passage. Again, if the answer comes from prior knowledge only, it is not counted as correct. For example, for the "Amelia Earhart" passage, one implicit question is, "Why do you think her plane was never found?" A student may answer, "because it burned up," which is a reasonable answer drawn from his/her background. However, the clues in the passage suggest that it crashed into an ocean and probably sank. When the student's answer to an implicit question obviously comes from background knowledge, its reasonableness can be acknowledged, and the examiner can then ask, "But what do the clues in the passage tell you?"

The pre-primer passages do not have implicit comprehension questions. However, the student may answer an explicit question by using information from the pictures. We have chosen to score such a response as a correct answer to an implicit question. For example, on "Just Like Mom," one question is, "Name one thing that the girl can do just like Mom." One of the most common responses was "water the flowers." That response comes from the fourth picture. However, the text says, "I can work at home." Thus, the child's response is an incorrect answer to the explicit question, but is counted as a *correct* implicit response. Another example on "People at Work," a question is, "What is one thing that people do at work?." A common response was "fix things." This is counted as an correct implicit response because although the text says "Other people make things at work," children interpret the picture as someone fixing the bicycle.

You must score the questions as you go along. The scores tell you when to move to higher passages and when to stop.

Criteria for Determining Reading Levels

Passages have five, six, eight, or ten questions. The following guide indicates the number of correct questions needed to attain an independent level (90% or above), an instructional level (70%–89%), and a frustration level (below 70%). The criteria for use on each passage is provided on the examiner's question page as well as below:

Five questions:	Independent level: 5 correct
	Instructional level: 4 correct
	Frustration level: 0–3 correct
Six questions:	Independent level: 6 correct
	Instructional level: 5 correct
	Frustration level: 0–4 correct
Eight questions:	Independent level: 8 correct
	Instructional level: 6–7 correct
	Frustration level: 0–5 correct
Ten questions:	Independent level: 9–10 correct
	Instructional level: 7–8 correct
	Frustration level: 0–6 correct

Analysis of a student's ability to answer explicit and implicit questions can provide valuable information. An examiner should analyze a student's performance at independent and instructional levels separately from that at frustration level. For each grouping, s/he should count the total number of explicit questions asked of the student and the total number answered correctly. To arrive at a percentage, s/he must divide the total correct by the total asked, repeating the procedure for implicit questions. A substantial difference between these two scores, such as 50% on several passages, may suggest that the student needs instruction in either remembering what the author stated explicitly in the text or in using clues in the text to make inferences, depending on which score is higher.

12 Administration and Scoring of the *Qualitative Reading Inventory–II*

Assessing Strategic Reading

Look-Backs: Locating Answers to Explicit Questions

Look-Backs: Arriving at Answers to Implicit Questions

Look-Backs: Assessing Student Awareness of Comprehension Roadblocks

Look-Backs: Assessing Vocabulary Knowledge

Using a Think-Aloud Procedure to Assess Comprehension

Assessing Note-Taking Ability

Assessing Use of Context

Assessing Listening Comprehension

The following procedures can offer valuable insights into a student's strengths and weaknesses in strategic reading. The examiner can choose to administer one or more of them in addition to or in lieu of the assessment measures explained in the preceding sections. The examiner must decide which procedures will offer the most meaningful information.

Look-Backs:
Locating Answers
to Explicit Questions

During the normal administration procedures, the examiner asks the student to answer questions without the benefit of the accompanying text. Afterwards, the examiner can give the student the text and ask if s/he can look back to locate answers that were unknown and/or correct incorrect answers. Such a procedure can roughly differentiate between comprehension and memory for what was read. If a student can locate answers and/or correct errors, s/he probably understood the text, at least after rereading it. The initial problem may have been one of memory or purpose. If, however, the student cannot locate or correct an answer, perhaps the problem lies with his/her basic understanding of what s/he read.

Look-Backs:
Arriving at Answers
to Implicit Questions

The examiner can use the same look-back procedure to determine if a student can locate and use the textual clues necessary to arrive at a correct answer to an implicit question. Answering implicit questions demands some background knowledge from the reader as well as identification of clues provided by the author. The examiner can probe to see if the student's inability to answer an implicit question is because of lack of background or lack of attention to the clues in the text. For example, the examiner can tell the student the correct answer and ask him/her to find the clue in the text. The examiner can also point out the clue and see if the student can use it to arrive at the correct answer.

Look-Backs:
Assessing Student
Awareness of
Comprehension
Roadblocks

The examiner can choose a passage that proved difficult to the student and ask the student to look back and indicate specific parts that s/he found especially troublesome. The examiner can either direct the student to indicate a specific word that s/he does not know or s/he can ask the subject to identify "something you found hard or something you didn't understand." Once the examiner isolates a segment of text, s/he can gently probe the student to ascertain that the chosen element was actually difficult and was not selected at random. If the student says that everything was hard, the examiner should reverse the procedure and ask him/her to find one or two things that were a bit easier than the rest.

Look-Backs:
Assessing Vocabulary
Knowledge

The examiner can ask the student to look back and define or explain certain key vocabulary words contained in a passage. This may be especially helpful if the student has evinced poor comprehension. The examiner can ascertain if the student knows the meaning of words that were pronounced correctly as well as words that were pronounced incorrectly during passage reading. After silent reading, the examiner can ask the student to define and pronounce certain key words contained in the passage. The student's inability to do either may be an indication of why his/her comprehension was low.

Using a Think-Aloud Procedure to Assess Comprehension

Think-alouds are a reader's verbalizations about the selection made before, during, and after reading. Think-alouds provide a way of "gathering information about individual readers' ongoing thinking processes and metacognitive behavior" (Brown and Lytle, 1988, p. 96). The examiner gives the student the title of the selection and asks him/her to predict or reflect on the topic and how s/he feels about it. Then the examiner asks the student to read the passage and stop after each sentence to "think out loud," sharing efforts to understand, judge, reason, and monitor. After the student completes the selection, the examiner asks him/her to talk about its content, structure, or difficulty level. The examiner can tape think-alouds for later analysis.

Assessing Note-Taking Ability

Once the examiner determines an instructional level, s/he can use a parallel passage to assess the student's ability to take notes. We recommend that s/he use expository text. This can be done in two ways. The examiner can give the student a copy of the passage and ask him/her to read with pencil in hand, underlining those parts of the selection that seem most important. Or the examiner can ask the student to read a selection and take notes on it as if studying for a test. Either procedure can identify the student who is unable to isolate the main ideas of a selection and/or engage in efficient note-taking procedures. The examiner may wish to map the student's note-taking efforts on the Retelling Scoring Sheet to note if the more important points are included.

Assessing Use of Context

The examiner can choose words that were unknown in the passage reading and use these to determine if the student can utilize the context of the passage to determine pronunciation, meaning, or both. The examiner can begin by asking the student what s/he does when faced with an unknown word. If the student indicates some use of context, the examiner can ask him/her to demonstrate the process. If the student does not indicate context usage as a strategy and/or is unable to demonstrate the process, the examiner can engage in some gentle probing by asking the student these questions:

1. Do any of the words in the sentence or passage suggest what this word could mean?
2. Do any clues such as endings or preceding words suggest that this word may be a noun, verb, etc.?
3. If you read the sentence and say "blank" when you come to the word, does the entire sentence give you some hints?

The examiner may wish to choose a word that the student knows and then ask these questions. The student can then imitate the examiner by using a known word before moving on to an unknown one.

Assessing Listening Comprehension

Often beginning readers or readers who have severe decoding problems cannot successfully read and comprehend material at the primer level. In such cases, it is wise to assess the level of material that the student can understand if the material is read to him/her. This will suggest if the student can profit from orally presented material at his/her grade level. An examiner can also find a listening level for students whose comprehension is severely below grade placement. In this case, a listening level can indicate whether or not the student can comprehend apart from reading.

Listening comprehension is evaluated in the same way as oral and silent reading. The only difference is that after assessing the student's prior knowledge, the examiner reads the passage to the student. The student retells what s/he heard and/or answers specific questions. It is most important to determine listening levels in familiar narrative text, although the examiner can also choose to determine listening levels in expository and unfamiliar text.

13 Summarizing the Results of the *Qualitative Reading Inventory–II*

Organizing the Data

The Student Profile Sheet
The Comparisons Sheet: Describing Specific Reading Behaviors
Word Identification
Comprehension

The major strength of the *QRI*–II is that it provides a profile of the strengths and needs of an individual reader across different types of text according to the student's prior knowledge. In order to facilitate such comparisons, we have provided two summary sheets: The Student Profile Sheet and the Comparisons Sheet (see Tables 13.1 and 13.2).

Organizing the Data

The Student Profile Sheet

The examiner should fill out the Student Profile Sheet using the following abbreviations:

Familiar: F   Unfamiliar: UF
Narrative: N   Expository: E
Independent: Ind   Instructional: Ins   Frustration: Fr

TABLE 13.1 Qualitative Reading Inventory–II

Student Profile Sheet

Name _____ Birthdate _____ Grade _____

Sex _____ Date of Test _____ Examiner _____

Word Identification

Grade									
Level/% Automatic									
Level/% Total									

Oral Reading

Passage Name									
Readability Level									
Passage Type									
Level/% Total Accuracy									
Level/% Total Acceptability									
Familiar/Unfamiliar									
# Explicit Correct									
# Implicit Correct									
Level/% Comprehension									
Rate									
Total Passage Level									

Silent Reading

Passage Name									
Readability Level									
Passage Type									
Familiar/Unfamiliar									
# Correct Explicit									
# Correct Implicit									
Level/% Comprehension									
Rate									

Obviously, the completeness of the Student Profile Sheet will depend upon the extent and complexity of the assessment. For some students, an examiner will enter data for only a few passages. Other students will be represented by a much more detailed profile sheet. In addition, examiners can choose not to fill in certain portions. For example, an examiner may choose to record levels, but not percentages, for Total Accuracy and/or Total Acceptability. An examiner may elect to determine levels from Total Acceptability only. In this case, the spaces for Total Accuracy would remain blank. Similarly, an examiner may elect to record the comprehension level without recording the number of explicit and implicit questions answered correctly. When recording the data, the examiner should:

1. Begin with the lowest level of list or passage administered and move to the right with successively higher levels.
2. Organize the passages into groupings: narrative, expository, familiar, unfamiliar.
3. When recording scores, record the information for familiar narratives first.
4. After listing results for familiar narratives, record scores for unfamiliar narratives.
5. Record familiar expository scores, then record unfamiliar expository scores.
6. If passages were administered to assess listening comprehension, group these to the far right on the Profile Sheet and draw a line separating them from passages administered orally or silently.

Section 14 contains an example of a completed Student Profile Sheet.

The Comparisons Sheet: Describing Specific Reading Behaviors

We have provided Table 13.2 to facilitate comparison of a student's reading ability across different contexts. The Comparisons Sheet is organized according to different questions that an assessment specialist might ask about a student. Answering these questions can provide important information for planning intervention instruction. The assessment specialist should complete the sheet by reporting the highest instructional levels attained by a student. If an instructional level is not available, the examiner can choose to report independent or frustration levels.

Word Identification

The Comparisons Sheet allows the examiner to describe the student's word-identification accuracy, word-identification automaticity, strategies used for word identification, and word identification in isolation and in context.

How Accurate Is the Student in Identifying Words? Total scores on the word lists and word-identification levels on oral passage reading will allow the examiner to ascertain the student's accuracy in identifying words. Accurate word identification is a critical component of skilled reading (Gough & Juel, 1991) and the majority of poor readers are deficient in this respect. The student's accuracy level should parallel his/her chronological grade placement. The greater the gap between word-identification accuracy and chronological grade placement, the more serious the reading problem.

TABLE 13.2 Comparisons: Describing Specific Reading Behaviors

Student _____

WORD IDENTIFICATION

How Accurate Is the Student in Identifying Words?
Words Lists Total Score: Level _____
Passage Reading
    Word Identification: Level _____

How Automatic Is the Student in Identifying Words?
Word Lists Timed Score: Level _____
Oral Passage Reading: WPM _____
Silent Passage Reading: WPM _____

What Strategies for Word Identification in Context Are Used by the Student?
Percent: Graphically Similar Miscues:
    Initial Position
    Final Position _____
Percent: Acceptable Miscues _____
Percent: Self-corrected Miscues _____

Is There a Difference Between a Student's Ability to Identify Words in Isolation and Words in Context?
Word Lists Total Score: Level _____
Passage Reading
    Word Identification: Level _____

COMPREHENSION

Which Types of Text Can the Student Handle Most Successfully?
Narrative Text: Level _____
Expository Text: Level _____
Text with Pictures: Level _____
Text without Pictures: Level _____

Which Modes of Reading Represent a Strength for the Student?
Oral Reading: Level _____
Silent Reading: Level _____

How Does the Student Perform in Familiar and Unfamiliar Text?
Familiar Text: Level _____
Unfamiliar Text: Level _____

What Is the Extent of the Student's Reading Problem?
Highest Instructional Level _____
Chronological Grade Placement _____

How Automatic Is the Student in Identifying Words? Reading fluency is dependent upon an extensive sight vocabulary or automaticity in identifying words. If a reader must pause and decode the majority of words, his/her fluency will suffer and comprehension will likely be hindered. The timed score on the word lists gives the examiner one measure of word-identification automaticity. If the level for words pronounced automatically on the word lists is lower than the total level for word identification, the subject may profit from procedures to increase automatic word identification. Reading rate attained on the passages is another measure that suggests automaticity of word identification. If a student reads very slowly, the examiner should recommend instructional interventions to increase fluency.

What Strategies for Word Identification Are Used by the Student? The results of miscue analysis can suggest strategies used by the student in identifying words. A high percentage of graphically similar words suggests that the student is paying attention to letter cues. Errors in word identification indicate that the student does not have an accurate representation of the target word in memory (Perfetti, 1991). The examiner can note which letter–sound matches are known and which ones need instructional emphasis. Self-corrected miscues or miscues that do not seriously change the meaning of the text indicate that the student is comprehending as s/he is reading. If a subject's comprehension is poor after reading, this may indicate that attention to word identification is disrupting the recall process.

Is There a Difference Between a Student's Ability to Identify Words in Context and Words in Isolation? The examiner should compare the student's highest instructional level for words recognized in isolation with those recognized when reading within the context of a passage. For many readers, the instructional levels attained on the word lists will closely parallel the instructional levels achieved for word accuracy in familiar text. However, some readers recognize far more words in context. If the oral reading of these students is fluent and expressive, a lower score on the list probably does not represent a serious area of concern. However, if oral reading is slow and halting, lower scores on the word lists could indicate lack of automaticity in word identification. Occasionally a student will have better word-identification scores in isolation than in context. This may be a function of classroom instruction that has focused on word lists. Also, less skilled readers may be less threatened by a word list than a passage.

Comprehension

The examiner can use the Comparisons Sheet to compare a student's comprehension in a variety of contexts. These comparisons are based upon total passage levels. For oral reading, the word-identification and comprehension levels together determine the total passage level (see Section 9). For silent reading, total passage levels are drawn from the comprehension score.

What Types of Text Can the Student Handle Most Successfully? The examiner should compare the student's levels in narrative and expository text. Many readers, especially those below fourth grade, will score a year or two below their familiar narrative level when asked to read expository text. Because content-area material is primarily exposition, the student will have difficulty comprehending this material. S/he will need instruction in expository text structure, including typical paragraph structure. For levels pre-primer through grade two, the examiner can also compare a student's performance in text with and without pictures. Emerging readers naturally depend upon a picture context for both word identification and comprehension. However, skilled readers are less dependent upon such contextual aids (Stanovich, 1980). A student whose success in word identification is dependent upon pictures needs to learn strategies for context-free and automatic decoding. A student whose success in comprehension is dependent upon pictures should be exposed to instruction in prereading activities such as prediction and to self-monitoring strategies during reading.

What Modes of Reading Represent a Strength for the Student? The examiner should compare the student's oral and silent reading comprehension. It is natural for young readers to do better in oral reading because of the stress on this mode during the early elementary grades. As the student moves through the grades, s/he must become increasingly efficient at silent reading. A middle-school student whose instructional level for oral reading is higher than for silent reading will be at a disadvantage in coping with the demands of textbook reading. Such a reader needs instruction and practice in silent reading.

How Does the Student Perform on Familiar and Unfamiliar Text? The examiner can compare levels in familiar versus unfamiliar text. For levels three through junior high, the *QRI*–II provides passages offering both familiar and unfamiliar content. Most readers will score at a higher level in familiar text. This will be true for both narrative and expository material. It is likely that a student may score a year below the familiar instructional level when reading unfamiliar material. A fifth-grade student reading at the fifth-grade level in familiar text but only at the third-grade level in unfamiliar material may have extreme difficulty with content area subjects where s/he is less likely to be familiar with the material.

What Is the Extent of the Students's Reading Problem? To identify a serious reading disability, the examiner can compare the student's highest instructional level with his/her chronological grade placement. Reading disability is generally defined as a serious discrepancy between a student's level of potential and the level at which s/he can read with some measure of success. Individually administered intelligence tests are valid measures of a student's potential; however, IQ scores are not available for all students who are given the *QRI*–II. In addition, a student who cannot keep up with his/her peers in the classroom is disabled in that situation, regardless of any potential assessed by an IQ test. Therefore, reading disability can be defined as a serious discrepancy between the chronological grade level of the student and the level at which a student can read familiar narrative material. A serious discrepancy is defined by Spache (1981) as:

> One year for first- through third-graders
> Two years for fourth- through sixth-graders
> Three years for seventh grade and above

The seriousness of the disability is obviously dependent upon the size of the discrepancy. For example, a third-grader reading at a primer level would be more disabled than one reading at a first-grade level. Another consideration is the grade level at which the student is reading. A student who cannot read primer material has not learned to read. A student who is having trouble at the second- or third-grade level may be able to read but lacks fluency and automaticity at that level. Children reading beyond the third-grade level may have learned to read, but they may not have learned how to read to learn. An older student who has not learned how to read despite years of instruction is obviously more disabled than one who knows how to read but cannot handle the demands of reading to learn.

14 Examples of Using the *Qualitative Reading Inventory–II*

Using the *QRI*–II in the Classroom to Estimate Reading Level

Connie
Joseph
Ann

Using the *QRI*–II for Reading Portfolios

Juanita
LaKendra

Using the *QRI*–II for Planning Intervention Instruction

Michelle
Alex
Peter
Jamie

Using the *QRI*–II in the Classroom to Estimate Reading Level

Connie

Connie is in fourth grade. Her teacher spent several weeks at the beginning of each school year observing the reading strengths and needs of the class. Then, in early October, she formed three reading groups. Each group read in different levels of basal texts and tradebooks. The teacher wanted to be sure that each child was appropriately placed and whenever she was unsure of placement, she used the *QRI*–II for further assessment. Connie's work suggested that she might be most comfortable in the middle group, however, the teacher suspected that Connie might be a better reader than her performance in the classroom indicated.

The teacher chose two passages from the *QRI*–II: the fourth-grade "Johnny Appleseed" and the fifth-grade "Martin Luther King." The concept-question task indicated that Connie was very familiar with Johnny Appleseed and she scored at an independent level for Total Accuracy and for comprehension. The teacher then asked Connie to read "Martin Luther King," another familiar passage. Connie scored at an independent level for word identification and at an instructional level for comprehension. The teacher placed Connie in the highest reading group.

Joseph

Joseph, a third-grader, transferred schools. His new classroom teacher utilized a literature study-group format for reading instruction, in which children read books of their choice, wrote personal reflections in literature logs, and engaged in group discussion with peers reading the same book. The teacher carefully monitored their text choice to ensure that materials were appropriate for all students. Joseph's records from his previous school indicated average progress in reading, although no reading level was recorded. Therefore, the teacher wanted an estimate of Joseph's reading level in order to assist him in selecting books.

The teacher chose a second-grade narrative from the QRI–II, "What Can I Get for My Toy?" For the third-grade selection, she chose "The Trip to the Zoo." Because Joseph seemed somewhat nervous at the prospect of reading alone to a new teacher, she asked him to read the second-grade passage first, hoping that he would experience success and become more comfortable with the assessment process. The concept question task indicated that trading toys was a familiar topic for Joseph and he scored at an instructional level for word identification as measured by Total Accuracy. He also scored at an instructional level for comprehension. The teacher next asked a more relaxed Joseph to read the third-grade selection. The topic was also familiar to him as suggested by the concept-question task and Joseph again achieved at an instructional level for both word identification and comprehension. However, because both scores were close to the lower limits for an instructional level, the teacher did not attempt a fourth-grade passage. The teacher then helped Joseph to choose suitable text for literature study-group activities although she suggested somewhat easier text for independent reading.

Ann

Ann, a sixth-grader, qualified for placement in a Learning Disabilities program as a result of Multidisciplinary Team (M-Team) Staffing. Her school places such students in the regular classroom, supported by a learning-disabilities specialist. In social studies and science, the classroom teacher presents concepts orally and through demonstration. Then students read assigned texts at their level. Ann's reading level as indicated by standardized tests administered during the M-Team Staffing was 4.7. In order to determine which text would be most appropriate for Ann, the learning-disabilities specialist asked Ann to read the third-grade passage "Wool: From Sheep to You." The concept-question task indicated that this was unfamiliar to Ann, however, this did not concern the specialist who realized that Ann would be required to read much unfamiliar content during the school year. Ann scored at an instructional level for both word identification and comprehension. The specialist then asked Ann to read a fourth-grade passage, "The City of Cahokia," another unfamiliar selection. Ann scored at an instructional level for word identification but placed at a frustration level for comprehension. Accordingly, the specialist gave Ann third-grade textbooks.

Using the *QRI*–II for Reading Portfolios

Juanita

Juanita is a fifth-grade student whose classroom teacher uses reading portfolios as a key component of his student assessment. At the beginning of the first semester, the teacher asked all students in the class to silently read the fifth-grade expository passage, "The Octopus." Without looking back at the passage, they wrote down what they recalled and answered the questions. The teacher then scored the written recall and questions according to the protocol sheets provided in the *QRI*–II. Juanita scored at a frustration level for comprehension and her recall was both sparse and inaccurate. The teacher then asked Juanita and other children like her who demonstrated poor comprehension to read the passage again. Each child orally read "The Octopus" individually to the teacher who scored their word-identification according to Total Accuracy. Juanita scored at an instructional level for word identification. The teacher then shared the protocols with Juanita and they discussed her strengths and needs. Juanita and her teacher decided that her goals for the coming semester would be to work on recalling main ideas and locating text cues to inference questions. The protocols, together with the teacher's and Juanita's notes from the conference, were dated and placed in her portfolio.

The teacher held conferences with Juanita's classmates in a similar fashion. He asked those whose word identification was below fifth grade to read easier passages until he located their word-identification instructional level. He then assessed their comprehension of this text. The teacher used his findings to set instructional objectives not only for individuals but also for the entire class.

After a semester of effort, Juanita again read "The Octopus" silently, wrote down her recall and answered the questions. Her recall was much more complete and her ability to answer questions placed her at an instructional level. Juanita's teacher asked her to also silently read another fifth-grade expository passage, "Getting Rid of Trash," and she performed similarly. Both Juanita and her teacher were pleased with her progress. All protocols were dated, clipped to the original set, and placed in Juanita's portfolio along with Juanita's own analysis of her efforts and progress.

LaKendra

LaKendra is a first-grader whose teacher used the *QRI*–II to maintain an ongoing record of LaKendra's developing word identification skills. At the beginning of the year, LaKendra read the pre-primer word list. Her protocol was scored, dated and placed in her portfolio. At that time, LaKendra knew only four words and scored at the frustration level.

LaKendra's teacher administered the pre-primer list on two other occasions during the first three months of first grade. When LaKendra approached an instructional level, her teacher asked her to read the pre-primer text with pictures, "Just Like Mom." LaKendra scored at a low instructional level (90%) for word identification. When asked to read the text without pictures, "Lost and Found," LaKendra met frustration.

LaKendra's teacher administered "Just Like Mom" and "Lost and Found" two additional times. By January, LaKendra had achieved a solid instructional level for word identification on pre-primer text with and without pictures. Her teacher then moved into primer level text and repeated the process. LaKendra's teacher placed all protocols, suitably dated, in LaKendra's portfolio along with other oral reading samples and observational comments. She used these to choose classroom reading activities for LaKendra, to fill out her progress report and to discuss her growth as a reader with her parents during conference times.

Using the *QRI*–II for Planning Intervention Instruction

Michelle

Michelle, a third-grader, was referred to the school reading specialist. Her teacher described Michelle as a capable decoder and a fluent, expressive oral reader. School records indicated that Michelle had done well in first and second grade. However, during the first semester of third grade, she began to experience difficulties. Although she was in the average reading group, her performance in reading class was inconsistent and her achievement in science and social studies activities was poor.

Word Identification

How Accurate Is the Student in Identifying Words? Because the reading specialist knew Michelle's present reading group placement and because she was described as a capable decoder and fluent oral reader, the *QRI*–II word lists were not administered either to evaluate word-identification ability or to suggest a starting point for passage administration. In order to ensure that Michelle met with initial success, the examiner first asked her to read a second-grade familiar narrative. She scored at an independent level for both word identification and comprehension. The examiner then asked Michelle to read the third-grade narrative "The Trip to the Zoo." The concept task indicated that this was a very familiar topic to Michelle. Michelle scored at an instructional level for word identification and comprehension.

How Automatic Is the Student in Identifying Words? On both the second- and third-grade passages, Michelle's oral reading rate was acceptable. She read both fluently and expressively suggesting that, at her level, automaticity of word identification was not a problem.

What Strategies for Word Identification Are Used by the Student? Michelle scored at a third-grade instructional level for word-identification. Because word identification accuracy did not seem to be a problem, the examiner chose not to analyze Michelle's miscues.

Is There a Difference Between a Student's Ability to Identify Words in Isolation and Words in Context? Again, because word identification was not a problem for Michelle, the examiner chose to ignore this question.

Comprehension

Which Types of Text Can the Student Handle Most Successfully? The examiner then asked Michelle to read a third-grade expository passage orally. The passage "Cats: Lions and Tigers in Your House," dealt with concepts familiar to Michelle. While Michelle's word-identification score placed her in the instructional range, she scored at a frustration level for comprehension. This suggested to the examiner that Michelle's problems might rest in the area of expository text.

Which Modes of Reading Represent a Strength for the Student? The examiner chose to verify Michelle's third-grade instructional level in silent-reading thinking that her problem might be due to poor silent reading strategies. However, Michelle silently read a familiar passage, "The Surprise," with acceptable rate and scored at an instructional level for comprehension.

How Does the Student Perform in Familiar and Unfamiliar Text? The examiner asked Michelle to orally read the third-grade passage "Wool." The concept-question task suggested that this represented an unfamiliar topic for Michelle. Again, her word-identification score was acceptable, but her comprehension score placed her at a frustration level.

Summary The results of the QRI–II suggest that Michelle is indeed a capable decoder and does not require any supportive instruction in this area. In addition, Michelle is able to comprehend familiar narrative text and there are no major differences in her ability to understand following oral or silent reading, However, Michelle experiences some difficulty in dealing with expository material and unfamiliar content at her grade level. As a result, Michelle may perform at a higher level in narrative reading than in content-area texts, and her inconsistent performance in class activities may be due to the structure of the specific selections. The results of the assessment suggest that Michelle could profit from supportive instruction in reading and understanding both expository and unfamiliar text.

Alex

Alex, a sixth-grader, was evaluated through M-Team Staffing. Norm-referenced instruments placed him at a low fourth-grade level for both word identification and comprehension. As a result, Alex qualified for Exceptional Educational Placement. The reading-assessment specialist administered portions of the QRI–II to plan a program of instruction for Alex.

Word Identification

How Accurate Is the Student in Identifying Words? The examiner chose to administer several word lists in order to determine strengths and needs in word identification. He presented the third- through fifth-grade lists. While Alex scored at a fourth-grade instructional level for the number of total words identified correctly, he met frustration with the fifth-grade list.

The examiner asked Alex to orally read a third-grade passage, "The Trip to the Zoo." The concept task indicated that a class trip was a familiar topic to Alex. He scored at an instructional level for both word identification and comprehension. However, when asked to read another familiar narrative, the fourth-grade "Johnny Appleseed," Alex met frustration for word identification and comprehension. This suggested to the examiner that the norm-referenced instruments previously administered had somewhat exaggerated Alex's reading level and that he should be provided with text at a difficulty level lower than fourth grade.

How Automatic Is the Student in Identifying Words? The examiner counted the number of words on the word lists that Alex identified automatically (that is, within one second). On all lists, Alex reached a frustration level if only automatic pronunciations were counted. In addition, Alex orally read the passages at an extremely slow rate, averaging 43 words per minute. All of this suggested to the examiner that Alex was still laboriously decoding every word and had not developed a workable sight vocabulary. Intervention instruction would need to focus upon activities to develop word-identification automaticity.

What Strategies for Word Identification Are Used by the Student? The examiner chose not to formally analyze Alex's miscues, although he noted an absence of self-corrections, which might suggest that attention to word identification was preventing Alex from attending to meaning.

Is There a Difference Between a Student's Ability to Identify Words in Isolation and Words in Context? The examiner noted that Alex scored at a higher instructional level on the isolated word lists than when reading the passage. Several words correctly identified on the fourth-grade list were mispronounced by Alex as he read "Johnny Appleseed." This pattern is not typical; many poor readers do better when reading passages as they utilize the context to help them identify unfamiliar words. Alex, however, seemed threatened by print. He commented several times about the length of the passages. This, coupled with his extremely slow rate, probably prevented Alex from effectively using context. The examiner noted that Alex's instructional intervention should center around passage reading, starting with short segments and gradually moving to those of increasing length.

Which Types of Text Can the Student Handle Most Successfully? Because Alex is a sixth-grader who will be mainstreamed for some content classes, the examiner asked him to read orally the third-grade expository passage, "Cats." The examiner felt it was necessary to determine any possible weakness in expository text inasmuch as Alex would be required to read much material of this type. Alex scored at a third-grade instructional level, the same attained when reading narrative text. This suggested that text structure was not a primary problem.

What Modes of Reading Represent a Strength for the Student? The examiner asked Alex to silently read a third-grade familiar passage, "The Surprise." He read it very quickly with a rate almost triple that of his oral reading rate. He met frustration for comprehension and was able to answer only two explicit questions. This suggested to the examiner that Alex was not really reading the passage but simply running his eyes over the page. Therefore, activities to ease Alex into silent reading were marked as a focus for instruction.

How Does the Student Perform in Familiar and Unfamiliar Text? Alex was not asked to read any unfamiliar text. He tired easily and asked repeatedly, "Aren't we done yet?" The examiner felt that any reading of unfamiliar text would not represent a valid assessment.

Summary As a result of the evaluation, the examiner identified several areas for instructional emphasis. Alex needs to develop accuracy in identifying words at higher levels of difficulty. Along with this, it is important that he become more automatic at word identification. Alex's intervention program should also stress silent reading as opposed to oral reading and avoid isolated word activities in favor of reading authentic passages.

Peter

Peter is in the second half of third grade. He was referred for M-Team Staffing assessment by his teacher who described him as "persistent and cooperative, but clearly the worst reader in the class." Peter had experienced reading difficulties since first grade and his parents had provided private tutoring to supplement the regular classroom instruction. As part of the M-Team, the reading-assessment specialist evaluated Peter's reading ability.

Word Identification

How Accurate Is the Student in Identifying Words? The examiner asked Peter to read the pre-primer word list and he scored at an instructional level. He achieved the same level on the primer list although, with a score of 70%, he was close to the cut-off. Peter met frustration with the first-grade words recognizing barely half of them.

The examiner asked Peter to read the pre-primer narrative passage without pictures, "Lost and Found." He scored at an instructional level for word identification. Peter offered a complete and accurate recall and achieved an instructional level for comprehension. Because he was so close to a frustration level on the primer list, the examiner then asked Peter to orally read the primer passage with pictures, "The Pig Who Learned to Read." Peter scored at an instructional level for word identification and comprehension. His recall, again complete, contained elements obviously drawn from the accompanying pictures. When asked to read the primer text without pictures, "The Trip," Peter's recall was sparse. He scored at a frustration level for word identification but at an instructional level for comprehension. The words he was able to identify carried enough of the text content for Peter to offer adequate answers to the questions. The examiner asked Peter to read the first-grade text with pictures, "The Bear and the Rabbit." Peter had so much difficulty and became so upset that the examiner stopped half way through the passage. The examiner noted that Peter was most comfortable identifying words at a pre-primer level but could handle primer text if given additional support such as pictures.

How Automatic Is the Student in Identifying Words? On the words lists, there was little difference between the total number of words identified correctly and the number of words pronounced automatically. When Peter knew a word, he seemed to know it automatically. However, when reading the passages, Peter's rate was very slow, fluctuating between 15–30 words per minute. Peter seemed very concerned about accurate pronunciation. Several times, he asked, "Did I say all the words right?" He also tended to pause quite a bit in order to check the accuracy of previously pronounced words and this obviously affected his rate.

What Strategies for Word Identification Are Used by the Student? The examiner formally analyzed Peter's miscues. The majority were graphically similar in the initial and final positions indicating that Peter was paying attention to letter–sound matching and word endings such as "ing" and "ed." However, there were few self-corrections or semantically acceptable miscues. Peter either knew the word or he didn't. If he didn't, he attempted to decode but usually ended with a nonword substitution or the substitution of a real word with similar beginning and ending letters such as "liked" for "looked." Peter clearly needs some workable strategies for identifying unfamiliar words and checking that the resulting pronunciation makes sense within the context of the passage.

Is There a Difference in the Student's Ability to Identify Words in Isolation and Words in Context? No difference was noted. Peter scored at the same level for both the word lists and the passages.

Comprehension

Which Types of Text Can the Student Handle Most Successfully? Peter was only asked to read narrative passages; however, they were presented with and without pictures. Peter was more successful with pictured text at the primer level, suggesting use of context. However, at the first-grade level, he met too many unfamiliar words, and pictures were of no help. This suggests that Peter can use contextual clues in those situations in which he can successfully identify most of the words.

Which Mode of Reading Represents a Strength for the Student? Because of Peter's low instructional level, he was not asked to read silently.

How Does the Student Perform on Familiar and Unfamiliar Text? Peter was not asked to read unfamiliar text, again because of his low reading level.

Summary Peter is an almost fourth-grader who is most comfortable at a pre-primer level but who can handle primer text if given pictorial support. His primary problem is that of word identification accuracy. When Peter knows a word, he pronounces it quickly. However, when meeting an unknown word, he lacks strategies for identifying the word or checking its semantic acceptability.

Jamie

Jamie was referred to a private Reading Clinic for evaluation of his reading ability. He had always experienced problems in school, and he had been retained in second grade. Presently a fifth-grader, Jamie had been tested several times for Exceptional Educational Placement but had never qualified. His parents intended to place him in another school and they wanted a complete evaluation of his reading to be part of his records. Figure 14.1 presents a summary of the results.

Word Identification

How Accurate Is the Student in Identifying Words? The reading-assessment specialist knew from information provided by Jamie's present school that he was reading at a third-grade level. The examiner asked Jamie to read the third-grade word list and he scored at an instructional level. He met frustration on the fourth-grade list but, with a score of 65%, was close to the cut-off. On the fifth-grade list, Jamie met frustration.

The examiner chose a third-grade familiar passage, "A Trip to the Zoo," for Jamie to read orally. He scored at an instructional level for word identification. On the fourth-grade passage, "Amelia Earhart," he also scored at an instructional level but met frustration for word identification on the fifth-grade "Christopher Columbus." Both the word lists and the passages suggest that Jamie's ability to accurately identify words is at a fourth-grade instructional level.

How Automatic Is the Student in Identifying Words? On the word lists, no differences were evident between the total number of words pronounced correctly and those pronounced automatically. Both seemed to present a weakness for Jamie. Jamie's rate on the passages ranged from 50–60 words per minute. He tended to read in a deliberate and monotone fashion, suggesting that his primary attention was directed toward word identification.

What Strategies for Word Identification Are Used by the Student? The examiner analyzed Jamie's miscues both at an instructional level (Figure 14.2) and at a frustration level (Figure 14.3). She chose to analyze miscues made on "The Trip to the Zoo" and "Amelia Earhart" as representative of a clear instructional level. Miscues made on "Christopher Columbus" reflected a clear frustration level. At an instructional level, 37% of Jamie's miscues were graphically similar in the initial position and 22% in the final position. Forty one percent were semantically acceptable and he self-corrected 19%. In frustration text, 68%

FIGURE 14.1 Qualitative Reading Inventory–II

Student Profile Sheet

Name Jamie   Birthdate 11/12   Grade 5 (retained)

Sex M   Date of Test 11/8   Examiner YC

Word Recognition

Grade	3	4	5						
Level/% Automatic	70 ins	55 fr	25 fr						
Level/% Total	85 ins	65 fr	40 fr						

Oral Reading

Passage Name	200	Amelia	Columbus		Beavers				
Readability Level	3	4	5		4				
Passage Type	N	N	N		E				
Level/% Total Accuracy	95 ins	95 ins	88 fr		95 ins				
Level/% Total Acceptability	96 ins	98 ins	91 fr		97 ins				
Familiar/Unfamiliar	f	f	f		f				
# Explicit Correct	4	4	3		2				
# Implicit Correct	3	3	2		0				
Level/% Comprehension	88 ins	75 ins	63 fr		25 fr				
Rate									
Total Passage Level	ins	ins	fr		fr				

Silent Reading

Passage Name	John A								
Readability Level	4								
Passage Type	N								
Familiar/Unfamiliar	f								
# Correct Explicit	3								
# Correct Implicit	2								
Level/% Comprehension	fr								
Rate									

FIGURE 14.2 Miscue Analysis Worksheet

Subject **Jamie**   Level of Miscues: Independent / **Instructional**   Frustrational

MISCUE	TEXT	GRAPHICALLY SIMILAR Initial	Final	Semantically Acceptable	Self-Corrected
class	classes	✓	✓		
then	when		✓		✓
grade	graders	✓		✓	
lots	lot	✓		✓	
teacher	teachers	✓		✓	
was	—				✓
Lopzek	Lopez	✓		✓	
into					
Mary	Maria	✓			✓
they	she				
—	that			✓	
—	of				
the	—			✓	
place	pace	✓	✓		✓
the	his			✓	
pioneer	pioneer	✓	✓		
—	too			✓	
ocean	—			✓	
do	be				
—	also			✓	
fly	flying	✓			
she	—				
also	as				
Column Total Total Miscues Column Total / Total Miscues = %		___ ___ ___	___ ___ ___	___ ___ ___	___ ___ ___

FIGURE 14.2 (Cont.) **Miscue Analysis Worksheet**

Subject _Jamie (cont.)_   **Level of Miscues:**   Independent / (Instructional)   **Frustrational**

MISCUE	TEXT	GRAPHICALLY SIMILAR Initial	Final	Semantically Acceptable	Self-Corrected
frightened	frightening	✓			
to	it				
fault	failure				✓
—	ocean			✓	
Column Total Total Miscues Column Total / Total Miscues = %		10 27 37%	6 27 22%	11 27 41%	5 27 19%

FIGURE 14.3 Miscue Analysis Worksheet

Subject _Jamie_   Level of Miscues: Independent/Instructional   (Frustrational)

MISCUE	TEXT	GRAPHICALLY SIMILAR Initial	Final	Semantically Acceptable	Self-Corrected
a	—				
determinded	determined	✓	✓		
—	an				
rou tee	route	✓	✓		
Indians	Indies	✓	✓		
was	world	✓			
for time	fortune	✓			
thor ree	theory	✓	✓		
—	the			✓	
me rit	merit	✓	✓		
careful	costly	✓			
fin ence	finance	✓	✓		
ex pen sion	expedition	✓	✓		
soap lies	supplies	✓	✓		
it	in	✓			✓
explored	unexplored	✓	✓		
solers	sailers	✓	✓		
the	—			✓	
—	too				
—	so				
mutter	mutiny	✓			
were	had				✓
finis shed	finished	✓	✓		
Column Total Total Miscues Column Total / Total Miscues = %		___ ___ ___	___ ___ ___	___ ___ ___	___ ___ ___

FIGURE 14.3 (Cont.)   Miscue Analysis Worksheet

Subject _Jamie (cont.)_   Level of Miscues: Independent/Instructional   (Frustrational)

MISCUE	TEXT	GRAPHICALLY SIMILAR Initial	Final	Semantically Acceptable	Self-Corrected
vorge	voyage	✓	✓		
—	he			✓	
treatened	threatened	✓	✓		
the jurney	—			✓	
front	farther	✓			✓
wel come	welcome	✓	✓		
clumed	claimed	✓	✓		
it	—			✓	
inhabitats	inhabitants	✓	✓		
the	he		✓		
men	mistakenly	✓			
rote	route	✓	✓		
of	—				
died	did	✓	✓		
Indians	Indies	✓	✓		
Column Total		26	20	5	5
Total Miscues		38	38	38	38
Column Total / Total Miscues = %		68%	53%	13%	8%

of Jamie's miscues were similar in the initial position and 56% in the final position. Thirteen percent were semantically acceptable and he only self-corrected 8%. When Jamie meets unfamiliar text, his primary strategy is to decode phonetically. Unfortunately, he does not check that the resulting pronunciation makes sense either as an actual word or in the context of the passage.

Is There a Difference Between a Student's Ability to Identify Words in Isolation and Words in Context? No differences were noted.

Comprehension

Which Types of Text Can the Student Handle Most Successfully? The examiner asked Jamie to read three narratives: "The Trip to the Zoo," "Amelia Earhart," and "Christopher Columbus." Jamie scored at an instructional level for both word identification and comprehension for the third- and fourth-grade texts. However, his retelling was extremely sparse and reflected only a few isolated ideas offered in a nonsequential manner. The examiner also asked Jamie to read the fourth-grade expository passage, "The Busy Beaver." Although Jamie achieved an instructional level for word identification, he met frustration for comprehension. This suggests that expository text may present more of a problem for Jamie than narrative.

Which Modes of Reading Represent a Strength for the Student? Jamie was asked to read the fourth-grade passage, "Johnny Appleseed," silently. He scored at the frustration level for comprehension, suggesting that silent reading may also pose a problem for Jamie.

How Does the Student Perform on Familiar and Unfamiliar Text? The examiner administered the concept-question task for "Sequoyah" and "The City of Cahokia." She had hoped that "Sequoyah" would prove unfamiliar to Jamie, so she could assess his ability to handle unfamiliar material in a narrative structure. Because Jamie seemed more comfortable with a narrative format, this would allow her to assess the effect of topic unfamiliarity upon word identification and comprehension. Unfortunately, Jamie had just completed a unit on Native Americans in social studies and he knew quite a bit about Sequoyah and the Cherokee nation. The concept task indicated that Cahokia was unfamiliar. However, because Jamie had experienced difficulty with expository structure in familiar text, that examiner did not feel that poor performance could be ascribed to lack of topic knowledge. Jamie was growing tired so the examiner ended the session.

Summary Jamie needs instruction in several areas. Word-identification accuracy was at a fourth-grade level, two years below Jamie's chronological grade placement if his retention in second grade is taken into account. His primary strategy for identifying unfamiliar words is to attempt to decode phonetically. Because he pays little attention to the resulting meaning, this practice does not work well for him. Jamie's slow reading rate suggests that he has not developed automaticity of word identification but, instead, is still decoding words he has met many times previously.

Jamie's ability to comprehend familiar narrative text is also two years below his grade placement with some problems suggested in silent reading. Expository text seems to present another problem for Jamie.

The examiner suggested a program centered around silent reading of expository text. In addition, she suggested instruction in word-identification strategies The examiner also recommended that Jamie engage in much silent reading of easy text in order to develop automaticity in word identification. Repeated reading of text was also suggested as a way of building reading fluency.

15 Test Materials

Subject Word Lists

Examiner Word Lists

Pre-Primer Level Passages

Lost and Found
Just Like Mom
People at Work
Examiner Copies

Primer Level Passages

A Trip
The Pig Who Learned to Read
Who Lives Near Lakes?
Living and Not Living
Examiner Copies

Level One Passages

Mouse in a House
The Bear and the Rabbit
Air
What You Eat
Examiner Copies

Level Two Passages

What Can I Get for My Toy?
Father's New Game
Whales and Fish
Seasons
Examiner Copies

Level Three Passages

The Trip to the Zoo
The Surprise
The Friend
Cats: Lions and Tigers in Your House
Where Do People Live?
Wool: From Sheep to You
Examiner Copies

Level Four Passages

Johnny Appleseed
Amelia Earheart
Sequoyah
The Busy Beaver
Saudi Arabia
The City of Cahokia
Examiner Copies

Level Five Passages

Martin Luther King, Jr.
Christopher Columbus
Margaret Mead
The Octopus
Getting Rid of Trash
Laser Light
Examiner Copies

Level Six Passages

Pele
Abraham Lincoln
Andrew Carnegie
Computers
Predicting Earthquakes
Ultrasound
Examiner Copies

Junior High Passages

Lewis and Clark
Ferdinand Magellan
Peter the Great
Fireworks
Diamonds
The City of Constantine
Examiner Copies

Subject Word List

can	mother
just	need
I	them
work	what
write	children
at	thing
with	was
my	animal
he	they
too	were
the	saw
in	want
she	every
other	went
make	like
place	from
go	said
to	live
many	comes
do	take

bear	morning
father	toy
find	room
rabbit	old
friend	trade
song	promise
thought	pieces
there	hatch
run	push
then	though
move	begins
group	food
eat	light
air	ends
bread	clue
have	breathe
wind	insects
get	weather
put	noticed
looked	money

Subject Word List

lunch	escape	attend
special	desert	protest
believe	crop	movement
claws	islands	sailor
lion	chief	month
rough	mounds	threatened
wear	busy	continue
tongue	pond	tales
crowded	signs	creature
wool	ocean	wavelengths
removed	pilot	laser
curious	fame	focuses
sheep	precious	arrested
electric	settlers	poison
worried	guarded	route
enemies	passenger	convince
hid	boundaries	giant
clothing	communicate	pollution
swim	adventurer	aluminum
entrance	invented	finance

sewed	commissioned
controlled	arduous
championships	tumultuous
messenger	navigated
fortune	straits
memories	initiated
abolish	skirmish
earthquake	laboriously
volunteers	reluctant
machines	sovereign
businesses	crucial
shrinking	tsar
research	parliament
abdomen	majestic
slavery	rebellion
howled	ammonium
homogenized	reign
connection	emperor
fashioned	meticulous
behavior	mantle

Examiner Word Lists

Pre-primer

	Identified Automatically	Identified
1. can	_____	_____
2. just	_____	_____
3. I	_____	_____
4. work	_____	_____
5. write	_____	_____
6. at	_____	_____
7. with	_____	_____
8. my	_____	_____
9. he	_____	_____
10. too	_____	_____
11. the	_____	_____
12. in	_____	_____
13. she	_____	_____
14. other	_____	_____
15. make	_____	_____
16. place	_____	_____
17. go	_____	_____
18. to	_____	_____
19. many	_____	_____
20. do	_____	_____

Total Correct Automatic _____ /20 = _____ %

Total Correct Identified _____ /20 = _____ %

Total Number Correct _____ /20 = _____ %

Primer

	Identified Automatically	Identified
1. mother	_____	_____
2. need	_____	_____
3. them	_____	_____
4. what	_____	_____
5. children	_____	_____
6. thing	_____	_____
7. was	_____	_____
8. animal	_____	_____
9. they	_____	_____
10. were	_____	_____
11. saw	_____	_____
12. want	_____	_____
13. every	_____	_____
14. went	_____	_____
15. like	_____	_____
16. from	_____	_____
17. said	_____	_____
18. live	_____	_____
19. comes	_____	_____
20. take	_____	_____

Total Correct Automatic _____ /20 = _____ %

Total Correct Identified _____ /20 = _____ %

Total Number Correct _____ /20 = _____ %

LEVELS		
Independent	Instructional	Frustration
18–20	14–17	below 14
90–100%	70–85%	below 70%

Examiner Word Lists

First

	Identified Automatically	Identified
1. bear	_____	_____
2. father	_____	_____
3. find	_____	_____
4. rabbit	_____	_____
5. friend	_____	_____
6. song	_____	_____
7. thought	_____	_____
8. there	_____	_____
9. run	_____	_____
10. then	_____	_____
11. move	_____	_____
12. group	_____	_____
13. eat	_____	_____
14. air	_____	_____
15. bread	_____	_____
16. have	_____	_____
17. wind	_____	_____
18. get	_____	_____
19. put	_____	_____
20. looked	_____	_____

Second

	Identified Automatically	Identified
1. morning	_____	_____
2. toy	_____	_____
3. room	_____	_____
4. old	_____	_____
5. trade	_____	_____
6. promise	_____	_____
7. pieces	_____	_____
8. hatch	_____	_____
9. push	_____	_____
10. though	_____	_____
11. begins	_____	_____
12. food	_____	_____
13. light	_____	_____
14. ends	_____	_____
15. clue	_____	_____
16. breathe	_____	_____
17. insects	_____	_____
18. weather	_____	_____
19. noticed	_____	_____
20. money	_____	_____

First

Total Correct Automatic _____ /20 = _____ %

Total Correct Identified _____ /20 = _____ %

Total Number Correct _____ /20 = _____ %

Second

Total Correct Automatic _____ /20 = _____ %

Total Correct Identified _____ /20 = _____ %

Total Number Correct _____ /20 = _____ %

LEVELS		
Independent	Instructional	Frustration
18–20	14–17	below 14
90–100%	70–85%	below 70%

Examiner Word Lists

Third

	Identified Automatically	Identified
1. lunch	_____	_____
2. special	_____	_____
3. believe	_____	_____
4. claws	_____	_____
5. lion	_____	_____
6. rough	_____	_____
7. wear	_____	_____
8. tongue	_____	_____
9. crowded	_____	_____
10. wool	_____	_____
11. removed	_____	_____
12. curious	_____	_____
13. sheep	_____	_____
14. electric	_____	_____
15. worried	_____	_____
16. enemies	_____	_____
17. hid	_____	_____
18. clothing	_____	_____
19. swim	_____	_____
20. entrance	_____	_____

Total Correct Automatic _____ /20 = _____ %

Total Correct Identified _____ /20 = _____ %

Total Number Correct _____ /20 = _____ %

Fourth

	Identified Automatically	Identified
1. escape	_____	_____
2. desert	_____	_____
3. crop	_____	_____
4. islands	_____	_____
5. chief	_____	_____
6. mounds	_____	_____
7. busy	_____	_____
8. pond	_____	_____
9. signs	_____	_____
10. ocean	_____	_____
11. pilot	_____	_____
12. fame	_____	_____
13. precious	_____	_____
14. settlers	_____	_____
15. guarded	_____	_____
16. passenger	_____	_____
17. boundaries	_____	_____
18. communicate	_____	_____
19. adventurer	_____	_____
20. invented	_____	_____

Total Correct Automatic _____ /20 = _____ %

Total Correct Identified _____ /20 = _____ %

Total Number Correct _____ /20 = _____ %

LEVELS		
Independent	Instructional	Frustration
18–20	14–17	below 14
90–100%	70–85%	below 70%

Examiner Word Lists

Fifth

	Identified Automatically	Identified
1. attend	_____	_____
2. protest	_____	_____
3. movement	_____	_____
4. sailor	_____	_____
5. month	_____	_____
6. threatened	_____	_____
7. continue	_____	_____
8. tales	_____	_____
9. creature	_____	_____
10. wavelengths	_____	_____
11. laser	_____	_____
12. focuses	_____	_____
13. arrested	_____	_____
14. poison	_____	_____
15. route	_____	_____
16. convince	_____	_____
17. giant	_____	_____
18. pollution	_____	_____
19. aluminum	_____	_____
20. finance	_____	_____

Total Correct Automatic _____ /20 = _____ %

Total Correct Identified _____ /20 = _____ %

Total Number Correct _____ /20 = _____ %

Sixth

	Identified Automatically	Identified
1. sewed	_____	_____
2. controlled	_____	_____
3. championships	_____	_____
4. messenger	_____	_____
5. fortune	_____	_____
6. memories	_____	_____
7. abolish	_____	_____
8. earthquake	_____	_____
9. volunteers	_____	_____
10. machines	_____	_____
11. businesses	_____	_____
12. shrinking	_____	_____
13. research	_____	_____
14. abdomen	_____	_____
15. slavery	_____	_____
16. howled	_____	_____
17. homogenized	_____	_____
18. connection	_____	_____
19. fashioned	_____	_____
20. behavior	_____	_____

Total Correct Automatic _____ /20 = _____ %

Total Correct Identified _____ /20 = _____ %

Total Number Correct _____ /20 = _____ %

LEVELS		
Independent	Instructional	Frustration
18–20	14–17	below 14
90–100%	70–85%	below 70%

Examiner Word Lists

Junior High

	Identified Automatically	Identified
1. commissioned	_____	_____
2. arduous	_____	_____
3. tumultuous	_____	_____
4. navigated	_____	_____
5. straits	_____	_____
6. initiated	_____	_____
7. skirmish	_____	_____
8. laboriously	_____	_____
9. reluctant	_____	_____
10. sovereign	_____	_____
11. crucial	_____	_____
12. tsar	_____	_____
13. parliament	_____	_____
14. majestic	_____	_____
15. rebellion	_____	_____
16. ammonium	_____	_____
17. reign	_____	_____
18. emperor	_____	_____
19. meticulous	_____	_____
20. mantle	_____	_____

Total Correct Automatic _____ /20 = _____ %

Total Correct Identified _____ /20 = _____ %

Total Number Correct _____ /20 = _____ %

LEVELS		
Independent	Instructional	Frustration
18–20	14–17	below 14
90–100%	70–85%	below 70%

Lost and Found

I lost my cat.

Where was she?

I looked inside the house.

I looked under the bed.

I looked outside too.

I lost my dog.

Where was he?

I looked inside the house.

I looked under the bed.

I looked outside too.

I found my cat.

I found my dog.

Where were they?

They were in the same place.

They were under the table.

Just Like Mom

I can write.

Just like Mom.

I can read.

Just like Mom.

I can go to work.

Just like Mom.

I can work at home.

Just like Mom.

I can work with numbers.

Just like Mom.

I can do lots of things.

Just like Mom.

People at Work

Some people work at home.

Other people go to work.

Why do people work?

People work to make money.

People work at many things.

Some people write at work.

Other people read at work.

Some people make things at work.

Other people sell things at work.

People work together.

Level: Pre-primer

Narrative

Concept Questions:

What does it mean when something is lost?

_____

_____

_____ (3-2-1-0)

What does it mean when something is found?

_____

_____

_____ (3-2-1-0)

What does "looking for something" mean to you?

_____

_____

_____ (3-2-1-0)

Score: _____ /9 = _____ %

_____ FAM _____ UNFAM

Prediction:

_____

_____

Lost and Found

I lost my cat.

Where was she?

I looked inside the house.

I looked under the bed.

I looked outside too.

I lost my dog.

Where was he?

I looked inside the house.

I looked under the bed.

I looked outside too.

I found my cat.

I found my dog.

Where were they?

They were in the same place.

They were under the table. (64 words)

Number of Total Miscues
(Total Accuracy): _____

Number of Meaning Change Miscues
(Total Acceptability): _____

Total Accuracy			Total Acceptability
0–1 miscue	_____	Independent	_____ 0–1 miscue
2–6 miscues	_____	Instructional	_____ 2–3 miscues
7+ miscues	_____	Frustration	_____ 4+ miscues

Rate: 64 x 60/ _____ seconds = _____ WPM

Retelling Scoring Sheet for Lost and Found

Events

_____ I lost my cat.
_____ Where was she?
_____ I looked
_____ inside the house.

____ I looked
____ under the bed.
____ I looked
____ outside too.
____ I lost my dog.
____ Where was he?
____ I looked
____ inside the house.
____ I looked
____ under the bed.
____ I looked
____ outside too.
____ I found my cat.
____ I found my dog.
____ Where were they?
____ They were in the same place.
____ They were under the table.

Questions for Lost and Found

1. What did the person in the story lose?
   Explicit: cat or dog

2. What else did the person in the story lose?
   Explicit: cat or dog, depending upon the answer above.

3. Where did the person in the story look?
   Explicit: inside the house; under the bed; or outside

4. Where else did the person in the story look?
   Explicit: inside the house; under the bed; or outside, depending upon the answer above

5. Where did the person find the dog and cat?
   Explicit: in the same place or under the table

Number Correct Explicit: _____

Total: _____

_____ Independent: 5 correct

_____ Instructional: 4 correct

_____ Frustration: 0–3 correct

Narrative

Concept Questions:

What is a Mom?

_____

_____

_____ (3-2-1-0)

What does "working at home" mean to you?

_____

_____

_____ (3-2-1-0)

What does "going to work" mean to you?

_____

_____

_____ (3-2-1-0)

Score: _____ /9 = _____ %

_____ FAM _____ UNFAM

Prediction:

_____

_____

Just Like Mom

I can write.

Just like Mom.

I can read.

Just like Mom.

I can go to work.

Just like Mom.

I can work at home.

Just like Mom.

I can work with numbers.

Just like Mom.

I can do lots of things.

Just like Mom. (44 words)

Number of Total Miscues
(Total Accuracy): _____

Number of Meaning Change Miscues
(Total Acceptability): _____

Total Accuracy			Total Acceptability
0–1 miscue	_____	Independent _____	0–1 miscue
2–4 miscues	_____	Instructional _____	2 miscues
5+ miscues	_____	Frustration _____	3+ miscues

Rate: 44 x 60/ _____ seconds = _____ WPM

Retelling Scoring Sheet for Just Like Mom

____ I can write.
____ Just like Mom.
____ I can read.
____ Just like Mom.
____ I can go to work
____ Just like Mom.
____ I can work
____ at home.
____ Just like Mom.
____ I can work
____ with numbers.
____ Just like Mom.
____ I can do lots
____ of things.
____ Just like Mom.

Questions for Just Like Mom

Note: If a question is answered with direct reference to pictures as opposed to text, score the answer as implicitly correct.

1. Name one thing the girl can do just like Mom.
   Explicit: write or read
   Implicit: water the flowers, work with the numbers

2. Name another thing the girl can do just like Mom.
   Explicit: read or write, depending on the answer above
   Implicit: same as #1

3. What can the girl work with just like Mom?
   Explicit: numbers
   Implicit: pencils, paper

4. Where can the girl work just like Mom?
   Explicit: at home or she can go to work
   Implicit: in the garden

5. Where is another place the girl can work just like Mom?
   Explicit: at home or at her workplace, depending on the answer above
   Implicit: same as #4

Number Correct Explicit: _____

Number Correct Implicit
    (from pictures): _____

     Total: _____

_____ Independent: 5 correct

_____ Instructional: 4 correct

_____ Frustration: 0–3 correct

Level: Pre-primer

Expository

Concept Questions:

Where do people work?

_____

_____

_____ (3-2-1-0)

Why do people work?

_____

_____

_____ (3-2-1-0)

What are different kinds of jobs?

_____

_____

_____ (3-2-1-0)

Score: _____ /9 = _____ %

_____ FAM _____ UNFAM

Prediction:

_____

_____

People at Work

Some people work at home.

Other people go to work.

Why do people work?

People work to make money.

People work at many things.

Some people write at work.

Other people read at work.

Some people make things at work.

Other people sell things at work.

People work together. (49 words)

Number of Total Miscues
(Total Accuracy): _____

Number of Meaning Change Miscues
(Total Acceptability): _____

Total Accuracy		**Total Acceptability**
0–1 miscue	_____ Independent _____	0–1 miscue
2–5 miscues	_____ Instructional _____	2 miscues
6+ miscues	_____ Frustration _____	3+ miscues
Rate: 49 x 60/_____ seconds =	_____ WPM	

Retelling Scoring Sheet for People at Work

Details

____ Some people work
____ at home.
____ Other people go to work.
____ Why do people work?
____ People work to make money.
____ People work
____ at many things.
____ Some people write
____ at work.

Level: Pre-primer

____ Other people read
____ at work.
____ Some people make things
____ at work.
____ Other people sell things
____ at work.
____ People work
____ together.

Questions for People at Work

Note: If a question is answered with direct reference to pictures as opposed to text, score the answer as implicitly correct.

1. Where do people work?
   Explicit: at home or they go to work

2. What is one thing that people do at work?
   Explicit: write; read; make things; or sell things
   Implicit: fix things

3. What is another thing that people do at work?
   Explicit: write; read; make things; or sell things, depending on answer above
   Implicit: fix things

4. What is another thing that people do at work?
   Explicit: write; read; make things; or sell things, depending on answers to previous questions
   Implicit: fix things

5. What is another thing that people do at work?
   Explicit: write; read; make things; or sell things, depending on answers to previous questions
   Implicit: fix things

Number Correct Explicit: _____

Number Correct Implicit
(from pictures): _____

Total: _____

_____ Independent: 5 correct

_____ Instructional: 4 correct

_____ Frustration: 0–3 correct

A Trip

It was a warm spring day.

The children were going on a trip.

The trip was to a farm.

The children wanted to see many animals.

They wanted to write down all they saw.

They were going to make a book for their class.

On the way to the farm the bus broke down.

The children thought their trip was over.

Then a man stopped his car.

He helped to fix the bus.

The bus started again.

The children said, "Yea!"

The children got to the farm.

They saw a pig.

They saw a hen and cows.

They liked petting the kittens.

They learned about milking cows.

They liked the trip to the farm.

They wanted to go again.

The Pig Who Learned to Read

Once there was a pig.

His name was Pete.

He lived on a farm.

He was not like other pigs.

He was special.

He wanted to learn to read.

His father said, "But pigs can't read!"

"I don't care," said Pete.

"I want to read."

One day Pete went to a boy who lived on the farm.

"Teach me to read," he said.

The boy said, "But you're a pig. I don't know if I can.

But I'll do what my mother and father did with me."

Every night before bed the boy read to the pig.

The pig loved the stories.

He liked one called "Pat the Bunny" best.

A week later Pete asked to take the book to the barn.

He looked at the words.

He thought about what the boy had said.

He did that every day.

One day he read a story to the boy.

He was so happy!

After that he read to the other animals every night.

The boy was happy too because he'd taught his first pig to read.

Who Lives Near Lakes?

Many animals live near lakes.

Turtles sit on rocks.

They like to be in the sun.

You can see ducks near a lake.

There may be baby ducks.

The babies walk behind the mother duck.

There are fish in lakes.

You can see them when they jump out of the water.

People live near lakes too.

They like to see the animals.

Living and Not Living

Some things around us live.

Others are not living.

Things that live need air.

Things that live need food.

Things that live need water.

Things that live move and grow.

Animals are living things.

Plants are living things.

Is paper living?

No, but it comes from something living.

Paper comes from trees.

Is a wagon living?

No, it moves but it is not living.

Level: Primer

Narrative

A Trip

It was a warm spring day. The children were going on a trip. The trip was to a farm. The children wanted to see many animals. They wanted to write down all they saw. They were going to make a book for their class. On the way to the farm the bus broke down. The children thought their trip was over. Then a man stopped his car. He helped to fix the bus. The bus started again. The children said, "Yea!" The children got to the farm. They saw a pig. They saw a hen and cows. They liked petting the kittens. They learned about milking cows. They liked the trip to the farm. They wanted to go again. (119 words)

Number of Total Miscues
(Total Accuracy): _____

Number of Meaning Change Miscues
(Total Acceptability): _____

Total Accuracy		Total Acceptability
0–2 miscues _____ Independent	_____	0–2 miscues
3–12 miscues _____ Instructional	_____	3–6 miscues
13+ miscues _____ Frustration	_____	7+ miscues

Rate: 119 x 60/_____ seconds = _____ WPM

Retelling Scoring Sheet for A Trip

Setting/Background

_____ The children were going on a trip
_____ to a farm.

Goal

_____ The children wanted to see animals
_____ and write down all they saw.
_____ They were going to make a book
_____ for their class.

Level: Primer

Events

____ On the way
____ to the farm
____ the bus broke down.
____ A man stopped his car.
____ The man helped
____ to fix the bus.
____ The children got to the farm.
____ They saw a pig
____ a hen
____ and cows.
____ They liked
____ petting kittens.
____ They learned
____ about milking cows.

Resolution

____ They liked their trip
____ and wanted to go again.

Other ideas recalled, including inferences

_____

Questions for A Trip

1. Where were the children going?
   Explicit: on a trip to a farm

2. What did they want to see?
   Explicit: many animals; or names of at least two types of animals

3. Who do you think went with the children on the trip?
   Implicit: their teacher. If the child says, "Bus driver," ask, "Who else went with them besides the bus driver?"

4. What happened on the way to the farm?
   Explicit: the bus broke down

5. What would have happened *to their trip* if the man hadn't stopped his car?
   Implicit: they wouldn't have gotten to the farm, they got to the farm late

6. What did the children learn at the farm?
   Explicit: about getting milk from cows. If the child says "About cows," say, "What about cows?"

Number Correct Explicit: _____

Number Correct Implicit: _____

Total: _____

_____ Independent: 6 correct

_____ Instructional: 4–5 correct

_____ Frustration: 0–3 correct

Narrative

<table>
<tr><td colspan="2">

Concept Questions:

What is doing something new?

_____

_____

_____ (3-2-1-0)

What is learning to read?

_____

_____

_____ (3-2-1-0)

What does it mean when people read stories to you?

_____

_____

_____ (3-2-1-0)

Score: _____ /9 = _____ %

_____ FAM _____ UNFAM

Prediction:

_____

_____

</td></tr>
</table>

The Pig Who Learned to Read

Once there <u>was</u> a pig. His name <u>was</u> Pete. He lived on a farm. He <u>was</u> not <u>like</u> other pigs. He <u>was</u> special. He wanted to learn to read. His father <u>said</u>, "But pigs can't read!" "I don't care," <u>said</u> Pete. "I <u>want</u> to read."

One day Pete <u>went</u> to a boy who lived on the farm. "Teach me to read," he <u>said</u>. The boy <u>said</u>, "But you're a pig. I don't know if I can. But I'll do <u>what</u> my <u>mother</u> and father did with me." <u>Every</u> night before bed the boy read to the pig. The pig loved the stories. He liked one called "Pat the Bunny" best. A week later Pete asked to take the book to the barn. He looked at the words. He thought about <u>what</u> the boy had <u>said</u>. He did that <u>every</u> day. One day he read a story to the boy. He was so happy! After that he read to the other <u>animals</u> <u>every</u> night. The boy <u>was</u> happy too because he'd taught his first pig to read. (176 words)

<table>
<tr><td colspan="4">

Number of Total Miscues
(Total Accuracy): _____

Number of Meaning Change Miscues
(Total Acceptability): _____

</td></tr>
<tr><td colspan="2">**Total Accuracy**</td><td colspan="2">**Total Acceptability**</td></tr>
<tr><td>0–4 miscues</td><td>_____ Independent</td><td>_____</td><td>0–4 miscues</td></tr>
<tr><td>5–18 miscues</td><td>_____ Instructional</td><td>_____</td><td>5–9 miscues</td></tr>
<tr><td>19+ miscues</td><td>_____ Frustration</td><td>_____</td><td>10+ miscues</td></tr>
<tr><td colspan="4">Rate: 176 x 60/_____ seconds = _____ WPM</td></tr>
</table>

Retelling Scoring Sheet for The Pig Who Learned to Read

Background/Setting

____ There was a pig
____ named Pete.

Goal

____ He wanted to learn
____ to read.
____ His father said,
____ "Pigs can't read."
____ Pete said,
____ "I don't care."

Events

____ He went to a boy
____ who lived on a farm.
____ He said,
____ "Teach me
____ to read."
____ The boy said,
____ I'll do
____ what my mother
____ and father did.
____ Every night
____ before bed,
____ the boy read
____ to the pig.
____ The pig loved the stories.
____ Pete took the book
____ to the barn.
____ He looked at the words
____ every day.
____ One day
____ the pig read a story
____ to the boy.
____ He was so happy.

Resolution

____ He read
____ to the animals
____ every night.
____ The boy was happy.
____ He taught the pig
____ to read.

Other ideas recalled, including inferences

_____

Questions for The Pig Who Learned to Read

1. Who was this story about?
   Explicit: Pete the pig

2. What did Pete want?
   Explicit: to learn to read

3. What did Pete do to get what he wanted?
   Explicit: he asked the boy who lived on the farm to teach him

4. Why was the boy unsure he could teach the pig to read?
   Implicit: because pigs didn't learn to read *or* because the boy had never taught anyone to read before

5. What did the boy do to teach Pete to read?
   Explicit: he read to him every night

6. What did the pig do in order to learn how to read?
   Implicit: he matched the words with what the boy had said. He did that every day.

Number Correct Explicit: _____

Number Correct Implicit: _____

Total: _____

_____ Independent: 6 correct

_____ Instructional: 4–5 correct

_____ Frustration: 0–3 correct

Level: Primer

Expository

Concept Questions:

What are animals who live near lakes?

_____

_____

_____ (3-2-1-0)

When do you see turtles outside?

_____

_____

_____ (3-2-1-0)

Why do people live near lakes?

_____

_____

_____ (3-2-1-0)

Score: _____ /9 = _____ %

_____ FAM _____ UNFAM

Prediction:

_____

_____

Who <u>Lives</u> Near Lakes?

Many <u>animals</u> <u>live</u> near lakes.

Turtles sit on rocks.

<u>They</u> <u>like</u> to be in the sun.

You can see ducks near a lake.

There may be baby ducks.

The babies walk behind the <u>mother</u> duck.

There are fish in lakes.

You can see <u>them</u> when <u>they</u> jump out of the water.

People <u>live</u> near lakes too.

<u>They</u> <u>like</u> to see the <u>animals</u>. (62 words)

Number of Total Miscues
(Total Accuracy): _____

Number of Meaning Change Miscues
(Total Acceptability): _____

Total Accuracy		Total Acceptability
0–1 miscues _____	Independent	_____ 0–1 miscues
2–6 miscues _____	Instructional	_____ 2–4 miscues
7+ miscues _____	Frustration	_____ 5+ miscues

Rate: 62 x 60/ _____ seconds = _____ WPM

Retelling Scoring Sheet for Who Lives Near Lakes?

Main Idea

____ Many animals live
____ near lakes.

Details

____ Turtles sit
____ on rocks.
____ They like to be in the sun.
____ You can see ducks
____ near a lake.
____ There may be baby ducks.
____ The babies walk
____ behind the mother duck.
____ There are fish
____ in lakes.
____ You can see them
____ when they jump
____ out of the water.

Level: Primer

____ People live near lakes too.
____ They like
____ to see the animals.

Questions for Who Lives Near Lakes?

1. What did the passage say turtles sit on?
   Explicit: rocks

2. When would turtles sit on rocks?
   Implicit: when it is sunny

3. Where do baby ducks walk?
   Explicit: behind the mother duck

4. What other animal besides a turtle and ducks does the passage talk about?
   Explicit: fish

5. When can you see fish?
   Explicit: when they jump out of the water

6. Why do people live near lakes?
   Implicit: they like to see animals

Number Correct Explicit: _____

Number Correct Implicit: _____

Total: _____

_____ Independent: 6 correct

_____ Instructional: 4–5 correct

_____ Frustration: 0–3 correct

Level: Primer

Expository

Concept Questions:

What do plants need to grow?

_____

_____

_____ (3-2-1-0)

What do living things do?

_____

_____

_____ (3-2-1-0)

What are things that have never been alive?

_____

_____

_____ (3-2-1-0)

Score: _____ /9 = _____ %

_____ FAM _____ UNFAM

Prediction:

_____

_____

Living and Not Living

Some <u>things</u> around us <u>live</u>.

Others are not living.

Things that <u>live</u> <u>need</u> air.

Things that <u>live</u> <u>need</u> food.

Things that <u>live</u> <u>need</u> water.

Things that live move and grow.

Animals are living <u>things</u>.

Plants are living <u>things</u>.

Is paper living?

No, but it <u>comes</u> <u>from</u> something living.

Paper <u>comes</u> <u>from</u> trees.

Is a wagon living?

No, it moves but it is not living. (**64 words**)

Number of Total Miscues
(Total Accuracy): _____

Number of Meaning Change Miscues
(Total Acceptability): _____

Total Accuracy		Total Acceptability
0–1 miscues _____	Independent _____	0–1 miscues
2–6 miscues _____	Instructional _____	2–3 miscues
7+ miscues _____	Frustration _____	4+ miscues
Rate: 64 x 60/ _____ seconds =	_____ WPM	

Retelling Scoring Sheet for Living and Not Living

Main Idea

____ Some things live.
____ Others are not living.

Details

____ Things that live
____ need air,
____ food,
____ and water.
____ They move
____ and grow.
____ Animals are living.

Level: Primer

____ Plants are living.
____ Paper is not living.
____ It comes from something living.
____ It comes from trees.
____ Your wagon is not living.

Other ideas recalled, including inferences

_____

Questions for Living and Not Living

1. Name two things that living things need.
   Explicit: air, food, water

2. What do living things do?
   Explicit: move and grow

3. What two things did your reading say were living things?
   Explicit: animals and plants

4. What causes a plant to die?
   Implicit: it doesn't have food or water or air

5. What living thing does paper come from?
   Explicit: trees

6. Why isn't a wagon that moves a living thing?
   Implicit: it does not grow

Number Correct Explicit: _____

Number Correct Implicit: _____

Total: _____

_____ Independent: 6 correct

_____ Instructional: 4–5 correct

_____ Frustration: 0–3 correct

Mouse in a House

Once there was a mouse.

He lived in a wall of an old house.

Each night the mouse went to the kitchen.

He wanted to find something to eat.

The man who lived in the house heard the mouse.

He knew the mouse lived in the wall.

But he didn't mind.

Then one day the man decided to sell the house.

He loved the old house.

But it was too big.

He put an ad in the paper.

It said, "100-year-old house for sale.

Call 224-3414."

Many people called and wanted to visit the house.

Two people came on Sunday.

They walked up the old stairs.

When they got to the top, the mouse ran down the wall.

He ran up and down the inside of the wall.

Up and down.

The people heard the mouse.

They said, "We don't want the house."

The mouse was very happy.

He was afraid that new people would try to get rid of him.

Every time someone visited the house, the mouse would do the same thing.

He would run up and down the wall between the first and second floor.

Every time the people left without buying the house.

Then a family came to see the house.

The house was just the right size for them.

When they walked up the stairs, the mouse ran up and down the wall.

They heard him and said, "Oh you have a mouse.

We love the house so much we'll buy it mouse and all."

The Bear and the Rabbit

Once there was a very big bear.

He lived in the woods.

He was sad because he didn't have anyone to play with.

He said to his father, "How can I find a friend?"

His father said, "By being you."

"But all the animals are afraid of me," said the bear.

"I can't even get near them."

But one day the bear was sitting by a river.

He was singing softly to himself.

A rabbit lived near the river.

He looked out of his hole when he heard the bear's song.

He thought, "Anyone who sings like that must be nice.

Maybe I don't need to be afraid of him.

It would be nice to have a friend."

The rabbit went and got his horn.

Very softly he began to play.

His music went well with the bear's song.

The bear looked around.

He couldn't see the rabbit.

Slowly, the rabbit walked up to the bear.

He kept playing and the bear kept singing.

They were both happy that they had found a friend.

And a bird joined in the song.

Air

Air is all around us.

But we can't see it.

How do we know it is there?

There are many ways.

We can see what air does.

Moving air is called wind.

Wind moves plants.

Wind moves dirt.

Strong winds can move heavy things.

Strong winds can even move a house.

We can weigh air.

We can weigh two balloons.

The one with a lot of air weighs more.

We can see what air does.

We can weigh air.

Then we know it is there.

What You Eat

People eat many kinds of food.

The different kinds of foods are called food groups.

There are four food groups.

One food group is the cereal and bread group.

Cereals and breads are foods made of grain.

It is good to eat them three times a day.

Another food group is the dairy group.

Milk and cheese are part of the dairy group.

You should have milk three times a day, too.

Another food group is fruit and vegetables.

Did you know that tomatoes are a fruit?

The fourth group is the meat group.

Meat, eggs, and fish are part of this group.

You should eat some of these foods every day.

Eating the right foods makes you grow and keeps you healthy.

Level: One

Narrative

Mouse in a House

Once there was a mouse. He lived in a wall of an old house. Each night the mouse went to the kitchen. He wanted to find something to eat. The man who lived in the house heard the mouse. He knew the mouse lived in the wall. But he didn't mind.

Then one day the man decided to sell the house. He loved the old house. But it was too big. He put an ad in the paper. It said, "100-year-old house for sale. Call 224-3414." Many people called and wanted to visit the house. Two people came on Sunday. They walked up the old stairs. When they got to the top, the mouse ran down the wall. He ran up and down the inside of the wall. Up and down. The people heard the mouse. They said, "We don't want the house." The mouse was very happy. He was afraid that new people would try to get rid of him.

Every time someone visited the house, the mouse would do the same thing. He would run up and down the wall between the first and second floor. Every time the people left without buying the house. Then a family came to see the house. The house was just the right size for them. When they walked up the stairs, the mouse ran up and down the wall. They heard him and said, "Oh, you have a mouse. We love the house so much we'll buy it, mouse and all." (254 words)

Number of Total Miscues
(Total Accuracy): _____

Number of Meaning Change Miscues
(Total Acceptability):_____

Total Accuracy			Total Acceptability
0–6 miscues	_____ Independent	_____	0–6 miscues
7–26 miscues	_____ Instructional	_____	7–13 miscues
27+ miscues	_____ Frustration	_____	14+ miscues

Rate: 254 x 60/_____ seconds = _____ WPM

Retelling Scoring Sheet for Mouse in a House

Setting/Background

____ There was a mouse.
____ He lived
____ in a wall
____ of a house.
____ Each night
____ the mouse went
____ to the kitchen
____ to find something to eat.
____ The man who lived in the house
____ heard the mouse.
____ He knew
____ that the mouse lived
____ in the wall.
____ He didn't mind.

Goal

____ The man decided
____ to sell the house.
____ The mouse was afraid
____ that the people would try
____ to get rid of him.

Events

____ The man put an ad
____ in the paper.
____ It said,
____ Call 224-3414.
____ Two
____ people came
____ on Sunday.
____ They walked up the stairs.
____ The mouse ran up
____ and down.
____ The people heard the mouse.
____ They said,
____ "We don't want the house."
____ When someone visited the house,
____ the mouse ran up
____ and down.

Resolution

____ A family came
____ to see the house.
____ The house was right
____ for them.
____ They said
____ "You have a mouse.
____ We love the house.
____ We'll buy the house
____ mouse and all."

Other ideas recalled, including inferences

_____

Questions for Mouse in a House

1. Where did the mouse live in the house?
   Explicit: in a wall

2. What did the old man decide to do?
   Explicit: sell the house

3. What did the mouse do when people came to visit the house?
   Explicit: run up and down the inside of the walls

4. How many floors did the house have?
   Implicit: two

5. Why didn't some people want to buy the house?
   Implicit: they didn't want a mouse in their house

6. Why did the last family buy the house even though it had a mouse?
   Explicit: it was the right size for them

Number Correct Explicit: _____

Number Correct Implicit: _____

Total: _____

_____ Independent: 6 correct

_____ Instructional: 4–5 correct

_____ Frustration: 0–3 correct

Level: One

Narrative

The Bear and the Rabbit

Once there was a very big bear. He lived in the woods. He was sad because he didn't have anyone to play with. He said to his father, "How can I find a friend?" His father said, "By being you." "But all the animals are afraid of me," said the bear. "I can't even get near them."

But one day the bear was sitting by a river. He was singing softly to himself. A rabbit lived near the river. He looked out of his hole when he heard the bear's song. He thought. "Anyone who sings like that must be nice. Maybe I don't need to be afraid of him. It would be nice to have a friend." The rabbit went and got his horn. Very softly he began to play. His music went well with the bear's song. The bear looked around. He couldn't see the rabbit. Slowly, the rabbit walked up to the bear. He kept playing and the bear kept singing. They were both happy that they had found a friend. And a bird joined in the song. (181 words)

Level: One

Retelling Scoring Sheet for The Bear and the Rabbit

Setting/Background

____ There was a bear
____ who was big.
____ He was sad
____ because he didn't have anyone
____ to play with.

Goal

____ He asked his father
____ "How can I find a friend?"

Events

____ His father said
____ "By being you."
____ "But all the animals are afraid of me,"
____ he said.
____ The bear was sitting
____ by the river.
____ He was singing
____ softly.
____ A rabbit lived there.
____ He looked out
____ of his hole
____ when he heard the song.
____ He thought
____ the bear was nice.
____ The rabbit went
____ and got his horn.
____ He began to play.
____ His music went well
____ with the bear's song.
____ The rabbit walked to the bear.
____ The bear kept singing.

Resolution

____ They were both happy
____ that they had found a friend.
____ A bird joined in.

Other ideas recalled including inferences

___

Questions for The Bear and the Rabbit

1. Why was the bear sad at the beginning of the story?
   Explicit: because he didn't have anyone to play with

2. Why did the father think that the bear could find a friend just by being himself?
   Implicit: the bear was nice and being nice makes friends

3. What was the bear doing as he sat by a river?
   Explicit: singing

4. What did the rabbit think when he heard the bear singing?
   Explicit: that the bear must be nice

Number Correct Explicit: _____

Number Correct Implicit: _____

Total: _____

_____ Independent: 6 correct

_____ Instructional: 4–5 correct

_____ Frustration: 0–3 correct

5. What did the rabbit do?
   Explicit: went and got his horn; played his horn

6. Why did the bear and the rabbit become friends?
   Implicit: because of their love of music

Level: One

Expository

Air

Air is all around us.

But we can't see it.

How do we know it is there?

There are many ways.

We can see what air does.

Moving air is called wind.

Wind moves plants.

Wind moves dirt.

Strong winds can move heavy things.

Strong winds can even move a house.

We can weigh air.

We can weigh two balloons.

The one with a lot of air weighs more.

We can see what air does.

We can weigh air.

Then we know it is there. (92 words)

Retelling Scoring Sheet for Air

Main Idea

____ Air is all around us.
____ But we can't see it.
____ How do we know it is there?
____ We can see
____ what air does.

Level: One

Details

____ Moving air
____ is called wind.
____ Wind moves plants.
____ Wind moves dirt.
____ Strong winds can move.
____ heavy things.
____ Strong winds can move a house.

Main Idea

____ We can weigh air.

Details

____ We can weigh
____ two balloons.
____ The one with lots of air
____ weighs more.

Main Idea Restatement

____ We can see what air does.
____ We can weigh air.
____ Then we know it is there.

Questions for Air

1. How do we know air is there?
   Explicit: we can see what air does; or air moves things (reader can answer things, dirt, plants, or houses); or we can weigh air

2. How else do we know air is there?
   Explicit: any other of the above answers

3. What does air move?
   Explicit: plants; or dirt; or houses

4. What else does air move?
   Explicit: any other of the above answers

5. How do we know that wind could move a car?
   Implicit: it can move heavy things; or it can move a house

6. Why does a flat tire weigh less that a tire that is not flat?
   Implicit: the flat tire does not have as much air

Number Correct Explicit: _____

Number Correct Implicit: _____

Total: _____

_____ Independent: 6 correct

_____ Instructional: 4–5 correct

_____ Frustration: 0–3 correct

Level: One

Expository

Concept Questions:

What are foods made from milk?

_____

_____

_____ (3-2-1-0)

What are foods made from grain?

_____

_____

_____ (3-2-1-0)

What are different kinds of meat?

_____

_____

_____ (3-2-1-0)

Score: _____ /9 = _____ %

_____ FAM _____ UNFAM

Prediction:

_____

_____

What You Eat

People eat many kinds of food.

The different kinds of foods are called food groups.

There are four food groups.

One food group is the cereal and bread group.

Cereals and breads are foods made of grain.

It is good to eat them three times a day.

Another food group is the dairy group.

Milk and cheese are part of the dairy group.

You should have milk three times a day, too.

Another food group is fruit and vegetables.

Did you know that tomatoes are a fruit?

The fourth group is the meat group.

Meat, eggs, and fish are part of this group.

You should eat some of these foods every day.

Eating the right foods makes you grow and keeps you healthy. (123 words)

Number of Total Miscues
(Total Accuracy): _____

Number of Meaning Change Miscues
(Total Acceptability): _____

Total Accuracy		Total Acceptability
0–3 miscues ____ Independent	____	0–3 miscues
4–12 miscues ____ Instructional	____	4–6 miscues
13+ miscues ____ Frustration	____	7+ miscues
Rate: 123 x 60/____ seconds =	____	WPM

Retelling Scoring Sheet for What You Eat

Main Idea

____ Different kinds of food are called food groups.

____ There are four food groups.

Details

____ One group is the cereal
____ and bread group.
____ Cereals
____ and breads are foods
____ made of grain.
____ It is good
____ to eat them
____ three times
____ a day.
____ Another group is the dairy group.
____ Milk
____ and cheese are part of this group.
____ You should have milk
____ three times
____ a day.
____ Another group is fruits
____ and vegetables.
____ Tomatoes are a fruit.
____ The fourth group is the meat group.
____ Meat,
____ eggs,
____ and fish are part of this group.
____ You should eat these
____ every day.
____ Eating foods
____ the right foods
____ makes you grow
____ and keeps you healthy.

Other ideas recalled, including inferences

_____

Questions for What You Eat

1. What food group does butter belong to?
   Implicit: dairy

2. What are cereals and breads made of?
   Explicit: grain

3. What two food groups should you have three times a day?
   Explicit: cereals and dairy

4. What kind of food is a tomato?
   Explicit: fruit

5. Name one member of the meat group other than meat.
   Explicit: eggs, fish

6. To what food group does a chicken belong?
   Implicit: meat

Number Correct Explicit: _____

Number Correct Implicit: _____

Total: _____

____ Independent: 6 correct

____ Instructional: 4–5 correct

____ Frustration: 0–3 correct

What Can I Get for My Toy?

It was a Saturday morning. John looked at the toys in his room. They were all old and he wanted something new. John went to his mother. "All my toys are old," he said. "I want something new to play with." His mother looked at him, "John, we don't have the money to buy you anything new. You'll have to find a way to make something new." John went back to his room and looked around at the toys. There were many toys that were fun. But he had played with them so much that they weren't fun anymore. Then he had an idea. His friend Chris wanted a truck just like his red truck. And John wanted a car like the one Chris got for his birthday. Maybe they could trade. John ran down the street to Chris's house. "Hey, Chris, would you trade your car for my truck?" "Sure," said Chris, "I'll trade. Later we can trade something else. That way we'll always have something new to play with."

Father's New Game

It was a cold winter day. Too cold for Mary and Susan to go outside. They wanted something interesting to do. They went to their father and asked if he would take them to a movie. He said, "I'm sorry girls. Someone is coming to see why the washer isn't working. If you'll play by yourselves for a while I'll think of a new game for you. But you must promise to stay in your room until I call you." "Okay," said Mary and Susan.

Father wrote notes on pieces of paper and left them around the house. Each note gave a clue as to where to find the next note. Just as the person came to look at the washer, father called to them. "Mary, Susan, you can come out now!" Then he went into the basement.

Mary and Susan came out of their room. They didn't see anything to play with. They thought that their Father had forgotten to think of a new game for them to play. Then Susan noticed a piece of paper on the floor. She picked it up and read it aloud, "I'm cold but I give off heat. I'm light when I'm open but dark when I'm closed. What am I? Open me and you'll find the next clue." The girls walked around their house thinking. They came into the kitchen and looked around. "That's it!" yelled Mary. "The refrigerator!" She opened the door and found the next clue taped to the inside of the door. The girls were off again in search for the next clue. After an hour they had found five clues. The person who had fixed the washer was just leaving as Susan found the last cue. It read, "Nice job, girls, let's go to a movie!"

Whales and Fish

Whales and fish both live in the water, but they are different in many ways. Whales are large animals that live in the water. Even though whales live in the water, they must come to the top of the water to get air. When they come to the top of the water, whales breathe in air through a hole in the top of their heads. At the same time they blow out old air. Whales don't get air like fish. Fish take in air from the water.

Mother whales give birth to live whales. The baby whale must come to the top of the water right away for air. The baby drinks milk from its mother for about a year. Then it finds its own food. Fish have babies in a different way. Most mother fish lay eggs. The babies are born when the eggs hatch. Right after they are born, the baby fish must find their own food.

Whales and fish are alike in some ways too. Whales and fish have flippers on their sides. They also have fins on their tails. Flippers and fins help whales and fish swim. Fins move and push the water away.

Seasons

There are four seasons in a year. They are spring, summer, fall, and winter. Each season lasts about three months. Spring is the season when new life begins. The weather becomes warmer. Warm weather, rain, and light make plants grow. Some plants which looked dead during the winter grow again. Tulips are plants which come up every spring.

Summer begins on June 20th for people who live in the United States. June 20th is the longest day of the year for us. We have more sunlight that day than on any other day. Insects come out in summer. One bug that comes out in summer likes to bite. The bite hurts and it itches. Do you know what that bug is? It's the deer fly.

Summer ends and fall begins during September. In fall we begin to get less light from the sun. In the North, leaves begin to die. When they die they turn brown. Then they fall off. Nuts fall from trees. They are saved by squirrels to eat in the winter.

Winter begins just a few days before Christmas. December 21st is the shortest day of the year for us. We have less light that day than on any other day. In winter many animals have to live on food that they stored during the fall. There are no green plants for the animals to eat. Winter ends when spring begins on March 20th. The seasons keep changing. Plant life begins and ends each year.

Level: Two

Narrative

What Can I Get for My Toy?

It was a Saturday morning. John looked at the toys in his room. They were all old and he wanted something new. John went to his mother. "All my toys are old," he said. "I want something new to play with." His mother looked at him. "John, we don't have the money to buy you anything new. You'll have to find a way to make something new." John went back to his room and looked around at the toys. There were many toys that were fun. But he had played with them so much that they weren't fun anymore. Then he had an idea. His friend Chris wanted a truck just like his red truck. And John wanted a car like the one Chris got for his birthday. Maybe they could trade. John ran down the street to Chris's house. "Hey, Chris, would you trade your car for my truck?" "Sure," said Chris. "I'll trade. Later we can trade something else. That way we'll always have something new to play with." (175 words)

Level: Two

Retelling Scoring Sheet for
What Can I Get for My Toy?

Setting/Background

____ John looked at his toys.
____ They were old.

Goal

____ John wanted something
____ that was new.

Events

____ John went to his mother.
____ "My toys are old,"
____ he said.
____ "I want something
____ new
____ to play with."
____ His mother looked
____ at John.
____ "We don't have money
____ to buy something
____ new."
____ John had played with his toys
____ so much
____ that they weren't fun
____ anymore.
____ His friend
____ Chris wanted a truck
____ just like his truck
____ his red truck
____ and John wanted a car
____ like Chris's car.
____ Maybe they could trade.
____ John ran
____ down the street
____ to Chris's house.
____ "Would you trade your car
____ for my truck?"
____ "Sure,"
____ said Chris.

Resolution

____ "We can trade something else
____ later.
____ We'll always have something
____ new
____ to play with."

Other ideas recalled, including inferences

_____

Questions for
What Can I Get for My Toy?

1. At the beginning of the story, what did John tell his mother he wanted?
   Explicit: something new to play with

2. Why did John want a new toy to play with?
   Implicit: because he had played with his old toys so much they weren't interesting to him any more; he got bored with them.
   Note: broken is not acceptable—the story discusses his boredom and that his toys were desired by another child

3. What did John's mother say when he asked her to buy something new for him?
Explicit: they didn't have the money to buy anything new; he'd have to make something new

4. What did John do to get what he wanted?
Explicit: he went to his friend's house and asked him to trade toys with him

5. Why was trading a good idea?
Implicit: the boys would always have something new to play with; boys had new toys without spending money

6. What did his friend suggest that they do?
Explicit: trade again later

7. In the future what must both boys have for trading to make them both happy?
Implicit: toys that the other boy wanted

8. When do you think that the boys will trade again?
Implicit: when they get bored with the toy they traded; later when they want a new toy again

Number Correct Explicit: _____

Number Correct Implicit: _____

Total: _____

_____ Independent: 8 correct

_____ Instructional: 6–7 correct

_____ Frustration: 0–5 correct

Level: Two

Narrative

Father's New Game

It was a cold winter day. Too cold for Mary and Susan to go outside. They wanted something interesting to do. They went to their father and asked if he would take them to a movie. He said, "I'm sorry girls. Someone is coming to see why the washer isn't working. If you'll play by yourselves for a while I'll think of a new game for you. But you must promise to stay in your room until I call you." "Okay," said Mary and Susan.

Father wrote notes on pieces of paper and left them around the house. Each note gave a clue as to where to find the next note. Just as the person came to look at the washer, Father called to them, "Mary, Susan, you can come out now!" Then he went into the basement. Mary and Susan came out of their room. They didn't see anything to play with. They thought that their Father had forgotten to think of a new game for them to play. Then Susan noticed a piece of paper on the floor. She picked it up and read it aloud. "I'm cold but I give off heat. I'm light when I'm open but dark when I'm closed. What am I? Open me and you'll find the next clue." The girls walked around their house thinking. They came into the kitchen and looked around. "That's it!" yelled Mary. "The refrigerator!" She opened the door and found the next clue taped to the inside of the door. The girls were off again in search for the next clue. After an hour they had found five clues. The person who had

Level: Two

fixed the washer was just leaving as Susan found the last <u>clue</u>. It read, "Nice job girls, let's go to a movie!" (298 words)

Number of Total Miscues
(Total Accuracy): _____

Number of Meaning Change Miscues
(Total Acceptability):_____

Total Accuracy				Total Acceptability
0–7 miscues	_____	Independent	_____	0–7 miscues
8–31 miscues	_____	Instructional	_____	8–16 miscues
32+ miscues	_____	Frustration	_____	17+ miscues

Rate: 298 x 60/_____ seconds = _____ WPM

Retelling Scoring Sheet for Father's New Game

Setting/Background

____ It was a cold day.
____ Too cold
____ for Mary
____ and Susan
____ to go outside.

Goal

____ They wanted something to do.

Events

____ They went to their father
____ and asked
____ if he would take them
____ to a movie.
____ He said,
____ "I'm sorry.
____ Someone is coming

____ to see
____ why the washer isn't working.
____ I'll think
____ of a game
____ a new game.
____ But you stay
____ in your room
____ until I call you."
____ Father wrote notes
____ on pieces
____ of paper
____ and left them
____ around the house.
____ Each note gave a clue
____ where to find the next note.
____ Father called to them,
____ "You can come out now."
____ Mary
____ and Susan came out
____ of their room.
____ Susan noticed a piece
____ of paper.
____ She read it.
____ They found the next clue
____ in the refrigerator.
____ They found clues.
____ five clues
____ The person who fixed the washer
____ was leaving
____ as Susan found the last clue.

Resolution

____ The last clue
____ read
____ "Nice job
____ girls.
____ Let's go
____ to the movies."

Other ideas recalled, including inferences

_____

Questions for Father's New Game

1. What kind of day was it?
   Explicit: very cold; winter

2. What did Mary and Susan want?
   Explicit: to go to a movie

3. Why couldn't their father take them to the movie when they asked to go?
   Implicit: their father needed to stay home to wait for someone to come to repair the washer

4. What did their father write in the notes he left them?
   Explicit: clues

5. Why did Mary and Susan think that father had forgotten to think up a new game?
   Implicit: when they came out of their room they didn't see anything; their dad wasn't there

6. Where did the first clue lead them?
   Explicit: to the refrigerator; if student says, "To the kitchen," ask, "Where in the kitchen?"

7. How did they know it was the refrigerator?
   Implicit: any of the clues—it was cold, but gave off heat; I'm light when I'm opened but dark when I'm closed

8. Why could they go to the movie when they found the last clue?
   Implicit: because the washer was fixed so their father could leave the house

Number Correct Explicit: _____

Number Correct Implicit: _____

Total: _____

_____ Independent: 8 correct

_____ Instructional: 6–7 correct

_____ Frustration: 0–5 correct

Level: Two

Expository

Concept Questions:

How do whales breathe?

_____

_____

_____ (3-2-1-0)

What does "baby animals staying with their mother" mean to you?

_____

_____

_____ (3-2-1-0)

How are baby fish born?

_____

_____

_____ (3-2-1-0)

Score: _____ /9 = _____ %

_____ FAM _____ UNFAM

Prediction:

_____

_____

Whales and Fish

Whales and fish both live in the water, but they are different in many ways. Whales are large animals that live in the water. Even though whales live in the water, they must come to the top of the water to get air. When they come to the top of the water, whales breathe in air through a hole in the top of their heads. At the same time they blow out old air. Whales don't get air like fish. Fish take in air from the water.

Mother whales give birth to live whales. The baby whale must come to the top of the water right away for air. The baby drinks milk from its mother for about a year. Then it finds its own food. Fish have babies in a different way. Most mother fish lay eggs. The babies are born when the eggs hatch. Right after they are born, the baby fish must find their own food.

Whales and fish are alike in some ways too. Whales and fish have flippers on their sides. They also have fins on their tails. Flippers and fins help whales and fish swim. Fins move and push the water away. (197 words)

Number of Total Miscues
(Total Accuracy): _____

Number of Meaning Change Miscues
(Total Acceptability): _____

Total Accuracy			Total Acceptability
0–2 miscues	_____ Independent	_____	0–2 miscues
3–19 miscues	_____ Instructional	_____	3–10 miscues
20+ miscues	_____ Frustration	_____	11+ miscues
Rate: 197 x 60/_____ seconds =	_____ WPM		

Retelling Scoring Sheet for Whales and Fish

Main Idea

____ Whales
____ and fish both live
____ in the water
____ but they are different
____ in many ways.

Details

____ Whales are large
____ animals.
____ They must come
____ to the top
____ of the water
____ to get air.
____ Whales breathe
____ in air
____ through a hole
____ in the top
____ of their heads.
____ At the same time,
____ they blow out
____ old air.
____ Fish take in air
____ from the water.
____ Mother whales give birth
____ to live whales.
____ The baby whale comes
____ to the top
____ of the water
____ right away
____ for air.
____ The baby drinks milk
____ from its mother
____ for about a year.
____ Most mother fish lay eggs.
____ The babies are born
____ when the eggs hatch,
____ Right after they are born
____ the baby fish must find their own food.

Main Idea

____ Whales
____ and fish are alike
____ in some ways too.

Details

____ Whales
____ and fish have flippers
____ on their sides.
____ They have fins
____ on their tails.
____ Flippers
____ and fins help whales
____ and fish swim.
____ Fins move
____ and push the water away.

Other ideas recalled, including inferences

_____

Questions for Whales and Fish

1. What is this passage mainly about?
   Implicit: How whales and fish are alike and different

2. Name one way that whales and fish are different.
   Explicit: whales breathe air and fish take in air from the water; whales give birth to live babies and fish lay eggs; baby whales get food from their mother and baby fish have to get it for themselves

3. Name another way that whales and fish are different.
   Explicit: any other of the above answers

4. What part of the whale is like our nose?
   Implicit: the air hole or the hole in the whale's head

5. Why does a baby whale stay with its mother for a year?
   Implicit: it gets food from its mother.

6. What part of whales and fish are alike?
   Explicit: fins or flippers.

7. Where are fins found on fish and whales?
   Explicit: on the tail

8. Why might a mother fish not know her baby?
   Implicit: the mother does not see the babies when they are born or the babies hatch from eggs.

Number Correct Explicit: _____

Number Correct Implicit: _____

Total: _____

_____ Independent: 8 correct

_____ Instructional: 6–7 correct

_____ Frustration: 0–5 correct

Level: Two

Expository

Seasons

There are four seasons in a year. They are spring, summer, fall, and winter. Each season lasts about three months. Spring is the season when new life begins. The weather becomes warmer. Warm weather, rain, and light make plants grow. Some plants which looked dead during the winter grow again. Tulips are plants which come up every spring.

Summer begins on June 20th for people who live in the United States. June 20th is the longest day of the year for us. We have more sunlight that day than on any other day. Insects come out in summer. One bug that comes out in summer likes to bite. The bite hurts and it itches. Do you know what that bug is? It's the deer fly.

Summer ends and fall begins during September. In fall we begin to get less light from the sun. In the North, leaves begin to die. When they die they turn brown. Then they fall off. Nuts fall from trees. They are saved by squirrels to eat in the winter.

Winter begins just a few days before Christmas. December 21st is the shortest day of the year for us. We have less light that day than on any other day. In winter many animals have to live on food that they stored during the fall. There are no green plants for the animals to eat. Winter ends when spring begins on March 20th. The seasons keep changing. Plant life begins and ends each year. (249 words)

Number of Total Miscues
(Total Accuracy): _____

Number of Meaning Change Miscues
(Total Acceptability):_____

Total Accuracy			Total Acceptability
0–6 miscues	_____ Independent	_____	0–6 miscues
7–26 miscues	_____ Instructional	_____	7–13 miscues
27+ miscues	_____ Frustration	_____	14+ miscues

Rate: 249 x 60/_____ seconds = _____ WPM

Retelling Scoring Sheet for Seasons

Main Idea

____ There are seasons
____ four seasons
____ in a year.

Details

____ They are spring,
____ summer,
____ fall,
____ and winter.

Main Idea

____ Spring is the season
____ when new life begins.

Details

____ The weather becomes warmer.
____ Rain
____ and light make plants grow.
____ Tulips come up
____ every spring.

Main Idea

____ Summer begins
____ on June 20.

Details

____ June 20 is the longest day
____ of the year.
____ Insects come out
____ in the summer.
____ One bug likes to bite.
____ It's the deer fly.

Main Idea

____ Fall begins
____ during September.

Details

____ We begin to get less light
____ from the sun
____ in the fall.
____ Leaves begin to die.
____ They turn brown.
____ Then they fall off.
____ Nuts are saved
____ by squirrels
____ to eat
____ in the winter.

Main Idea

____ Winter begins
____ a few days
____ before Christmas.

Details

____ December 21 is the shortest day
____ of the year.
____ Animals have to live on food
____ that they stored
____ during the fall.

Other ideas recalled, including inferences

_____

Questions for Seasons

1. How long does each season usually last?
   Explicit: three months

2. What are the conditions needed for flowers to come up in spring?
   Implicit: warm weather, rain, or light

3. Which day has more sunlight than any other?
   Explicit: June 20

4. According to your reading, what insect's bite makes you itch?
   Explicit: deer fly

5. How do you know that fall is coming even if the weather is warm?
   Explicit: there is less daylight; the leaves turn brown

6. Why do leaves die in the fall even when the weather is warm?
   Implicit: there is less light

7. About when in September does fall begin?
   Implicit: around September 20th

8. Why do squirrels save nuts for eating in winter?
   Implicit: Food is scarce

Number Correct Explicit: _____

Number Correct Implicit: _____

Total: _____

_____ Independent: 8 correct

_____ Instructional: 6–7 correct

_____ Frustration: 0–5 correct

The Trip to the Zoo

The day was bright and sunny. Carlos and Maria jumped out of bed and dressed in a hurry. They didn't want to be late for school today. It was a special day because their classes were going to the zoo. When they got to school, all of the children were waiting outside to get on the bus. When everyone was there, the second and third graders got on the bus and rode to the zoo. On the bus, the children talked about the zoo animals that they liked the best. Joe and Carlos wanted to see the lion, king of the beasts. Maria and Angela wanted to see the chimps. Maria thought they acted a lot like people.

When they got to the zoo, their teachers divided the children into four groups. One teacher, Mr. Lopez, told them if anyone got lost, to go to the ice cream stand. Everyone would meet there at noon. Maria went with the group to the monkey house where she spent a long time watching the chimps groom each other. She wrote down all the ways that the chimps acted like people. Her notes would help her write a good report of what she liked best at the zoo.

Carlos went with the group to the lion house. He watched the cats pace in front of the glass. Carlos was watching a lion so carefully that he didn't see his group leave. Finally, he noticed that it was very quiet in the lion house. He turned around and didn't see anyone. At first he was worried. Then he remembered what Mr. Lopez had said. He traced his way back to the entrance and found a map. He followed the map to the ice cream stand, just as everyone was meeting there for lunch. Joe smiled and said, "We thought that the lion had you for lunch!"

The Surprise

It was Jackie's birthday. Her mother and grandmother were trying to decide what to get her. They wanted to surprise her with a special present, but they didn't have a lot of money. Her mother and grandmother went downtown on the bus to look around. First, they saw a blue sweater. It would look beautiful on Jackie, but it wasn't special. Then they saw some ice skates. Jackie wanted some new skates, but these skates cost too much. They didn't know what to do. They were about to start home when they saw a pet store! That was it! Jackie had wanted a puppy for a long time. But she and her mother had lived in a place that didn't want dogs. Now she and her mother and grandmother lived in a house. Her mother and grandmother went into the store. They saw a white poodle that cost $25. They paid $5.00 for a black puppy and brought it home with them. They hid the puppy. When Jackie got home from school, she went to her room to put away her books. She heard a noise from her closet. When she opened up the closet, there sat the black puppy with a sign around its neck. It said, "Happy Birthday, Jackie! Love, Mama and Grandma."

The Friend

Once upon a time there was a boy named Mark. Mark loved to go to the ocean and play his flute. One day he was playing his flute when a school of dolphins swam by. They leaped in the air every 30 seconds. Mark could almost predict when they would leap again. He watched them for a long time because he was so interested in their play. That day he decided that he wanted to learn more about dolphins.

Mark went to the library. The next weekend he took a boat and rowed out about as far as he had seen the dolphins before. He started playing his flute trying to mimic the pulsed sounds he had heard on tapes of dolphin sounds. He had learned that they make two kinds of pulsed sounds. One kind is called sonar and is used to locate dolphins and objects. The other kind of sound is a burst pulse which tells the emotional state of the dolphin. Mark was trying to mimic sonar. Soon, about 400 yards away, he saw the roll of the dolphins. The boat bounced in the waves as the dolphins came closer. They seemed to be curious about the sounds coming from the boat. Suddenly, the boat tipped sharply and Mark fell out. Somehow he held onto his flute. Mark was a good swimmer, but he was too far from land to swim. The only thing to do was to try to mimic the sound of a dolphin in trouble. Maybe then the dolphins would help him to land. Kicking strongly, he kept himself up above the water. He blew high burst pulse sounds. Just when he was about to go underwater, he felt a push against his leg. Again and again a dolphin pushed him. She managed to keep his face above water as she gently pushed him to shore. Mark couldn't believe what was happening. He got safely to shore, although the boat was never seen again. As he sat on the beach, still shaking from fear, he realized that he had reached his goal. He had surely learned a lot about dolphins that day!

Cats: Lions and Tigers in Your House

House cats, lions, and tigers are part of the same family. When animals are part of the same family, they are alike in many ways. House cats are like lions and tigers in many ways, too. When kittens are first born, they drink milk from their mothers. Lions and tigers drink milk from their mothers, too. When kittens are born, they have claws, just like big cats. Claws are used by lions, tigers, and kittens to help them keep away enemies. As kittens get bigger, they learn to hunt from their mother. House cats hunt in the same way that lions and tigers do. They hide and lie very still. When the animal they are hunting comes close, they jump on it and grab it by the back of the neck. Cats kill other animals by shaking them and breaking their necks.

Lions, tigers, and house cats show when they are afraid in the same ways, too. Their fur puffs up, making them look bigger. They hiss and spit, too. Those are their ways of saying, "I'm afraid, don't come closer."

A cat's tongue has many uses. Because it is rough with little bumps on it, it can be used as a spoon. A cat drinks milk by lapping it. Because of the bumps the milk stays on the tongue until the cat can swallow it. If you feel the top of a cat's tongue, it is rough. This makes the tongue good for brushing the cat's hair. Lions and tigers clean themselves with their tongues just like house cats do.

Where Do People Live?

People live in different places. Some people live in a city. Others live in the country. Still other people live in between the city and the country. They live in suburbs. Why do people live in these different places?

People live in the city to be near their jobs. Cities have lots of factories, schools, and offices. People work in these buildings. If people don't want to drive a long way to their jobs, they live in the city. There are many other things to do in the city. Cities have museums and zoos. They also have many movie theaters.

People live in the country to be close to their jobs, too. Many people who live in the country are farmers. They plant crops on their land. They may sell their crops or may use them to feed the animals that live on the farm. Farmers raise cows, pigs, and chickens. The main food that these animals eat is grain. There are other things to do in the country. You can find a river to fish in. Or take walks in the woods. The life in the country is quiet.

People live in between the country and the city. They live in suburbs. Some people think that people who live in the suburbs have the best of both worlds. They live close to their jobs in the city. The suburbs are quieter than the city. They often have many movie theaters, too. It doesn't take as long to go to either the city or the country. The suburbs are more crowded than the country but less crowded than the city. Where people live depends upon what they like most.

Wool: From Sheep to You

Do you have a sweater? Do you know what it is made from? One fiber used to make sweaters is wool. Do you know where wool comes from? It comes from a sheep. However, many things must be done before the wool on a sheep can be woven or knitted to make clothing for you.

First, the wool must be removed from the sheep. People shear the wool off the sheep with electric clippers somewhat like a barber uses when he gives haircuts. Like our hair, the sheep's wool will grow back again. Most sheep are shorn only once a year. After the wool is removed, it must be washed very carefully to get out all the dirt. When the locks of wool dry, they are combed or carded to make all the fibers lie in the same direction. It is somewhat like combing or brushing your hair. Then the wool is formed into fine strands. These can be spun to make yarn. The yarn is knitted or woven into fabric. The fabric is made into clothing.

Yarn can also be used to knit sweaters by hand. Sweaters made from wool are very warm. They help keep you warm even when they are damp. Just think, the sweater you wear on a winter day may once have been on a sheep.

Level: Three

Narrative

Concept Questions:

What is a class trip?

_____

_____

_____(3-2-1-0)

What does "taking notes" mean to you?

_____

_____

_____(3-2-1-0)

What does "being by yourself" mean to you?

_____

_____

_____(3-2-1-0)

Why do people use maps?

_____

_____

_____(3-2-1-0)

Score: _____ /12 = _____ %

_____ FAM _____ UNFAM

Prediction:

_____

_____

The Trip to the Zoo

The day was bright and sunny. Carlos and Maria jumped out of bed and dressed in a hurry. They didn't want to be late for school today. It was a special day because their classes were going to the zoo. When they got to school, all of the children were waiting outside to get on the bus. When everyone was there, the second and third graders got on the bus and rode to the zoo. On the bus, the children talked about the zoo animals that they liked the best. Joe and Carlos wanted to see the lion, king of the beasts. Maria and Angela wanted to see the chimps. Maria thought they acted a lot like people.

When they got to the zoo, their teachers divided the children into four groups. One teacher, Mr. Lopez, told them if anyone got lost to go to the ice cream stand. Everyone would meet there at noon. Maria went with the group to the monkey house where she spent a long time watching the chimps groom each other. She wrote down all the ways that the chimps acted like people. Her notes would help her write a good report of what she liked best at the zoo.

Carlos went with the group to the lion house. He watched the cats pace in front of the glass. Carlos was watching a lion so

Level: Three

carefully that he didn't see his group leave. Finally, he noticed that it was very quiet in the lion house. He turned around and didn't see anyone. At first he was worried. Then he remembered what Mr. Lopez had said. He traced his way back to the entrance and found a map. He followed the map to the ice cream stand, just as everyone was meeting there for lunch. Joe smiled and said, "We thought that the lion had you for lunch!" (312 words)

Number of Total Miscues
(Total Accuracy): _____

Number of Meaning Change Miscues
(Total Acceptability): _____

Total Accuracy		Total Acceptability
0–7 miscues ____Independent	____	0–7 miscues
8–32 miscues ____Instructional	____	8–17 miscues
33+ miscues ____Frustration	____	18+ miscues

Rate: 312 x 60/_____ seconds = _____WPM

Retelling Scoring Sheet for The Trip to the Zoo

Setting/Background
____ Carlos
____ and Maria jumped
____ out of bed.
____ They didn't want
____ to be late
____ for school.
____ Their classes were going
____ to the zoo.
____ The second
____ and third graders
____ got on the bus
____ and rode
____ to the zoo.
____ They talked
____ about the animals
____ they liked best.

Goal
____ Carlos wanted
____ to see the lion.
____ Maria wanted
____ to see the chimps.

Events
____ Their teacher told them
____ their teacher Mr. Lopez
____ if anyone got lost
____ to go
____ to the ice cream stand
____ where everyone would meet
____ at noon.
____ Maria went
____ to the monkey house.
____ She wrote down all the ways
____ that chimps acted like people.
____ Her notes would help her
____ write a report.
____ Carlos went
____ to the lion house.

Problem
____ Carlos was watching a lion
____ so carefully
____ he didn't see his group
____ leave.
____ He noticed
____ that it was quiet.
____ He turned around

The Trip to the Zoo   171

Level: Three

____ and didn't see anyone.
____ He remembered
____ what Mr. Lopez said.
____ He traced his way
____ to the entrance
____ and found a map.
____ He followed the map
____ to the ice cream stand.

Resolution

____ Everyone was there
____ for lunch.
____ They thought
____ the lion had Carlos
____ for lunch.

Other ideas recalled, including inferences

_____

Questions for The Trip to the Zoo

1. Why was it a special day for Carlos and Maria?
   Explicit: their classes were going to the zoo

2. What grades were Carlos and Maria in?
   Implicit: second and third

3. What animal did Carlos want to see?
   Explicit: lions

4. Why was Maria watching the chimps so carefully?
   Implicit: so she could write a report for school

5. How did Carlos get separated from his group?
   Explicit: he was watching the lions so carefully he didn't see his group leave

6. What made Carlos realize that his classmates had left the lion house?
   Implicit: it was quiet—he didn't hear any talking—he turned around and no one was there

7. Where did Carlos find the map?
   Explicit: at the zoo entrance

8. Why did Carlos go to get a map from the zoo entrance?
   Implicit: to help him find his way to the ice cream stand

Number Correct Explicit: _____

Number Correct Implicit: _____

Total: _____

____ Independent: 8 correct

____ Instructional: 6–7 correct

____ Frustration: 0–5 correct

Level: Three

Narrative

The Surprise

It was Jackie's birthday. Her mother and grandmother were trying to decide what to get her. They wanted to surprise her with a special present, but they didn't have a lot of money. Her mother and grandmother went downtown on the bus to look around. First, they saw a blue sweater. It would look beautiful on Jackie, but it wasn't special. Then they saw some ice skates. Jackie wanted some new skates, but these skates cost too much. They didn't know what to do. They were about to start home when they saw a pet store! That was it! Jackie had wanted a puppy for a long time. But she and her mother had lived in a place that didn't want dogs. Now she and her mother and grandmother lived in a house. Her mother and grandmother went into the store. They saw a white poodle that cost $25. They paid $5.00 for a black puppy and brought it home with them. They hid the puppy. When Jackie got home from school, she went to her room to put away her books. She heard a noise from her closet. When she opened up the closet, there sat the black puppy with a sign around its neck. It said, "Happy Birthday, Jackie! Love, Mama and Grandma." (217 words)

Level: Three

Retelling Scoring Sheet for The Surprise

Setting/Background

____ It was a birthday
____ Jackie's birthday.
____ Her mother
____ and grandmother were trying
____ to decide
____ what to get her.

Goal

____ They wanted
____ to surprise her
____ with a present
____ a special present
____ but they didn't have a lot
____ of money.

Events

____ Her mother
____ and grandmother went downtown
____ on a bus
____ to look around.
____ They saw a sweater
____ a blue sweater

____ but it wasn't special.
____ They saw skates
____ ice skates
____ that Jackie wanted
____ but they cost too much.
____ They were about to start home
____ when they saw a store
____ a pet store.
____ Jackie wanted a puppy
____ but they had lived
____ in a place
____ that didn't want dogs.
____ Now they lived in a house.
____ They saw a poodle
____ a white poodle
____ that cost $25.
____ Her mother
____ and grandmother paid $5.00
____ for a puppy
____ a black puppy.
____ They brought it home.
____ They hid the puppy.

Resolution

____ When Jackie got home
____ from school
____ she went to her room.
____ She heard a noise
____ from her closet.
____ When she opened the closet
____ there sat the puppy
____ black puppy
____ with a sign
____ around its neck
____ that said
____ "Happy Birthday, Jackie
____ Love, Mama
____ and Grandma."

Other ideas recalled, including inferences

_____

Level: Three

Questions for The Surprise

1. What day was it?
   Explicit: Jackie's birthday

2. What problem did Jackie's mother and grandmother have?
   Implicit: they didn't have much money and they wanted a special present; they didn't know what to get her

3. Why didn't they buy ice skates for Jackie?
   Explicit: they cost too much

4. What did they buy for Jackie?
   Explicit: a puppy

5. Why didn't they buy the poodle?
   Implicit: It cost too much. If student says, "It cost $25," say, "So why didn't they pay the $25?"

6. Why can Jackie have a puppy now?
   Implicit: she and her mother live in a house. If student says, "They used to live where they couldn't have one," say, "Why can they have one now?"

7. Why did her mother and grandmother decide to hide the puppy in Jackie's bedroom closet?
   Implicit: because Jackie would go to her room after school. If student says, "So Jackie would be surprised," say, "Why did they pick the closet?"

8. What did the puppy have around its neck?
   Explicit: a sign

Number Correct Explicit: _____

Number Correct Implicit: _____

Total: _____

_____ Independent: 8 correct

_____ Instructional: 6–7 correct

_____ Frustration: 0–5 correct

Level: Three

Narrative

The Friend

Once upon a time there was a boy named Mark. Mark loved to go to the ocean and play his flute. One day he was playing his flute when a school of dolphins swam by. They leaped in the air every 30 seconds. Mark could almost predict when they would leap again. He watched them for a long time because he was so interested in their play. That day he decided that he wanted to learn more about dolphins. Mark went to the library.

The next weekend he took a boat and rowed out about as far as he had seen the dolphins before. He started playing his flute trying to mimic the pulsed sounds he had heard on tapes of dolphin sounds. He had learned that they make two kinds of pulsed sounds. One kind is called sonar and is used to locate dolphins and objects. The other kind of sound is a burst pulse which tells the emotional state of the dolphin. Mark was trying to mimic sonar. Soon, about 400 yards away, he saw the roll of the dolphins. The boat bounced in the waves as the dolphins came closer. They seemed to be curious about the sounds coming from the boat. Suddenly, the boat tipped sharply and Mark fell out. Somehow he held onto his flute. Mark was a good swimmer, but he was too far from land to <u>swim</u>. The only thing to do was to try to mimic the sound of a dolphin in trouble. Maybe then the dolphins would help him to land. Kicking strongly, he kept himself up above the water. He blew high burst pulse sounds. Just when he was about to go underwater, he felt a push against his leg. Again and again a dolphin pushed him. She managed to keep his face above water as she gently pushed him to shore. Mark couldn't <u>believe</u> what was happening. He got safely to shore, although the boat was never seen again. As he sat on the beach, still shaking from fear, he realized that he had reached his goal. He had surely learned a lot about dolphins that day! (357 words)

Number of Total Miscues
(Total Accuracy): _____

Number of Meaning Change Miscues
(Total Acceptability): _____

Total Accuracy		**Total Acceptability**
0–8 miscues	_____ Independent _____	0–8 miscues
9–37 miscues	_____ Instructional _____	9–19 miscues
38+ miscues	_____ Frustration _____	20+ miscues
Rate: 357 x 60/	_____ seconds =	_____ WPM

Retelling Scoring Sheet for The Friend

Setting/Background

____ There was a boy
____ named Mark.
____ Mark loved
____ to go
____ to the ocean
____ and play his flute.
____ A school
____ of dolphins swam by.
____ They leaped
____ every 30 seconds.

Goal

____ Mark wanted
____ to learn more
____ about dolphins.

Events

____ Mark went to the library.
____ He took a boat
____ and rowed out
____ where he had seen the dolphins.
____ He played his flute
____ to mimic sounds
____ pulsed sounds
____ of dolphins.
____ One sound is sonar
____ and is used to locate things.
____ Another kind is a pulse
____ burst pulse
____ which tells the emotional state
____ of the dolphin.
____ Mark saw the roll
____ of the dolphins.
____ The boat bounced
____ in the waves
____ as the dolphins came closer.
____ The boat tipped.
____ Mark fell out.
____ He held onto his flute.
____ Mark was a good swimmer
____ but he was too far

____ from land.
____ He tried
____ to mimic the sound
____ of the dolphin
____ in trouble
____ so the dolphin would help him.
____ Kicking
____ strongly
____ he kept himself
____ above water.
____ He blew sounds.
____ A dolphin pushed him
____ to shore.

Resolution

____ He got safely
____ to shore.
____ He realized
____ he had learned a lot
____ about dolphins.

Other ideas recalled, including inferences

_____

Questions for The Friend

1. What instrument did Mark play?
   Explicit: the flute

2. Where did Mark go to learn more about dolphins?
   Explicit: the library

3. How did Mark learn about the dolphin sounds?
   Implicit: he read about them, he listened to tapes; If student says, "He went to the library," ask, "How did that help him learn about dolphins?"

4. What two kinds of sounds do dolphins make?
   Explicit: sonar, or sounds to locate objects, and burst pulse, or sounds to indicate emotions

5. Why was Mark trying to mimic sonar?
   Implicit: to see if the dolphins would come to him

6. Why did the boat tip over?
   Implicit: the dolphins came close enough to cause waves

<table>
<tr><td>Number Correct Explicit: _____</td></tr>
<tr><td>Number Correct Implicit: _____</td></tr>
<tr><td>**Total:** _____</td></tr>
<tr><td>_____ Independent: 8 correct</td></tr>
<tr><td>_____ Instructional: 6–7 correct</td></tr>
<tr><td>_____ Frustration: 0–5 correct</td></tr>
</table>

7. What did Mark do to save himself?
   Implicit: he tried to make a burst pulse sound like a dolphin in trouble, hoping a dolphin would come to help him. Note: If student says, "He kicked strongly," ask "What other thing did Mark do?"

8. How did Mark get to shore?
   Explicit: a dolphin pushed him to shore

Level: Three

Expository

Cats: Lions and Tigers in Your House

House cats, lions, and tigers are part of the same family. When animals are part of the same family, they are alike in many ways. House cats are like lions and tigers in many ways, too. When kittens are first born, they drink milk from their mothers. Lions and tigers drink milk from their mothers, too. When kittens are born, they have claws just like big cats. Claws are used by lions, tigers, and kittens to help them keep away enemies. As kittens get bigger, they learn to hunt from their mother. House cats hunt in the same way that lions and tigers do. They hide and lie very still. When the animal they are hunting comes close, they jump on it and grab it by the back of the neck. Cats kill other animals by shaking them and breaking their necks.

Lions, tigers, and house cats show when they are afraid in the same ways, too. Their fur puffs up, making them look bigger. They hiss and spit, too. Those are their ways of saying, "I'm afraid, don't come closer."

A cat's tongue has many uses. Because it is rough with little bumps on it, it can be used as a spoon. A cat drinks milk by lapping it. Because of the bumps the milk stays on the tongue until the cat can swallow it. If you feel the top of a cat's tongue, it is rough. This makes the <u>tongue</u> good for brushing the cat's hair. Lions and tigers clean themselves with their <u>tongues</u> just like house cats do. (261 words)

Number of Total Miscues
(Total Accuracy): _____

Number of Meaning Change Miscues
(Total Acceptability):_____

Total Accuracy			**Total Acceptability**
0–6 miscues	_____ Independent	_____	0–6 miscues
7–27 miscues	_____ Instructional	_____	7–14 miscues
28+ miscues	_____ Frustration	_____	15+ miscues
Rate: 261 x 60/_____ seconds =		_____ WPM	

Retelling Scoring Sheet for
Cats: Lions and Tigers in Your House

Main Idea

____ Cats,
____ lions,
____ and tigers
____ are part of the same family.
____ They are alike
____ in many ways.

Details

____ When kittens are first born,
____ they drink milk
____ from their mothers.
____ Lions
____ and tigers
____ drink milk
____ from their mothers.
____ Kittens have claws.

____ Lions,
____ tigers,
____ and kittens use claws
____ to keep away enemies.
____ Cats hunt
____ in the same way
____ that lions
____ and tigers do.
____ They jump on the animal
____ and grab it
____ by the neck.
____ Cats kill animals
____ by breaking their necks.
____ When lions,
____ tigers,
____ and cats are afraid,
____ their fur puffs up.
____ They hiss
____ and spit.
____ Because a cat's tongue is rough
____ with bumps,
____ it can be used
____ as a spoon.
____ A cat drinks milk
____ by lapping it.
____ Because of the bumps,
____ the milk stays
____ on the tongue
____ until the cat can swallow it.
____ Lions
____ and tigers clean themselves
____ with their tongues
____ just like cats.

Other ideas recalled, including inferences

_____

Level: Three

Questions for
Cats: Lions and Tigers in Your House

1. What is this passage mostly about?
   Implicit: that cats, lions, and tigers are alike in many ways

2. How are lions, tigers, and cats alike?
   Explicit: any one of the ways presented in the story: milk from their mothers as babies; they have claws; the way they hunt; the way they show fear; the uses of their tongues

3. What is another way that lions, tigers, and cats are alike?
   Explicit: any other of the above responses

4. What is still another way that lions, tigers, and cats are alike?
   Explicit: any other of the above responses

5. What do you think a cat would do if you cornered it?
   Implicit: it would hiss, spit, or puff up

6. Why is it important for cats to have claws when they're born?
   Implicit: for protection from their enemies

7. Why is the top of a cat's tongue rough?
   Implicit: because of the bumps on it; or so it can drink

8. Why doesn't milk fall off a cat's tongue?
   Explicit: because of the bumps which make cups on the tongue

Number Correct Explicit: _____

Number Correct Implicit: _____

Total: _____

_____ Independent: 8 correct

_____ Instructional: 6–7 correct

_____ Frustration: 0–5 correct

Level: Three

Expository

Where Do People Live?

People live in different places. Some people live in a city. Others live in the country. Still other people live in between the city and the country. They live in suburbs. Why do people live in these different places?

People live in the city to be near their jobs. Cities have lots of factories, schools, and offices. People work in these buildings. If people don't want to drive a long way to their jobs, they live in the city. There are many other things to do in the city. Cities have museums and zoos. They also have many movie theaters.

People live in the country to be close to their jobs, too. Many people who live in the country are farmers. They plant crops on their land. They may sell their crops or may use them to feed the animals that live on the farm. Farmers raise cows, pigs, and chickens. The main food that these animals eat is grain. There are other things to do in the country. You can find a river to fish in. Or take walks in the woods. The life in the country is quiet.

People live in between the country and the city. They live in suburbs. Some people think that people who live in the suburbs have the best of both worlds. They live close to their jobs in the city. The suburbs are quieter than the city. They often have many movie theaters, too. It doesn't take as long to go to either the city or the country. The suburbs are more <u>crowded</u> than the country but less <u>crowded</u> than the city. Where people live depends upon what they like most. (288 words)

Number of Total Miscues
(Total Accuracy): _____

Number of Meaning Change Miscues
(Total Acceptability):_____

Total Accuracy			Total Acceptability
0–7 miscues	_____ Independent	_____	0–7 miscues
8–30 miscues	_____ Instructional	_____	8–15 miscues
31+ miscues	_____ Frustration	_____	16+ miscues
Rate: 288 x 60/_____ seconds =		_____ WPM	

Retelling Scoring Sheet for Where Do People Live?

Main Idea

____ People live
____ in different places.

Details

____ Some people live
____ in the city.
____ Others live
____ in the country.
____ Others live
____ in the suburbs.

Main Idea

____ People live
____ in the city
____ to be near their jobs.

Details

____ Cities have factories,
____ schools,
____ and offices.
____ People work
____ in these buildings.
____ There are many things
____ to do in the city.
____ Cities have museums,
____ and zoos.
____ They have theaters
____ movie theaters.

Main Idea

____ People live
____ in the country
____ to be close to their jobs.

Details

____ Many people are farmers.
____ They plant crops.
____ Farmers raise cows,
____ pigs,
____ and chickens.
____ The food that these animals eat
____ is grain.
____ There are other things
____ to do in the country.
____ You can find a river
____ to fish in
____ or take walks
____ in the woods.
____ The life in the country
____ is quiet.

Main Idea

____ Some people think
____ that people who live in the suburbs
____ have the best of both worlds.

Details

____ They live close to their jobs
____ in the city.
____ The suburbs are quieter
____ than the city.
____ The suburbs are more crowded
____ than the country
____ but less crowded
____ than the city.

Other ideas recalled, including inferences

_____

Questions for Where Do People Live?

1. What is this passage mostly about?
   Implicit: why people live where they do

2. Why do people live in the city?
   Explicit: to be near their jobs

3. Why do people want to live close to their jobs?
   Implicit: so they don't have to drive far to work; so they don't have to get up so early to go to work

4. Why would someone who isn't a farmer like to live in the country?
   Implicit: they like the quiet life; they like to fish or take walks; they don't like noise, crowds, etc.

5. What is one thing that the passage says you can do in the country besides farm?
   Explicit: take walks, or fish

6. What crop would be planted by farmers who raise animals?
   Implicit: grain

7. How do the city and suburbs differ?
   Explicit: the suburbs are less crowded than the city or quieter

8. According to the passage why do people choose different places to live?
   Explicit: it depends on what they like most

Number Correct Explicit: _____

Number Correct Implicit: _____

Total: _____

_____ Independent: 8 correct

_____ Instructional: 6–7 correct

_____ Frustration: 0–5 correct

Expository

Concept Questions:

What are sheep used for?

_____

_____

_____ (3-2-1-0)

What is wool used for?

_____

_____

_____ (3-2-1-0)

What is yarn used for?

_____

_____

_____ (3-2-1-0)

Why do people get haircuts?

_____

_____

_____ (3-2-1-0)

Score: _____ /12 = _____ %

_____ FAM _____ UNFAM

Prediction:

_____

_____

Wool: From Sheep to You

Do you have a sweater? Do you know what it is made from? One fiber used to make sweaters is wool. Do you know where wool comes from? It comes from a sheep. However, many things must be done before the wool on a sheep can be woven or knitted to make clothing for you.

First, the wool must be removed from the sheep. People shear the wool off the sheep with electric clippers somewhat like a barber uses when he gives haircuts. Like our hair, the sheep's wool will grow back again. Most sheep are shorn only once a year. After the wool is removed, it must be washed very carefully to get out all the dirt. When the locks of wool dry, they are combed or carded to make all the fibers lie in the same direction. It is somewhat like combing or brushing your hair. Then the wool is formed into fine strands. These can be spun to make yarn. The yarn is knitted or woven into fabric. The fabric is made into clothing.

Yarn can also be used to knit sweaters by hand. Sweaters made from wool are very warm. They help keep you warm even when they are damp. Just think, the sweater you wear on a winter day may once have been on a sheep. (221 words)

Level: Three

Number of Total Miscues
(Total Accuracy): _____

Number of Meaning Change Miscues
(Total Acceptability): _____

Total Accuracy				Total Acceptability
0–5 miscues	_____	Independent	_____	0–5 miscues
6–23 miscues	_____	Instructional	_____	6–12 miscues
24+ miscues	_____	Frustration	_____	13+ miscues

Rate: 221 x 60/_____ seconds = _____ WPM

Retelling Scoring Sheet for Wool: From Sheep to You

Main Idea

____ Many things have to be done
____ before wool can be woven
____ or knitted
____ to make clothing.

Details

____ Wool is a fiber
____ used to make sweaters.
____ It comes from a sheep.
____ The wool must be removed
____ from the sheep.
____ People shear the wool
____ off the sheep
____ with clippers
____ electric clippers
____ like a barber uses.
____ The wool will grow back again.
____ Most sheep are shorn
____ once a year.
____ After the wool is removed,
____ it must be washed
____ very carefully
____ to get out the dirt.

____ When the locks are dry,
____ they are combed
____ to make the fibers
____ lie in the same direction.
____ It is like combing
____ or brushing
____ your hair.
____ Then the wool is formed
____ into strands.
____ These can be spun
____ to make yarn.
____ The yarn is knitted
____ or woven into fabric.
____ The fabric is made
____ into clothing
____ and knitted
____ into sweaters.
____ Sweaters made
____ from wool
____ are very warm
____ even when they are damp.

Other ideas recalled, including inferences

_____

Questions for Wool: From Sheep to You

1. What is this passage mainly about?
   Implicit: how wool is made; what you do to wool in order to use it

Level: Three

2. What is the first step in the making of wool?
   Explicit: cutting it off the sheep

3. What do people use to cut wool off sheep?
   Explicit: electric clippers; electric scissors (*electric* must be in the answer)

4. Why can sheep give wool for many years?
   Implicit: because it grows back after it is cut off

5. What is done to the wool after it is washed and dried?
   Explicit: it is combed

6. What happens to wool fibers after they are combed?
   Explicit: the fibers lie in the same direction

7. What two different things can people do with the wool yarn?
   Implicit: knit; weave into fabric; make into clothing

8. Why would it be good to wear a wool sweater out in the snow?
   Implicit: it would keep you warm even when it's damp. Note: If the student omits the idea of dampness and only says, "It would keep you warm," ask, "Why would it be especially warm in the snow?"

Number Correct Explicit: _____	
Number Correct Implicit: _____	
Total: _____	
_____ Independent:	8 correct
_____ Instructional:	6–7 correct
_____ Frustration:	0–5 correct

Johnny Appleseed

John Chapman was born in 1774 and grew up in Massachusetts. He became a farmer and learned how to grow different kinds of crops and trees. John especially liked to grow and eat apples. Many people were moving west at that time. They were heading for Ohio and Pennsylvania. John knew that apples were a good food for settlers to have. Apple trees were strong and easy to grow. Apples could be eaten raw and they could be cooked in many ways. They could also be dried for later use. So in 1797, John decided to go west. He wanted to plant apple trees for people who would build their new homes there.

John first gathered bags of apple seeds. He got many of his seeds from farmers who squeezed apples to make a drink called cider. Then, in the spring, he left for the western frontier. He planted seeds as he went along. Also, he gave them to people who knew how valuable apple trees were.

John walked many miles in all kinds of weather. He had to cross dangerous rivers and find his way through strange forests. Often he was hungry, cold, and wet. Sometimes he had to hide from unfriendly Indians. His clothes became ragged and torn. He used a sack for a shirt, and he cut out holes for the arms. He wore no shoes. But he never gave up. He guarded his precious seeds and carefully planted them where they had the best chance of growing into strong trees.

John's fame spread. He was nicknamed Johnny Appleseed. New settlers welcomed him and gratefully accepted a gift of apple seeds. Many legends grew up about Johnny Appleseed which were not always true. However, one thing is true. Thanks to Johnny Appleseed, apple trees now grow in parts of America where they once never did.

From *America's History* by B. B. Armbruster, C. L. Mitsakas, and V. R. Rogers, copyright © 1986 by Schoolhouse Press. Reprinted by permission of the publisher.

Amelia Earhart

Amelia Earhart was an adventurer and a pioneer in the field of flying. She did things no other woman had ever done before.

During World War I, Earhart worked as a nurse. She cared for pilots who had been hurt in the war. Earhart listened to what they said about flying. She watched planes take off and land. She knew that she, too, must fly.

In 1928, Earhart was the first woman to cross the Atlantic in a plane. But someone else flew the plane. Earhart wanted to be more than just a passenger. She wanted to fly a plane across the ocean herself. For four years, Earhart trained to be a pilot. Then, in 1932, she flew alone across the Atlantic to Ireland. The trip took over fourteen hours.

Flying may seem easy today. However, Earhart faced many dangers. Airplanes had just been invented. They were much smaller than our planes today. Mechanical problems happened quite often. There were also no computers to help her. Flying across the ocean was as frightening as sailing across it had been years before. Earhart knew the dangers she faced. However, she said, "I want to do it because I want to do it. Women must try to do things as men have tried. When they fail, their failure must be a challenge to others."

Earhart planned to fly around the world. She flew more than twenty thousand miles. Then, her plane disappeared somewhere over the huge Pacific Ocean. People searched for a long time. Finally they gave up. Earhart and her plane were never found.

Adapted from *Scott, Foresman Social Studies, Grade 4: Regions of Our Country and Our World* (Glenview, Ill.: Scott. Foresman and Co., 1983), p. 83.

Sequoyah

Sequoyah was a Cherokee Indian who lived in Tennessee in the 1800s. One day he met some Americans who were not Indians. He noticed that they looked at something he had never seen before, large white leaves with black marks on them. It seemed to Sequoyah as if the marks were talking to the people.

Sequoyah decided he would try to create talking leaves for the Cherokee people. He spent all of his time working. He drew his signs and pictures on tree bark. He thought the people would be excited about what he was trying to do but they were not. Once, when he was away from home, his wife burned the talking leaves. She did not realize they were important, and others in the village agreed.

Sequoyah continued to work on his signs. When he finished, he had eighty-six signs. Now the time had come to test the signs. Sequoyah and his daughter attended a meeting with Cherokee leaders from many villages. Sequoyah was sent out of the lodge. The chiefs gave messages to his daughter. She wrote down whatever they said. Sequoyah was called back into the lodge. He took the paper and read aloud what was written. It was exactly what the chiefs had said. It worked! Now the Cherokee had a written language all their own.

Within months, hundreds of Cherokee knew the new language. Soon the Cherokee nation had a newspaper and many books. Cherokees from different regions could now communicate with one another. Sequoyah became a great hero. He had given the Cherokee a wonderful gift, the written word.

Adapted from *Scott, Foresman Social Studies, Grade 4: Regions of Our Country and Our World* (Glenview, Ill.: Scott, Foresman and Co., 1983), p. 53.

The Busy Beaver

Have you ever heard someone say "busy as a beaver"? Beavers are very busy animals and they are master builders. This furry animal spends its life working and building. As soon as a beaver leaves its family, it has much work to do.

First, the beaver must build a dam. It uses sticks, leaves, and mud to block a stream. The beaver uses its two front teeth to get the sticks. The animal uses its large flat tail to pack mud into place. A pond forms behind the dam. The beaver spends most of its life near this pond.

In the middle of the beaver's pond is a large mound. This mound of mud and twigs is the beaver's lodge or house. The beaver's family is safe in the lodge because it is well hidden. The doorway to the lodge is under the water. After the lodge is built, the beaver still cannot rest. More trees must be cut down to be used as food for the coming winter. Sometimes there will be no more trees around the pond. Then the beaver has to find trees elsewhere. These trees will have to be carried to the pond. The beaver might build canals leading deep into the forest.

All this work changes the land. As trees are cut down, birds, squirrels, and other animals may have to find new homes. Animals that feed on trees lose their food supply. The pond behind the dam floods part of the ground. Animals that used to live there have to move. However, the new environment becomes a home for different kinds of birds, fish, and plants. All this happens because of the very busy beaver.

Adapted from M. R. Cohen, B. J. Del Giorno, J. D. Harlan, A. J. McCormack, and J. R. Staver, *Scott Foresman Science, Grade 4* (Glenview, Ill.: Scott, Foresman and Co., 1984), p. 287.

Saudi Arabia

Saudi Arabia is a large country. It is about the size of the United States east of the Mississippi River. But it is a country that has not one lake or river!

The capital is a city of both new and old. There are air-conditioned buildings and high-rise apartments. There are also old buildings made of mud brick. Families often sleep on the roofs at night to escape the heat. They don't worry that it will rain. Saudi Arabia has very dry, very hot weather. Where do people find water? They dig wells deep into the earth. The capital, a city of many people, is watered by many of these wells.

Outside the capital lies the world's largest sand desert. Strong winds blow the sand. From the air, the sand dunes look like waves of a great tan ocean. On the ground, the feel of sand covers everything. A few islands of palm trees spring up out of the desert. They mean only one thing, water. These islands of life are the oases of Saudi Arabia which form around the springs or wells. Many people live near the oases in low mud houses. They plant gardens and orchards and raise camels.

Many groups of people live on the desert itself. They are the Bedouin who move from place to place in search of food and water for their animals. The Bedouin depend on camels and goats for milk and meat. They use the animals' hair to make rugs and cloth for tents. The Bedouin know no boundaries. The open desert has been their home for generations.

Adapted from *Scott, Foresman Social Studies, Grade 4: Regions of Our Country and Our World* (Glenview, Ill.: Scott, Foresman and Co., 1983), pp. 244–245

The City of Cahokia

Cahokia was once a city in what is now the state of Illinois. Nobody lives in Cahokia now. There are no buildings. How did people find out about Cahokia?

Cahokia was discovered because of a group of mounds or hills. These hills did not look like regular hills. It seemed that people might have built them.

Archaeologists dug into the hills. They discovered a buried city. They found remains of large buildings. Between the hills, they found many smaller buildings. Some contained small rooms without any windows. In the middle of the buildings was a large open space. A large circle of post holes was found. A thick post fence was around the hills and the houses.

Archaeologists learned about Cahokia by studying all the facts. Cahokia was a busy city about a thousand years ago. Many of the people were farmers. They probably grew corn, beans, and squash. The city had a strong government. A strong government would be needed to build the hills and the fence. Archaeologists think the circle of holes might have been a huge calendar. It would tell the direction of the sun. The sun told people when to plant and harvest.

The people of Cahokia probably gathered together in large groups. Perhaps they prayed or listened to their leaders. That was what the large open space might have been used for. Cahokia might have had enemies. They built the fence to keep them out.

We don't know everything about Cahokia. However, thanks to archaeologists, we know it is more than a few strange hills.

Adapted from *Scott, Foresman Social Studies, Grade 4: Regions of Our Country and Our World* (Glenview, Ill.: Scott, Foresman and Co., 1983), pp. 22–24.

Level: Four

Narrative

Johnny Appleseed

John Chapman was born in 1774 and grew up in Massachusetts. He became a farmer and learned how to grow different kinds of crops and trees. John especially liked to grow and eat apples. Many people were moving west at that time. They were heading for Ohio and Pennsylvania. John knew that apples were a good food for settlers to have. Apple trees were strong and easy to grow. Apples could be eaten raw and they could be cooked in many ways. They could also be dried for later use. So in 1797, John decided to go west. He wanted to plant apple trees for people who would build their new homes there.

John first gathered bags of apple seeds. He got many of his seeds from farmers who squeezed apples to make a drink called cider. Then, in the spring, he left for the western frontier. He planted seeds as he went along. Also, he gave them to people who knew how valuable apple trees were.

John walked many miles in all kinds of weather. He had to cross dangerous rivers and find his way through strange forests. Often he was hungry, cold, and wet. Sometimes he had to hide from unfriendly Indians. His clothes became ragged and torn. He used a sack for a shirt, and he cut

Level: Four

out holes for the arms. He wore no shoes. But he never gave up. He guarded his precious seeds and carefully planted them where they had the best chance of growing into strong trees.

John's fame spread. He was nicknamed Johnny Appleseed. New settlers welcomed him and gratefully accepted a gift of apple seeds. Many legends grew up about Johnny Appleseed which were not always true. However, one thing is true. Thanks to Johnny Appleseed, apple trees now grow in parts of America where they once never did. (308 words)

From *America's History* by B. B. Armbruster, C. L. Mitsakas and V. R. Rogers, copyright © 1986 by Schoolhouse Press. Reprinted by permission of the publisher.

Number of Total Miscues
(Total Accuracy): _____

Number of Meaning Change Miscues
(Total Acceptability): _____

Total Accuracy		Total Acceptability
0–7 miscues	_____ Independent _____	0–7 miscues
8–32 miscues	_____ Instructional _____	8–16 miscues
32+ miscues	_____ Frustration _____	17+ miscues

Rate: 308 x 60/_____ seconds = _____ WPM

Retelling Scoring Sheet for Johnny Appleseed

Setting/Background

____ John Chapman was born
____ in 1774.
____ He became a farmer
____ and grew crops.
____ John liked
____ to grow
____ and eat apples.
____ People were moving west.
____ Apples were a good food
____ for settlers to have.

Goal

____ John decided
____ to go west.
____ He wanted
____ to plant apple trees.

Events

____ John got many seeds
____ from farmers
____ who squeezed apples
____ to make a drink
____ called cider.
____ He left
____ for the frontier.
____ He planted seeds
____ as he went along.
____ He gave them away.
____ John walked miles.
____ He crossed rivers
____ and went through forests.
____ He was hungry
____ and wet.
____ He had to hide
____ from Indians
____ unfriendly Indians.
____ His clothes were torn.
____ He used a sack
____ for a shirt

Level: Four

____ and he cut out holes
____ for the arms.
____ He wore no shoes.

Resolution

____ John's fame spread.
____ He was nicknamed
____ Johnny Appleseed
____ Settlers accepted seeds
____ gratefully.
____ Thanks to Johnny Appleseed
____ trees grow
____ in many parts
____ of America.

Other ideas recalled, including inferences

_____

Questions for Johnny Appleseed

1. What was John Chapman's main goal?
   Implicit: to plant apple trees across the country

2. Why did John choose apples to plant instead of some other fruit?
   Implicit: the trees were easy to grow, the fruit could be used in a lot of ways; he especially liked apples

3. Where did John get most of his seeds?
   Explicit: from farmers; or from people who made cider

4. Why would John be able to get so many seeds from cider makers?
   Implicit: cider is a drink and you don't drink seeds; apples have a lot of seeds and you don't use seeds in cider

5. How do we know that John cared about planting apple trees?
   Implicit: he suffered hardships; he guarded the apple seeds carefully

6. How did John get to the many places he visited?
   Explicit: he walked

7. Name one hardship John suffered.
   Explicit: being hungry, cold, wet, lost, in danger from unfriendly Indians

8. Why should we thank Johnny Appleseed?
   Explicit: apples now grow in parts of America where they once never did

---

Number Correct Explicit: _____

Number Correct Implicit: _____

Total: _____

_____ Independent: 8 correct

_____ Instructional: 6–7 correct

_____ Frustration: 0–5 correct

Level: Four

Narrative

Amelia Earhart

Amelia Earhart was an adventurer and a pioneer in the field of flying. She did things no other woman had ever done before.

During World War I, Earhart worked as a nurse. She cared for pilots who had been hurt in the war. Earhart listened to what they said about flying. She watched planes take off and land. She knew that she, too, must fly.

In 1928, Earhart was the first woman to cross the Atlantic in a plane. But someone else flew the plane. Earhart wanted to be more than just a passenger. She wanted to fly a plane across the ocean herself. For four years, Earhart trained to be a pilot. Then, in 1932, she flew alone across the Atlantic to Ireland. The trip took over fourteen hours.

Flying may seem easy today. However, Earhart faced many dangers. Airplanes had just been invented. They were much smaller than our planes today. Mechanical problems happened quite often. There were also no computers to help her. Flying across the ocean was as frightening as sailing across it had been years before. Earhart knew the dangers she faced. However, she said, "I want to do it because I want to do it. Women must try to do things as men have tried. When they fail, their failure must be a challenge to others."

Earhart planned to fly around the world. She flew more than twenty thousand miles. Then, her plane disappeared somewhere over

Level: Four

the huge Pacific Ocean. People searched for a long time. Finally they gave up. Earhart and her plane were never found. (263 words)

Adapted from *Scott, Foresman Social Studies, Grade 4: Regions of Our Country and Our World* (Glenview, Ill.: Scott, Foresman and Co., 1983), p. 83.

Number of Total Miscues
(Total Accuracy): _____

Number of Meaning Change Miscues
(Total Acceptability):_____

Total Accuracy			Total Acceptability
0–6 miscues	_____ Independent	_____	0–6 miscues
7–27 miscues	_____ Instructional	_____	7–14 miscues
28+ miscues	_____ Frustration	_____	15+ miscues

Rate: 263 x 60/_____ seconds = _____ WPM

Retelling Scoring Sheet for Amelia Earhart

Setting/Background

____ Amelia Earhart was an adventurer.
____ During World War I
____ she was a nurse.
____ She cared for pilots
____ who had been hurt.
____ Earhart watched planes
____ take off
____ and land.

Goal

____ She knew
____ that she must fly.

____ Earhart was the first woman
____ to cross
____ the Atlantic
____ in a plane.
____ Someone else flew the plane.
____ Earhart wanted to be more
____ than a passenger.
____ She wanted
____ to fly a plane
____ across the ocean.

Events

____ Earhart trained
____ to be a pilot.
____ In 1932
____ she flew
____ alone
____ across the Atlantic
____ to Ireland.
____ Earhart faced dangers.
____ Airplanes were smaller.
____ Problems happened often.
____ There were no computers.
____ Earhart said
____ Women must try
____ to do things
____ as men have tried.
____ Earhart planned
____ to fly
____ around the world.

Resolution

____ Her plane disappeared
____ over the ocean.
____ Pacific Ocean
____ People searched
____ for a long time.
____ They gave up.
____ Earhart
____ and her plane were
____ never found.

Other ideas recalled, including inferences

_____

Level: Four

Questions for Amelia Earhart

1. What was Amelia Earhart's main goal?
   Implicit: to fly; to do things that were challenging

2. When Amelia Earhart first crossed the Atlantic in a plane, what was her role?
   Explicit: she was a passenger

3. How long did it take Amelia Earhart when she flew alone across the Atlantic?
   Explicit: over fourteen hours

4. Why would flying *alone* across the Atlantic be an especially dangerous thing to do?
   Implicit: it was a long trip; there was no one to help with problems; there was no one to help her stay awake or give her a break

5. What was one of the dangers of flying in those early days?
   Explicit: small planes; mechanical problems; no computers

6. How do we know Amelia Earhart believed in equal rights for women?
   Implicit: she said women should try to do things just as men have tried

7. What was Amelia Earhart trying to do when her plane disappeared?
   Explicit: fly around the world

8. Why do you think her plane was never found?
   Implicit: probably sank in the ocean; ocean was so big; plane was very small

Number Correct Explicit: _____

Number Correct Implicit: _____

Total: _____

_____ Independent: 8 correct

_____ Instructional: 6–7 correct

_____ Frustration: 0–5 correct

Narrative

Concept Questions:

Who was Sequoyah?

_____

_____

_____ (3-2-1-0)

What are alphabets used for?

_____

_____

_____ (3-2-1-0)

Why do people write?

_____

_____

_____ (3-2-1-0)

What does "finishing something that is difficult" mean to you?

_____

_____

_____ (3-2-1-0)

Score: _____ /12 = _____ %

_____ FAM _____ UNFAM

Prediction:

_____

_____

Sequoyah

Sequoyah was a Cherokee Indian who lived in Tennessee in the 1800s. One day he met some Americans who were not Indians. He noticed that they looked at something he had never seen before, large white leaves with black marks on them. It seemed to Sequoyah as if the marks were talking to the people.

Sequoyah decided he would try to create talking leaves for the Cherokee people. He spent all of his time working. He drew his signs and pictures on tree bark. He thought the people would be excited about what he was trying to do but they were not. Once, when he was away from home, his wife burned the talking leaves. She did not realize they were important, and others in the village agreed.

Sequoyah continued to work on his signs. When he finished, he had eighty-six signs. Now the time had come to test the signs. Sequoyah and his daughter attended a meeting with Cherokee leaders from many villages. Sequoyah was sent out of the lodge. The chiefs gave messages to his daughter. She wrote down whatever they said. Sequoyah was called back into the lodge. He took the paper and read aloud what was written. It was exactly what the chiefs had said. It worked! Now the Cherokee had a written language all their own.

Within months, hundreds of Cherokee knew the new language. Soon the Cherokee nation had a newspaper and many books. Cherokees from different regions could now communicate with one another. Sequoyah became a great hero. He had given the Cherokee a wonderful gift, the written word. (266 words)

Adapted from *Scott, Foresman Social Studies, Grade 4: Regions of Our Country and Our World* (Glenville, Ill.: Scott, Foresman and Co., 1983), p. 53.

Number of Total Miscues
(Total Accuracy): _____

Number of Meaning Change Miscues
(Total Acceptability):_____

Total Accuracy		Total Acceptability
0–6 miscues _____	Independent	0–6 miscues
7–27 miscues _____	Instructional _____	7–14 miscues
28+ miscues _____	Frustration _____	15+ miscues

Rate: 266 x 60/_____ seconds = _____ WPM

Retelling Scoring Sheet for Sequoyah

Setting/Background

____ Sequoyah was an Indian
____ a Cherokee Indian.

____ He met some Americans
____ who were not Indians.
____ They looked at leaves
____ large leaves
____ white leaves
____ with marks on them
____ black marks.
____ It seemed to Sequoyah
____ as if the marks were talking
____ to the people.

Goal

____ Sequoyah decided
____ he would create leaves
____ talking leaves
____ for the people
____ the Cherokee people.

Events

____ He drew his signs
____ and pictures
____ on tree bark.
____ When he was away
____ his wife burned the leaves.
____ She did not realize
____ they were important.
____ Sequoyah continued to work.
____ When he finished
____ he had signs.
____ eighty-six signs.
____ The time had come
____ to test the signs.
____ Sequoyah
____ and his daughter attended a meeting
____ with leaders
____ Cherokee leaders.
____ Sequoyah was sent out
____ of the lodge.
____ The chiefs gave messages
____ to his daughter.
____ She wrote down what they said.
____ Sequoyah was called back.
____ He read what was written
____ exactly what the chiefs said.

Level: Four

Resolution

____ The Cherokee had a language
____ a written language
____ all their own.
____ The nation had a newspaper
____ and books.
____ Cherokees could communicate with
       Cherokees
____ from different regions.
____ Sequoyah became a great hero.
____ He gave a gift
____ a wonderful gift
____ to the Cherokee,
____ the written word.

Other ideas recalled, including inferences

_____

Questions for Sequoyah

1. What was Sequoyah's main goal?
   Implicit: he wanted to make a written
   language for his people; he wanted to create
   talking leaves

2. What might have been the objects that
   Sequoyah thought were large white leaves
   with black marks?
   Implicit: white paper with black
   letters/words

3. What did Sequoyah use to draw on?
   Explicit: tree bark

4. Why did Sequoyah's wife burn his signs?
   Explicit: she didn't know they were
   important

5. How do we know that Sequoyah did not
   easily give up?
   Implicit: he kept on working even when his
   signs were burned and others did not agree
   with him

6. Who tested the signs with Sequoyah and his
   daughter?
   Explicit: Cherokee chiefs

7. What did the Cherokee nation do with their
   new language?
   Explicit: make newspapers and books

8. Why was the written word an important gift
   for the Cherokee?
   Implicit: Cherokees from different regions
   could now keep in touch

Number Correct Explicit: _____

Number Correct Implicit: _____

Total: _____

_____ Independent: 8 correct

_____ Instructional: 6–7 correct

_____ Frustration: 0–5 correct

Level: Four

Expository

Concept Questions:

What is a beaver?

_____

_____

_____ (3-2-1-0)

What are dams built by beavers?

_____

_____

_____ (3-2-1-0)

What are problems caused by beavers?

_____

_____

_____ (3-2-1-0)

How do beavers protect their young?

_____

_____

_____ (3-2-1-0)

Score: _____ /12 = _____ %

_____ FAM _____ UNFAM

Prediction:

_____

_____

The Busy Beaver

Have you ever heard someone say "busy" as a beaver"? Beavers are very busy animals and they are master builders. This furry animal spends its life working and building. As soon as a beaver leaves its family, it has much work to do.

First, the beaver must build a dam. It uses sticks, leaves, and mud to block a stream. The beaver uses its two front teeth to get the sticks. The animal uses its large flat tail to pack mud into place. A pond forms behind the dam. The beaver spends most of its life near this pond.

In the middle of the beaver's pond is a large mound. This mound of mud and twigs is the beaver's lodge or house. The beaver's family is safe in the lodge because it is well hidden. The doorway to the lodge is under the water. After the lodge is built, the beaver still cannot rest. More trees must be cut down to be used as food for the coming winter. Sometimes there will be no more trees around the pond. Then the beaver has to find trees elsewhere. These trees will have to be carried to the pond. The beaver might build canals leading deep into the forest.

All this work changes the land. As trees are cut down, birds, squirrels, and other animals may have to find new homes. Animals that feed on trees lose their food supply. The pond behind the dam floods part of the ground. Animals that used to live there have to move. However, the new environment becomes a home for different kinds of birds, fish, and plants. All this happens because of the very <u>busy</u> beaver. (281 words)

Adapted from M. R. Cohen, B. J. Del Giorno, J. D. Harlan, A. J. Mccormack, and J. R. Staver, *Scott, Foresman Science, Grade 4* (Glenview, Ill.: Scott, Foresman and Co., 1984), p. 287.

Number of Total Miscues
(Total Accuracy): _____

Number of Meaning Change Miscues
(Total Acceptability): _____

Total Accuracy				**Total Acceptability**
0–7 miscues	_____	Independent	_____	0–7 miscues
8–29 miscues	_____	Instructional	_____	8–15 miscues
30+ miscues	_____	Frustration	_____	16+ miscues

Rate: 281 x 60/_____ seconds = _____ WPM

Retelling Scoring Sheet for The Busy Beaver

Main Idea

____ Have you heard
____ "busy as a beaver?"
____ Beavers are animals
____ busy animals
____ and builders
____ master builders.

Details

____ As soon as a beaver leaves its family,
____ it has much work to do.

____ The beaver builds a dam.
____ It uses sticks,
____ leaves,
____ and mud
____ to block a stream.
____ The beaver uses its teeth
____ its front teeth
____ to get sticks.
____ The animals uses its tail
____ to pack mud.
____ A pond forms
____ behind the dam.
____ The beaver spends its life
____ near the pond.
____ The beaver's home is a mound
____ in the pond.
____ The family is safe
____ because the lodge is well hidden.
____ The doorway
____ to the lodge
____ is under the water.
____ Trees are cut down
____ to be used as food
____ for the winter.
____ Sometimes there will be no trees
____ around the pond.
____ The beaver has to find trees
____ and carry them
____ to the pond.
____ The beaver might build canals.

Main Idea

____ This changes the land.

Details

____ As trees are cut,
____ birds,
____ squirrels,
____ and animals have to find new homes.
____ Animals lose their food supply.
____ The pond floods the land.
____ Animals have to move.
____ A new environment becomes home
____ for different birds
____ and fish.

Other ideas recalled, including inferences

_____

Questions for The Busy Beaver

1. What is the passage mainly about?
   Implicit: how a beaver keeps busy; what a beaver does

2. According to the passage, what are the beaver's front teeth used for?
   Explicit: to get the sticks

3. Describe the beaver's tail.
   Explicit: large and flat

4. Why does the beaver build a dam?
   Implicit: to make a pond or to make a place for his lodge

5. What is the beaver's lodge or house made of?
   Explicit: mud and sticks

6. Why is the doorway to the beaver's house under the water?
   Implicit: it is safer and more hidden; so enemies can't get in

7. What does the beaver eat during the winter?
   Explicit: trees

8. Why might some people dislike beavers?
   Implicit: they change the land by flooding; they drive out animals; they cut down too many trees

Number Correct Explicit: _____

Number Correct Implicit: _____

Total: _____

_____ Independent: 8 correct

_____ Instructional: 6–7 correct

_____ Frustration: 0–5 correct

Level: Four

Expository

Saudi Arabia

Saudi Arabia is a large country. It is about the size of the United States east of the Mississippi River. But it is a country that has not one lake or river!

The capital is a city of both new and old. There are air-conditioned buildings and high-rise apartments. There are also old buildings made of mud brick. Families often sleep on the roofs at night to escape the heat. They don't worry that it will rain. Saudi Arabia has very dry, very hot weather. Where do people find water? They dig wells deep into the earth. The capital, a city of many people, is watered by many of these wells.

Outside the capital lies the world's largest sand desert. Strong winds blow the sand. From the air, the sand dunes look like waves of a great tan ocean. On the ground, the feel of sand covers everything. A few islands of palm trees spring up out of the desert. They mean only one thing, water. These islands of life are the oases of Saudi Arabia which form around the springs or wells. Many people live near the oases in low mud houses. They plant gardens and orchards and raise camels.

Many groups of people live on the desert itself. They are the Bedouin who move from place to place in search of food and water for

Level: Four

their animals. The Bedouin depend on camels and goats for milk and meat. They use the animals' hair to make rugs and cloth for tents. The Bedouin know no boundaries. The open desert has been their home for generations. (265 words)

Adapted from *Scott, Foresman Social Studies, Grade 4: Regions of Our Country and Our World* (Glenview, Ill.: Scott, Foresman and Co., 1983), p. 244–245.

Number of Total Miscues
(Total Accuracy): _____

Number of Meaning Change Miscues
(Total Acceptability): _____

Total Accuracy			Total Acceptability
0–6 miscues	_____	Independent _____	0–6 miscues
7–27 miscues	_____	Instructional _____	7–14 miscues
28+ miscues	_____	Frustration _____	15+ miscues
Rate: 265 x 60/_____ seconds =		_____ WPM	

Retelling Scoring Sheet for Saudi Arabia

Main Idea

____ Saudi Arabia is a country
____ a large country.

Details

____ It is the size
____ of the U.S.
____ east of the Mississippi.
____ It does not have one lake
____ or river.

Main Idea

____ The capital is a city of
____ old
____ and new.

Details

____ There are buildings
____ air-conditioned buildings
____ and apartments
____ high-rise apartments.
____ There are buildings
____ old buildings
____ made of brick
____ mud brick.
____ Families sleep
____ on roofs
____ at night
____ to escape the heat.
____ They don't worry
____ about rain.
____ Saudi Arabia has dry weather
____ and hot weather.
____ People find water
____ by digging wells
____ deep
____ in the earth.

Main Idea

____ Outside the capital
____ is a desert
____ the world's largest desert.

Details

____ Islands are on the desert
____ islands of palm trees.
____ They mean water.
____ They are oases
____ which form around springs
____ or wells.
____ People live near the oases
____ in houses
____ mud houses.
____ People live on the desert.
____ They are the Bedouin

____ who move

____ in search of food

____ and water

____ for their animals.

____ The Bedouin depend on camels

____ and goats

____ for milk

____ and meat.

____ They use the animals' hair

____ to make rugs

____ and cloth.

Other ideas recalled, including inferences

_____

Questions for Saudi Arabia

1. What is this passage mainly about?
   Implicit: how the people of Saudi Arabia live; what Saudi Arabia is like

2. Describe the weather of Saudi Arabia.
   Explicit: very hot and dry

3. Where do the people of Saudi Arabia get water?
   Explicit: from wells and/or springs

4. Why are cities in Saudi Arabia built near wells?
   Implicit: there is little water; they need water

5. What kind of houses would you find by an oasis in Saudi Arabia?
   Explicit: low, mud houses

6. What animals do the Bedouin people depend on for meat and milk?
   Explicit: goats and camels

7. Why don't Bedouin live in the cities of Saudi Arabia?
   Implicit: they raise animals; they like to wander

8. Why wouldn't swimming be a popular sport in Saudi Arabia?
   Implicit: there isn't enough water for pools; there are no lakes or rivers

Number Correct Explicit: _____

Number Correct Implicit: _____

Total: _____

_____ Independent: 8 correct

_____ Instructional: 6–7 correct

_____ Frustration: 0–5 correct

Level: Four

Expository

The City of Cahokia

Cahokia was once a city in what is now the state of Illinois. Nobody lives in Cahokia now. There are no buildings. How did people find out about Cahokia?

Cahokia was discovered because of a group of <u>mounds</u> or hills. These hills did not look like regular hills. It seemed that people might have built them.

Archaeologists dug into the hills. They discovered a buried city. They found remains of large buildings. Between the hills, they found many smaller buildings. Some contained small rooms without any windows. In the middle of the buildings was a large open space. A large circle of post holes was found. A thick post fence was around the hills and the houses.

Archaeologists learned about Cahokia by studying all the facts. Cahokia was a <u>busy</u> city about a thousand years ago. Many of the people were farmers. They probably grew corn, beans, and squash. The city had a strong government. A strong government would be needed to build the hills and the fence. Archaeologists think the circle of holes might have been a huge calendar. It would tell the direction of the sun. The sun told people when to plant and harvest.

The people of Cahokia probably gathered together in large groups. Perhaps they prayed or listened to their leaders. That was what the large open space might have been used for. Cahokia might have had enemies. They built the fence to keep them out.

We don't know everything about Cahokia. However, thanks to archaeologists, we know it is more than a few strange hills. (260 words)

Adapted from *Scott, Foresman Social Studies, Grade: Regions of Our Country and Our World* (Glenview, Ill.: Scott, Foresman and Co., 1983), pp. 22–24.

Number of Total Miscues
(Total Accuracy): _____

Number of Meaning Change Miscues
(Total Acceptability): _____

Total Accuracy			Total Acceptability
0–6 miscues	_____	Independent	_____ 0–6 miscues
7–27 miscues	_____	Instructional	_____ 7–14 miscues
28+ miscues	_____	Frustration	_____ 15+ miscues

Rate: 260 x 60/_____ seconds = _____ WPM

Retelling Scoring Sheet for The City of Cahokia

Main Idea

____ Cahokia was discovered
____ because of mounds
____ or hills.

Details

____ Cahokia was once a city
____ in Illinois.
____ Nobody lives in Cahokia.
____ The mounds did not look
____ like regular hills.
____ Archaeologists dug
____ into the hills.

Main Idea

____ They discovered a city
____ a buried city.

Details

____ They found remains
____ of buildings.
____ Some contained rooms
____ without windows.
____ In the middle of the buildings
____ they found a space
____ a large space.
____ They found a circle
____ of holes.
____ They found a fence
____ around the hills
____ and houses.

Main Idea

____ Archaeologists learned
____ about Cahokia
____ by studying the facts.

Details

____ Cahokia was busy
____ a thousand
____ years ago.
____ The people were farmers.
____ They grew corn,
____ beans,
____ and squash.
____ The city had a government
____ a strong government
____ The circle was a calendar.
____ It told the direction
____ of the sun.

Level: Four

_____ The sun told people
_____ when to plant
_____ and harvest.
_____ The people gathered together.
_____ They prayed
_____ or listened to their leaders.
_____ That was what the space was for.
_____ Cahokia had enemies.
_____ They built the fence
_____ to keep them out.

Other ideas recalled, including inferences

_____

Questions for The City of Cahokia

1. What is this passage mainly about?
   Implicit: what the city of Cahokia was like

2. What led to the discovery of Cahokia?
   Explicit: the hills or mounds

3. What was unusual about some of the rooms?
   Implicit: they didn't have windows

4. What did the people of Cahokia probably grow?
   Explicit: corn, beans, or squash

5. How do you think archaeologists knew that the people were farmers?
   Implicit: they probably found remains of tools

6. What do the archaeologists think the huge calendar may have been used for?
   Explicit: to tell the direction of the sun; to tell when to plant and harvest

7. Why did the people build a fence around the city?
   Explicit: to keep out enemies

8. What is the job of an archaeologist?
   Implicit: to study lost cities and people

Number Correct Explicit: _____

Number Correct Implicit: _____

Total: _____

_____ Independent: 8 correct

_____ Instructional: 6–7 correct

_____ Frustration: 0–5 correct

Martin Luther King, Jr.

When Martin Luther King, Jr., was a boy, many laws would not allow black people to go to the same places as whites. Some people thought blacks were not as good as whites. Black children could not attend some schools, and certain restaurants had signs that said "whites only." Blacks could not sit in the front of a bus and, if a bus got crowded, they had to give up their seat to a white person. King did not agree with laws like these for he believed that all people are equal. He did not think that skin color should keep people apart. Laws separating blacks and whites were unjust, and King decided to protest such laws.

Many people organized to help him. King said that they must protest in a peaceful way. King told his followers to "meet hate with love." In Montgomery, Alabama, Rosa Parks, a black woman, was arrested and fined for not giving up her seat to a white man on a bus. King led the movement to protest this action. Thousands of people refused to ride the buses. The bus companies began to lose money. In time the law was changed. King traveled to many cities. He talked to the people and led them in peaceful marches.

More and more people heard about King's peaceful protests and joined him. King led a march to our center of government, Washington, D.C., to ask that the unjust laws be changed. Finally, the United States Supreme Court agreed with King. The laws separating blacks and whites were changed. King was given the Nobel Peace Prize for his work. Today people still admire King because he fought for justice in a peaceful way. January 15 was named as a national holiday in honor of Martin Luther King, Jr.

From *Holt Social Studies, Our World, Our Regions, and Our History,* edited by JoAnn Cangemi, copyright © 1983, by Holt, Rinehart and Winston, Inc. Reprinted by permission of the publisher.

Christopher Columbus

Christopher Columbus was determined to find an all-water route to the East Indies. Discovering this would bring him fame and fortune. However, Columbus also believed that the world was round. Many people laughed at this idea. They thought the world was flat. Columbus hoped to prove his theory. He would sail west in order to reach the East.

King Ferdinand and Queen Isabella of Spain thought Columbus's idea had merit. However, Spain was fighting a costly war. Columbus had to wait seven long years. Then they gave him money to finance the expedition. It was easy to buy ships and supplies. It was more difficult to find sailors who were willing to join him. Finally, in 1492, he set sail on the uncharted, unexplored Atlantic Ocean. Columbus had ninety sailors and three ships. His ships were the Nina, the Pinta, and the Santa Maria.

After they had been out of sight of land for a month, the sailors became frightened. They did not really believe the earth was round. They were afraid to sail too far to the edge. No one had ever sailed out so far upon the "Sea of Darkness." The sailors talked of mutiny. Columbus tried to convince them that they had nothing to fear. He reminded them of the gold they would get if they finished the voyage and he told them they would be famous. But still the sailors threatened to take over and turn back.

Just when it seemed they would go no farther, branches and leaves were seen in the water. The sailors felt much better and agreed to continue sailing. Then on October 12, 1492, the welcome call was heard that land had been sighted. Columbus claimed the new land for Spain and named the inhabitants Indians. He mistakenly thought he had found a new route to the East. In fact, Columbus died believing he had reached the Indies.

Adapted from *The United States and Its Neighbors* by T. M. Helmus, V. E. Arnsdorf, E. A. Toppin, and N. J. G. Pounds. Copyright © 1984, by Silver, Burdett and Ginn, Inc. Used with permission.

Margaret Mead

Margaret Mead had always been interested in the ways of life of people from other lands. When Mead went to college, she took a class in anthropology. This is the study of how different people live. Mead decided to make this her career. She wanted to study primitive people before modern ways of living destroyed their culture.

Mead realized that living with a people is the only effective way to learn about them. She chose a village in Samoa to investigate. Several islands make up Samoa which is in the Pacific Ocean. Mead worked hard to prepare for Samoa. She studied languages like the Samoan language. She read everything she could about the Samoan people. She read about their food and how they built their homes. She read about their ceremonies, their past history, and their taboos. But she wanted to learn much more.

Finally Mead arrived in Samoa. At first life was difficult for her. She was alone. She was not fluent in the Samoan language. She lived in a house with no walls and no electricity or gas. It had no running water and no bathroom. One day she said to herself, "I can't go on," in Samoan. Then she thought that maybe she could continue after all. Mead became fluent in the Samoan language, and the people soon regarded her as one of the village. She listened to their talk, their jokes, and their gossip. They told her their problems. Mead felt that being a woman assisted her in learning more about the lives of these people. Instead of having to go on hunts with the men, Mead stayed with the women. She observed the children play and learned how food was prepared. She made efforts to get the older people to recount tales of the past.

Mead learned many things from the Samoan people. She always took notes and kept careful records. These notes were used to write her first book which was called *Coming of Age in Samoa*. It made her famous. Mead spent the rest of her life studying and writing about primitive ways of life that no longer exist today.

Adapted from *The People of Tiegs-Adams: People and Their Heritage* series, Copyright © 1983, by Silver, Burdett & Ginn, Inc. Used with permission.

The Octopus

Some people think of the octopus as a giant creature. They have seen this in science fiction movies. They think the octopus is a mean creature who attacks people and other animals. The octopus is really a shy animal. It is usually quite small.

The octopus has eight arms. Its name tells us this because "octo" means eight. The octopus uses its arms to walk on the ocean floor. Its arms are also used to capture crabs. Crabs are its favorite food. The octopus bites into the crab with its strong beak. This sends poison into the crab's body.

The octopus protects itself in three ways. First, when frightened, the octopus can push water from its body in a powerful stream. This action pushes the octopus forward very rapidly. This allows it to escape.

Second, the body of the octopus has a special sac or pouch that holds a dark, inklike fluid. When an enemy comes close, the octopus squirts some of this fluid. It then swims away. All that the predator sees is a dark cloud in the water where the octopus was. Meanwhile, the octopus has escaped.

Finally, the octopus's body changes color when the octopus is excited or frightened. Suppose an octopus sees a crab. Patches of pink, purple, or blue will appear on the octopus's skin. Suppose the octopus sees an enemy. The octopus will completely change color. Then it seems to disappear into the background of its hiding place. It is hard for the predator to find the octopus.

Adapted from M. R. Cohen, B. J. Del Giorno, J. D. Harlan, A. J. McCormack, and J. R. Staver, *Scott, Foresman Science, Grade 5* (Glenview, Ill.: Scott, Foresman and Co., 1984), p. 31.

Getting Rid of Trash

In the past, when people wanted to get rid of their trash, they just threw it out. Sometimes they threw it into the streets or alleys, and sometimes they packed it into a wagon and dumped it near the edge of town. Open dumping caused many problems. The trash was ugly and often smelled. It attracted rats and other animals that carried diseases.

Over the years people have changed the way they get rid of trash. Now trash is often crushed and put in open places. A layer of trash is dumped and smashed down. Then it is covered with dirt. Another layer of trash is dumped and covered with dirt. This way of getting rid of trash is called landfill. Buildings can be built on landfill.

Burning trash is another way of getting rid of it; however, this often adds to air pollution. Today we have new furnaces for burning trash which are called incinerators. These new incinerators have scrubbers on their chimneys which cut down on air pollution. The new incinerators also gather some of the heat let off by burning trash. This energy can be used to heat homes and businesses.

There is another way of dealing with trash. It is recycling or changing waste products so they can be used again. We can do this with paper, glass, or aluminum. Glass can be crushed, melted down, and then made into new jars and bottles. This cuts down on the amount of trash. It also takes less energy to recycle glass and cans than to make new ones.

Adapted from M. R. Cohen, B. J. Del Giorno, J. D. Harlan, A. J. McCormack, and J. R. Staver, *Scott, Foresman Science, Grade 5* (Glenview, Ill.: Scott, Foresman and Co., 1984), pp. 374–376.

Laser Light

Scientists have found a new kind of light. This light is called laser light. Lasers are being used in medicine, industry, and science research.

How is laser light different from other kinds of light? White light actually contains all the colors of the rainbow. And the "red" light in a traffic signal contains red light of many different wavelengths. But the waves of laser light are all the same wavelength. So the light from a laser is one pure color. Another difference between laser light and other light is that a laser makes a thin beam of light that travels only in one direction. Finally, the waves of laser light are all lined up. Because the waves of laser light are the same length, travel in one direction, and all line up, a beam of laser light can be very powerful. A laser beam can even drill holes in metal. A lens focuses the laser beam to hit the point where the hole is to be drilled.

Laser light is useful in many ways. Laser beams can be used to carry radio and telephone messages. Lasers can even prevent some people from going blind. A person's eye is often damaged in an accident. Doctors use laser beams to reattach the retina. Lasers can be used to burn out tumors without a lot of bleeding. Lasers are also used to cut cloth for clothes. Every year new uses for laser light are being discovered. This new light in our life will continue to help us in many ways.

Adapted from M. R. Cohen, B. J. Del Giorno, J. D. Harlan, A. J. McCormack, and J. R. Staver, *Scott, Foresman Science, Grade 5* (Glenview, Ill.: Scott, Foresman and Co., 1984), p. 289.

Narrative

Concept Questions:

Who was Martin Luther King?

_____

_____

_____ (3-2-1-0)

What is racism?

_____

_____

_____ (3-2-1-0)

What is Washington D.C.?

_____

_____

_____ (3-2-1-0)

What does "equal rights for blacks" mean to you?

_____

_____

_____ (3-2-1-0)

Score: _____ /12 = _____ %

_____ FAM _____ UNFAM

Prediction:

_____

_____

Martin Luther King, Jr.

When Martin Luther King, Jr., was a boy, many laws would not allow black people to go to the same places as whites. Some people thought blacks were not as good as whites. Black children could not attend some schools, and certain restaurants had signs that said "white only." Blacks could not sit in the front of a bus and, if a bus got crowded, they had to give up their seat to a white person. King did not agree with laws like these for he believed that all people are equal. He did not think that skin color should keep people apart. Laws separating blacks and whites were unjust, and King decided to protest such laws.

Many people organized to help him. King said that they must protest in a peaceful way. King told his followers to "meet hate with love." In Montgomery, Alabama, Rosa Parks, a black woman, was arrested and fined for not giving up her seat to a white man on a bus. King led the movement to protest this action. Thousands of people refused to ride the buses. The bus companies began to lose money. In time the law was changed. King traveled to many cities. He talked to the people and led them in peaceful marches.

More and more people heard about King's peaceful protests and joined him. King led a march to our center of government, Washington, D.C., to ask that the unjust laws be changed. Finally, the United States

Level: Five

Supreme Court agreed with King. The laws separating blacks and whites were changed. King was given the Nobel Peace Prize for his work. Today people still admire King because he fought for justice in a peaceful way. January 15 was named as a national holiday in honor of Martin Luther King, Jr. (297 words)

From *Holt Social Studies, Our World, Our Regions, and Our History,* edited by JoAnn Cangemi, copyright © 1983 by Holt, Rinehart and Winston, Inc. Reprinted by permission of the publisher.

Number of Total Miscues
(Total Accuracy): _____

Number of Meaning Change Miscues
(Total Acceptability): _____

Total Accuracy			Total Acceptability
0–7 miscues	_____ Independent	_____	0–7 miscues
8–31 miscues	_____ Instructional	_____	8–16 miscues
32+ miscues	_____ Frustration	_____	17+ miscues
Rate: 297 x 60/_____ seconds =		_____ WPM	

Retelling Scoring Sheet for Martin Luther King, Jr.

Setting/Background

____ When Martin Luther King, Jr., was a boy
____ laws would not allow blacks
____ to go to the same places
____ as whites.
____ People thought
____ blacks weren't as good
____ as whites.

____ Black children could not attend some schools.
____ Certain restaurants had signs
____ that said
____ "whites only."
____ Blacks could not sit
____ in front
____ of a bus.
____ If the bus got crowded
____ they had to give up their seat
____ to a white.

Goal

____ King did not agree
____ with these laws.
____ He believed
____ that all people are equal.
____ He decided
____ to protest these laws.

Events

____ King said
____ they must protest
____ in a peaceful way.
____ In Alabama
____ Rosa Parks was arrested
____ for not giving up her seat
____ to a white man.
____ King led a movement
____ to protest this action.
____ Thousands refused
____ to ride the buses.
____ The bus company lost money.
____ The law was changed.
____ King led a march
____ to our center of government,
____ Washington, D.C.,
____ to ask
____ that the laws be changed.
____ the unjust laws

Resolution

____ The Supreme Court agreed.
____ The laws were changed
____ laws separating blacks and whites.

Level: Five

____ King was given a prize
____ the Nobel Peace Prize
____ for his work.
____ People still admire King.
____ January 15 was named
____ as a holiday
____ a national holiday
____ in honor of King.

Other ideas recalled, including references

_____

Questions for Martin Luther King, Jr.

1. What was Martin Luther King's main goal?
   Implicit: he wanted equality for black people

2. Why had people made laws separating blacks and whites?
   Implicit: they thought blacks were not as good as whites

3. In some cities, what did blacks have to do on a crowded bus?
   Explicit: give up their seat to a white person

4. Why was Rosa Parks arrested?
   Explicit: she refused to give up her seat

5. What did many people do to protest Rosa Park's arrest?
   Explicit: they refused to ride the buses

6. What happened when people refused to ride the buses?
   Implicit: the law was changed. If the student says, "the bus companies lost money," ask "what happened because of that"?

7. Why was Washington, D.C., an important place to protest unjust laws?
   Implicit: it is where the President and government officials are so they would see the protest

8. Name one way in which Martin Luther King was honored for his work.
   Explicit: the Nobel Prize; or the national holiday

Number Correct Explicit: _____

Number Correct Implicit: _____

Total: _____

_____ Independent: 8 correct

_____ Instructional: 6–7 correct

_____ Frustration: 0–5 correct

Level: Five

Narrative

Christopher Columbus

Christopher Columbus was determined to find an all-water route to the East Indies. Discovering this would bring him to fame and fortune. However, Columbus also believed that the world was round. Many people laughed at this idea. They thought the world was flat. Columbus hoped to prove his theory. He would sail west in order to reach the East.

King Ferdinand and Queen Isabella of Spain thought Columbus's idea had merit. However, Spain was fighting a costly war. Columbus had to wait seven long years. Then they gave him money to finance the expedition. It was easy to buy ships and supplies. It was more difficult to find sailors who were willing to join him. Finally, in 1492, he set sail on the uncharted, unexplored Atlantic Ocean. Columbus had ninety sailors and three ships. His ships were the Nina, the Pinta, and the Santa Maria.

After they had been out of sight of land for a month, the sailors became frightened. They did not really believe the earth was round. They were afraid to sail too far to the edge. No one had ever sailed out so far upon the "Sea of Darkness." The sailors talked of mutiny. Columbus tried to convince them that they had nothing to fear. He reminded

Level: Five

them of the gold they would get if they finished the voyage and he told them they would be famous. But still the sailors threatened to take over and turn back.

Just when it seemed they would go no farther, branches and levels were seen in the water. The sailors felt much better and agreed to continue sailing. Then on October 12, 1942, the welcome call was heard that land had been sighted. Columbus claimed the new land for Spain and named the inhabitants Indians. He mistakenly thought he had found a new route to the East. In fact, Columbus died believing he had reached the Indies. (317 words)

Adapted from *The United States and Its Neighbors* by T. M. Helmus, V. E. Arnsdorf, E. A. Toppin, and N. J. G. Pounds. © Copyright 1984, by Silver, Burdett and Ginn, Inc. Used with permission.

Number of Total Miscues
(Total Accuracy): _____

Number of Meaning Change Miscues
(Total Acceptability): _____

Total Accuracy			Total Acceptability
0–7 miscues	_____ Independent	_____	0–7 miscues
8–33 miscues	_____ Instructional	_____	8–17 miscues
34+ miscues	_____ Frustration	_____	18+ miscues

Rate: 317 x 60/_____ seconds = _____ WPM

Retelling Scoring Sheet for Christopher Columbus

Setting/Background
_____ Columbus believed
_____ that the world was round.
_____ People thought
_____ the world was flat.
_____ Columbus hoped
_____ to prove his theory.

Goal
_____ Columbus was determined
_____ to find a route
_____ an all-water route
_____ to the Indies.
_____ He would sail west
_____ to reach the East.

Events
_____ Spain was fighting a war.
_____ Columbus had to wait
_____ for years.
_____ The King Ferdinand
_____ and Queen Isabella gave him money.
_____ It was easy
_____ to buy ships
_____ and supplies.
_____ It was difficult
_____ to find sailors.
_____ In 1492
_____ he set sail.
_____ Columbus had sailors
_____ 90 sailors and ships,
_____ three ships,
_____ the Nina,
_____ the Pinta,
_____ and the Santa Maria.
_____ The sailors were afraid
_____ to sail too far
_____ to the edge.
_____ Columbus tried to convince them
_____ that they had nothing to fear.
_____ Columbus reminded them

____ of the gold
____ they would get.
____ He told them
____ they would be famous.
____ But the sailors threatened
____ to take over
____ and turn back.
____ Just when it seemed
____ they would go no farther,
____ branches
____ and leaves were seen
____ in the water.
____ The sailors felt better
____ and agreed
____ to continue.

Resolution

____ Land was sighted.
____ Columbus claimed the land
____ for Spain.
____ He named the inhabitants
____ Indians.
____ Columbus died
____ believing
____ he had reached the Indies.

Other ideas recalled, including inferences

_____

Questions for Christopher Columbus

1. What was Christopher Columbus's main goal?
   Implicit: to prove the world was round; to sail west to get to the East Indies

2. How long did Christopher Columbus have to wait before he got the money from the king and queen of Spain?
   Explicit: seven years

3. Why was it more difficult to get sailors than ships and supplies?
   Implicit: people did not believe the world was round; the Atlantic was uncharted and unknown. If student says, "Sailors were afraid," ask, "Why?"

4. Why did the sailors become frightened after being out of sight of land for a month?
   Explicit: they didn't believe the earth was round and they didn't want to sail close to the edge

5. Why did many people of that time call the Atlantic Ocean a "Sea of Darkness"?
Implicit: no one knew much about it; they thought they would die if they sailed too far.

6. How did Christopher Columbus try to convince the sailors to continue the voyage?
Explicit: he said there was nothing to fear; he said they would be rich and famous

7. What did the sailors see that made them agree to continue sailing?
Explicit: branches and leaves in the water

8. Why did Christopher Columbus name the inhabitants of the new lands Indians?
Implicit: he thought he had reached the Indies

Number Correct Explicit: _____

Number Correct Implicit: _____

Total: _____

_____ Independent: 8 correct

_____ Instructional: 6–7 correct

_____ Frustration: 0–5 correct

Level: Five

Narrative

Margaret Mead

Margaret Mead had always been interested in the ways of life of people from other lands. When Mead went to college, she took a class in anthropology. This is the study of how different people live. Mead decided to make this her career. She wanted to study primitive people before modern ways of living destroyed their culture.

Mead realized that living with a people is the only effective way to learn about them. She chose a village in Samoa to investigate. Several islands make up Samoa which is in the Pacific Ocean. Mead worked hard to prepare for Samoa. She studied languages like the Samoan language. She read everything she could about the Samoan people. She read about their food and how they built their homes. She read about their ceremonies, their past history, and their taboos. But she wanted to learn much more.

Finally Mead arrived in Samoa. At first life was difficult for her. She was alone. She was not fluent in the Samoan language. She lived in a house with no walls and no electricity or gas. It had no running water and no bathroom. One day she said to herself, "I can't go on," in Samoan. Then she thought that maybe she could continue after all. Mead became fluent in the Samoan language, and the people soon regarded her as one of the village. She listened to their talk, their jokes, and their gossip. They told her their problems. Mead felt that being a woman assisted her in learning more about the lives of these people. Instead of having to go on hunts with the men, Mead stayed with the women. She observed the children play and learned how food was prepared. She made efforts to get the older people to recount <u>tales</u> of the past.

Mead learned many things from the Samoan people. She always took notes and kept careful records. These notes were used to write her first book which was called *Coming of Age in Samoa*. It made her famous. Mead spent the rest of her life studying and writing about primitive ways of life that no longer exist today. (357 words)

Adapted from *The People of Tiegs-Adams: People and Their Heritage* series, © Copyright, 1983, by Silver, Burdett & Ginn, Inc. Used with permission.

Number of Total Miscues (Total Accuracy): _____			
Number of Meaning Change Miscues (Total Acceptability):_____			
Total Accuracy		**Total Acceptability**	
0–5 miscues	_____ Independent	_____	0–8 miscues
9–37 miscues	_____ Instructional	_____	9–19 miscues
38+ miscues	_____ Frustration	_____	20+ miscues
Rate: 357 x 60/_____ seconds =		_____ WPM	

Retelling Scoring Sheet for Margaret Mead

Background/Setting

____ When Margaret Mead went to college
____ she took a class
____ in anthropology.
____ She decided to make this her career.

Goal

____ She wanted to study people
____ primitive people.
____ She chose a village
____ in Samoa
____ to investigate.
____ Islands make up Samoa
____ which is in the Pacific Ocean.

Events

____ Margaret Mead studied languages
____ like the Samoan language.
____ She read everything she could
____ about the Samoan people.
____ She read
____ about their food,
____ and how they built their homes.
____ She arrived in Samoa.
____ Life was difficult.
____ She lived
____ in a house
____ with no walls
____ with no electricity.
____ She said,
____ "I can't go on"
____ in Samoan.
____ Then she thought
____ that she could continue.
____ The people regarded her
____ as one of the village.
____ She listened
____ to their jokes,
____ their gossip.
____ Instead of having to go
____ on hunts
____ with the men

____ Margaret Mead stayed
____ with the women.
____ She observed the children
____ play
____ and learned
____ how food was prepared.

Resolutions

____ She wrote a book
____ called *Coming of Age in Samoa.*
____ It made her famous.

Other ideas recalled, including inferences

_____

Questions for Margaret Mead

1. What was Margaret Mead's main goal?
   Implicit: to study primitive people

2. What people did Margaret Mead choose to investigate?
   Explicit: people in Samoa

3. Name one thing Margaret Mead read about to prepare her for Samoa.
   Explicit: homes; food; ceremonies; its history; taboos

4. Give one reason why life in Samoa was difficult at first.
   Explicit: she was alone; there were no walls, electricity, running water, bathroom; she was not fluent in the language

5. What made Margaret Mead decide she would be able to stay in Samoa?
   Implicit: when she talked to herself in Samoan and realized she knew the language

6. Why was Margaret Mead able to learn a lot about the family life of the Samoans?
   Implicit: she stayed with the women and children; the women and children talked to her

7. Why did Margaret Mead want to hear the stories of the Samoans' past?
   Implicit: she wanted to learn as much about them as she could

8. What did Margaret Mead do with the notes and records she kept?
   Explicit: she wrote a book

Number Correct Explicit: _____

Number Correct Implicit: _____

Total: _____

_____ Independent: 8 correct

_____ Instructional: 6–7 correct

_____ Frustration: 0–5 correct

Expository

Concept Questions:

What is an octopus?

_____

_____

_____ (3-2-1-0)

Why does an animal attack another animal?

_____

_____

_____ (3-2-1-0)

What are animal defenses?

_____

_____

_____ (3-2-1-0)

What is animal camouflage?

_____

_____

_____ (3-2-1-0)

Score: _____ /12 = _____ %

_____ FAM _____ UNFAM

Prediction:

_____

_____

The Octopus

Some people think of the octopus as a giant creature. They have seen this in science fiction movies. They think the octopus is a mean creature who attacks people and other animals. The octopus is really a shy animal. It is usually quite small.

The octopus has eight arms. Its name tells us this because "octo" means eight. The octopus uses its arms to walk on the ocean floor. Its arms are also used to capture crabs. Crabs are its favorite food. The octopus bites into the crab with its strong beak. This sends poison into the crab's body.

The octopus protects itself in three ways. First, when frightened, the octopus can push water from its body in a powerful stream. This action pushes the octopus forward very rapidly. This allows it to escape.

Second, the body of the octopus has a special sac or pouch that holds a dark, inklike fluid. When an enemy comes close, the octopus squirts some of this fluid. It then swims away. All that the predator sees is a dark cloud in the water where the octopus was. Meanwhile, the octopus has escaped.

Finally, the octopus's body changes color when the octopus is excited or frightened. Suppose an octopus sees a crab. Patches of pink, purple, or blue will appear on the octopus's skin. Suppose the octopus sees an enemy. The octopus will completely change color. Then it seems to disappear into the background of its hiding place. It is hard for the predator to find the octopus. (254 words)

Adapted from M. R. Cohen, B. J. Del Giorno, J. D. Harlan, A. J. McCormack, and J. R. Staver, *Scott, Foresman Science, Grade 5* (Glenview, Ill.: Scott, Foresman and Co., 1984), p. 31.

Number of Total Miscues
(Total Accuracy): _____

Number of Meaning Change Miscues
(Total Acceptability):_____

Total Accuracy			Total Acceptability
0–6 miscues	_____	Independent _____	0–6 miscues
7–26 miscues	_____	Instructional _____	7–13 miscues
27+ miscues	_____	Frustration _____	14+ miscues

Rate: 254 x 60/_____ seconds = _____ WPM

Retelling Scoring Sheet for The Octopus

Main Idea

____ Some people think
____ the octopus is a giant creature
____ and a mean creature.
____ They have seen this
____ in movies
____ science fiction movies.
____ The octopus is shy
____ and small.

Details

____ The octopus has eight arms.
____ Octo means "eight."
____ It uses its arms
____ to walk

____ and capture crabs.
____ Crabs are its food
____ its favorite food.
____ The octopus bites
____ into the crab.
____ This sends poison
____ into the crab's body.
____ The octopus protects itself
____ in three ways.
____ First,
____ when frightened,
____ the octopus can push water
____ from its body.
____ This action pushes the octopus
____ forward
____ very rapidly.
____ This allows it
____ to escape.
____ Second,
____ the octopus has a sac
____ that holds a liquid
____ an inklike liquid.
____ When an enemy comes close,
____ the octopus squirts fluid.
____ It swims away.
____ The predator sees a cloud
____ a dark cloud.
____ The octopus has escaped.
____ Finally,
____ the octopus changes color
____ when it is excited
____ or scared.
____ Suppose the octopus sees a crab.
____ Pink patches,
____ purple patches,
____ or blue patches
____ appear.
____ If the octopus sees an enemy,
____ the octopus will change color
____ completely.
____ It seems to disappear
____ into the background.

Other ideas recalled, including inferences

_____

Level: Five

Questions for The Octopus

1. What is this passage mainly about?
   Implicit: what the octopus is like; how it behaves

2. What is the favorite food of the octopus?
   Explicit: crabs

3. How does the octopus move forward very rapidly when it is frightened?
   Explicit: it pushes water from its body

4. What does the inklike fluid do to the water?
   Explicit: it changes it into a dark cloud

5. What is one color that an octopus can change to?
   Explicit: pink, purple, or blue

6. Why doesn't an octopus completely change color when it sees a crab?
   Implicit: it is excited, not frightened

7. What color does an octopus probably become when it sees an enemy?
   Implicit: a dark blue or brown or black; it camoflages itself with the background

8. Why might the shy octopus attack another creature?
   Implicit: for food

Number Correct Explicit: _____

Number Correct Implicit: _____

Total: _____

_____ Independent: 8 correct

_____ Instructional: 6–7 correct

_____ Frustration: 0–5 correct

Expository

Concept Questions:

What does "getting rid of trash" mean to you?

_____

_____

_____ (3-2-1-0)

What are the purposes of recycling?

_____

_____

_____ (3-2-1-0)

What happens after products are recycled?

_____

_____

_____ (3-2-1-0)

What is landfill?

_____

_____

_____ (3-2-1-0)

Score: _____ /12 = _____ %

_____ FAM _____ UNFAM

Prediction:

_____

_____

Getting Rid of Trash

In the past, when people wanted to get rid of their trash, they just threw it out. Sometimes they threw it into the streets or alleys, and sometimes they packed it into a wagon and dumped it near the edge of town. Open dumping caused many problems. The trash was ugly and often smelled. It attracted rats and other animals that carried diseases.

Over the years people have changed the way they get rid of trash. Now trash is often crushed and put in open places. A layer of trash is dumped and smashed down. Then it is covered with dirt. Another layer of trash is dumped and covered with dirt. This way of getting rid of trash is called landfill. Buildings can be built on landfill.

Burning trash is another way of getting rid of it; however, this often adds to air pollution. Today we have new furnaces for burning trash which are called incinerators. These new incinerators have scrubbers on their chimneys which cut down on air pollution. The new incinerators also gather some of the heat let off by burning trash. This energy can be used to heat homes and businesses.

There is another way of dealing with trash. It is recycling or changing waste products so they can be used again. We can do this with paper, glass, or aluminum. Glass

Level: Five

can be crushed, melted down, and then made into new jars and bottles. This cuts down on the amount of trash. It also takes less energy to recycle glass and cans than to make new ones. (261 words)

Adapted from M. R. Cohen, B. J. Del Giorno, J. D. Harlan, A. J. McCormack, and J. R. Staver, *Scott, Foresman Science, Grade 5* (Glenview, Ill.: Scott, Foresman and Co., 1984), pp. 374–376

Number of Total Miscues
(Total Accuracy): _____

Number of Meaning Change Miscues
(Total Acceptability):_____

Total Accuracy			Total Acceptability
0–6 miscues	_____ Independent	_____	0–6 miscues
7–27 miscues	_____ Instructional	_____	7–14 miscues
28+ miscues	_____ Frustration	_____	15+ miscues

Rate: 261 x 60/_____ seconds = _____ WPM

Retelling Scoring Sheet for Getting Rid of Trash

Main Idea

____ In the past
____ when people got rid of trash
____ they threw it out.

Details

____ They threw it
____ into streets
____ or alleys
____ or dumped it
____ near the edge
____ of town.

____ Dumping caused problems.
____ The trash was ugly
____ and smelled.
____ It attracted rats
____ and animals carrying diseases.

Main Idea

____ A way of getting rid of trash
____ is landfill.

Details

____ Trash is crushed
____ and put in open places.
____ A layer is dumped
____ and smashed down.
____ It is covered
____ with dirt.
____ Another layer of trash is dumped
____ and covered
____ with dirt.
____ Buildings can be built on landfill.

Main Idea

____ Burning is another way
____ of getting rid of trash.

Details

____ This added to pollution.
____ Furnaces burn trash
____ called incinerators.
____ They have scrubbers
____ to cut down pollution.
____ They gather heat.
____ This energy can heat homes
____ and businesses.

Main Idea

____ Recycling gets rid of trash.

Details

____ We do this with paper,
____ glass,
____ or aluminum.
____ Glass can be melted

Getting Rid of the Trash

233

_____ and made into jars
_____ and bottles.
_____ It takes less energy
_____ to recycle glass
_____ and cans
_____ than to make new ones.

Other ideas recalled, including inferences

_____

Questions for Getting Rid of Trash

1. What is this passage mainly about?
   Implicit: different ways to get rid of trash

2. What was one problem caused by open dumping?
   Explicit: bad smells, diseased animals, ugly sights

3. Why is trash crushed before it is placed in a landfill?
   Implicit: it takes up less space/land

4. Landfills get rid of trash. What other use do they have?
   Implicit: you can build on them

5. What is put on incinerator chimneys to cut down on pollution?
   Explicit: scrubbers

6. What can the heat let off by burning trash be used for?
   Explicit: heating homes and businesses

7. Name one product that can be recycled.
   Explicit: glass; paper; aluminum

8. Why might recycled cans and bottles be cheaper than new ones?
   Implicit: used less energy so they probably cost less

Number Correct Explicit: _____

Number Correct Implicit: _____

Total: _____

_____ Independent: 8 correct

_____ Instructional: 6–7 correct

_____ Frustration: 0–5 correct

Expository

Concept Questions:

What is laser light?

_____

_____

_____ (3-2-1-0)

What are things that light can go through?

_____

_____

_____ (3-2-1-0)

Why does bleeding stop?

_____

_____

_____ (3-2-1-0)

What do artists make?

_____

_____

_____ (3-2-1-0)

Score: _____ /12 = _____ %

_____ FAM _____ UNFAM

Prediction:

_____

_____

Laser Light

Scientists have found a new kind of light. This light is called laser light. Lasers are being used in medicine, industry, and science research.

How is laser light different from other kinds of light? White light actually contains all the colors of the rainbow. And the "red" light in a traffic signal contains red light of many different wavelengths. But the waves of laser light are all the same wavelength. So the light from a laser is one pure color. Another difference between laser light and other light is that a laser makes a thin beam of light that travels only in one direction. Finally, the waves of laser light are all lined up. Because the waves of laser light are the same length, travel in one direction, and all line up, a beam of laser light can be very powerful. A laser beam can even drill holes in metal. A lens focuses the laser beam to hit the point where the hole is to be drilled.

Laser light is useful in many ways. Laser beams can be used to carry radio and telephone messages. Lasers can even prevent some people from going blind. A person's eye is often damaged in an accident. Doctors use laser beams to reattach the retina. Lasers can be used to burn out tumors without a lot of bleeding. Lasers are also used to cut cloth for clothes. Every year new uses for laser light are being discovered. This new light in our life will continue to help us in many ways. (257 words)

Adapted from M. R. Cohen, B. J. Del Giorno, J. D. Harlan, A. J. McCormack, and J. R. Staver, *Scott, Foresman Science, Grade 5* (Glenview, Ill.: Scott, Foresman and Co., 1984), p. 289.

Number of Total Miscues
(Total Accuracy): _____

Number of Meaning Change Miscues
(Total Acceptability): _____

Total Accuracy			Total Acceptability
0–6 miscues	_____ Independent	_____	0–6 miscues
7–26 miscues	_____ Instructional	_____	7–14 miscues
27+ miscues	_____ Frustration	_____	15+ miscues
Rate: 257 x 60/_____ seconds =		_____ WPM	

Retelling Scoring Sheet for Laser Light

Main Idea

____ Scientists have found a new kind
____ of light
____ called laser light.

Details

____ Lasers are used in medicine,
____ industry,
____ and science.

Main Idea

____ Laser light is different
____ from other kinds of light.

Details

____ White light
____ contains all the colors
____ of the rainbow.
____ Red light
____ in a traffic signal
____ contains different wavelengths.
____ Waves of laser light
____ are the same wavelength.
____ Laser light is one color.
____ A laser makes a beam
____ that travels
____ in one direction.
____ Waves of laser light are lined up.
____ Laser beam is very powerful.
____ It can drill holes
____ in metal.

Main Idea

____ Laser light is useful
____ in many ways.

Details

____ Laser beams carry
____ radio
____ and telephone messages.
____ They can prevent blindness.
____ They can reattach a retina
____ or burn out tumors
____ without a lot of bleeding.
____ Lasers cut cloth.
____ Every year
____ new uses
____ are being discovered.

Other ideas recalled, including inferences

_____

Questions for Laser Light

1. What is this passage mainly about?
   Implicit: how laser light works; how laser light is used

2. What colors are contained in white light?
   Explicit: all the colors of the rainbow

3. In what direction do the waves of laser light travel when compared to other types of light?
   Explicit: in one direction; they all go the same way

4. If a laser beam hits a solid object, what happens to the object?
   Implicit: a hole is made in it

5. What is used to focus the laser beam so it strikes a certain point?
   Explicit: a lens

6. What kinds of messages can laser beams carry?
   Explicit: telephone or radio

7. Why would laser surgery be safer than surgery that uses a knife?
   Implicit: there would be less bleeding

8. How might a sculptor use laser light?
   Implicit: to sculpt metal or stone or wood.

Number Correct Explicit: _____

Number Correct Implicit: _____

Total: _____

_____ Independent: 8 correct

_____ Instructional: 6–7 correct

_____ Frustration: 0–5 correct

Pele

Pele was born in the South American country of Brazil. He lived in a small village and his family was very poor. But Pele had a dream. He wanted to become a professional soccer player. He could not afford a soccer ball so he fashioned one. He took an old sock, stuffed it with newspapers and sewed it together with string. It was a poor substitute, but it was better than nothing. Pele and his friends formed their own team. They did not have enough money to purchase shoes but that did not stop them. They played barefoot and became known as the "barefoot team."

Pele and his friends saved their money, and eventually the team was able to get a regular ball and shoes. Pele discovered that the ball could be better controlled when he wore shoes. Pele and his team practiced continuously. They soon began playing older and more established teams from the big cities. The team began to win most of its games. Pele was the star of the team. People thought this was amazing because he was only eleven years old!

Pele's skill at soccer came to the attention of influential people and when he was fifteen, he was signed by the Santos team. Pele led the Santos team to many championships. He also led the Brazilian national team to three world championships. Pele also holds many records and has scored over twelve hundred goals in his career as a professional player.

Pele decided to retire in 1974. Then he changed his mind and came to the United States where he joined the New York Cosmos. Soccer had not been very popular in the United States up to this point, but Pele's presence had a dramatic effect. Crowds at games doubled and tripled as people came to see the famous and exciting Pele. Games began to be shown on television. Soccer gained in popularity and many children in the United States began to play soccer. Soccer is now one of the most popular sports in the United States, due in part to the dream of a young boy in Brazil.

From *Holt Social Studies, Our World, Our Regions, and Our History,* edited by JoAnn Cangemi, copyright © 1983 by Holt, Rinehart and Winston, Inc. Reprinted by permission of the publisher.

Abraham Lincoln

When Abraham Lincoln was nineteen years old, he visited the city of New Orleans. He saw things he would never forget. He saw black people being sold in slave markets. They were chained together and treated like animals. Lincoln watched little children being sold to strangers and taken away from their parents. Lincoln was heartbroken and these memories stayed with him for the rest of his life. Although slavery was allowed in many states of the Union, Lincoln believed that it was wrong and he was not afraid to say so.

In 1858, Lincoln ran for the United States Senate against Stephen Douglas. There was much talk about slavery. Should the owning of slaves be allowed in new states that were just coming into the Union? Douglas said that the decision to own slaves was up to each individual person. Lincoln said that slavery must not be allowed to spread because it was wrong. But he knew that it would not be easy to end slavery in those states which had allowed it for so many years. Lincoln believed it was important to keep the United States strong. He felt that slavery weakened the country. In one speech, he said the country could not last half slave and half free. He said, "A house divided against itself cannot stand." Lincoln lost the election to the Senate, but he became well known for his views. In 1860 he ran for president of the United States.

The slave states opposed Lincoln as president. They did not want to abolish slavery. They threatened to leave the Union if Lincoln was elected. When he became president, the slave states carried out their threat. A terrible war broke out between the northern and southern states. At times, members of the same family were fighting against one another.

In 1863, Lincoln gave an order called the Emancipation Proclamation which ended slavery. The war finally ended two years later. The southern states once more became part of the Union, but slavery was no longer allowed. No more would little children be torn from their parents and sold to strangers. Abraham Lincoln had achieved his goal.

Andrew Carnegie

Andrew Carnegie was the son of Scottish immigrants. One of his first jobs was as a messenger boy. He earned $2.50 a week! At the age of eighteen, Carnegie got a job on the Pennsylvania Railroad. He soon realized that iron was not a good construction material for the railroad. Iron rails tended to crack and often had to be replaced. The weight of a train weakened iron bridges. Carnegie felt that steel would be a stronger building material. He decided to find ways to increase the production of steel.

Carnegie carefully saved his money and used it to become part owner of a small iron company. Eventually he acquired the ownership of several more companies. But making steel was slow and costly. Then Carnegie learned about the Bessemer process. Using this method, steel could be made quickly and on a large scale. Carnegie decided to risk all. He built a huge steel mill. He bought iron and coal mines as well as ships and trains for transport. By 1900, three million tons of steel were produced by Carnegie's mills each year, and his fortune was worth two hundred and fifty million.

Carnegie accomplished his dream, that of increasing steel production, and, in doing so, he developed and shaped the United States steel industry. In 1901, at the peak of his career, Carnegie sold his business and retired. He then spent much of his time and money in helping others and started more than two thousand libraries in the United States and around the world. Carnegie can truly be called the Man of Steel.

From *Holt Social Studies, Our World, Our Regions, and Our History,* edited by JoAnn Cangemi, copyright © 1983 by Holt, Rinehart and Winston, Inc. Reprinted by permission of the publisher.

Computers are machines that help solve problems, but they can't do anything without directions from humans. People give computers information. Then they tell them what to do with it. Computers cannot come up with any new information, but they can save much work and time.

For example, you could store all the information in the phone book in a computer's memory. Then you could ask the computer to tell you all the names of people living on one single street. If you lived in a big city, it might take days or even weeks for you to come up with all the names. But the computer could do it in seconds!

The first computers were huge. One filled up the floor of a large office building. The machines were very costly. Only big industries could buy them. But because computers could save so much time, other businesses wanted them. So scientists found a way to make computers smaller and cheaper by inventing chips. Chips made it possible to store more information in less space.

Today a computer can fit on the top of a table. They are still shrinking in size and price. More businesses use them. Hospitals use them to keep track of billing. Stores use them to make check-outs easier and faster. Families use computers too. Many students have computers at home that help them with their homework. Computer games are very popular. A computer can help to keep track of a family's expenses. Someday every family may have a home computer.

Adapted from M. R. Cohen, B. J. Del Giorno, J. D. Harlan, A. J. McCormack, and J. R. Staver, *Scott, Foresman Science, Grade 5* (Glenview, Ill.: Scott, Foresman and Co., 1984), pp. 348–349.

Predicting Earthquakes

Some scientists think that certain animals know when an earthquake is coming. They sense the earthquake days or hours before it happens. In some cases, animal behavior has predicted a coming earthquake.

Before the Chinese earthquake in February of 1975, people noted animals doing strange things. Birds suddenly flew away. They would not return to their nests. Chickens refused to enter their coops. Rats ran around bumping into things. Well-trained police dogs howled and would not obey their masters. They kept sniffing the ground.

What might these animals know that we do not? Perhaps they can sense some of the changes that happen in the earth before an earthquake. Certain animals might hear low booms that come before an earthquake. Perhaps they can smell certain gases that escape from the earth.

Scientists wanted to study the possible connection between animal behavior and earthquakes. They set up a project in California. It ran for three years. Over a thousand volunteers took part. The volunteers watched animals and called the project every day to report on their actions. During the project at least thirteen earthquakes were recorded. Some were bigger than others. The volunteers saw an unusually high amount of strange behavior before seven of the earthquakes. Someday we may use animals to warn people of an earthquake. If this happens, we can thank the efforts of scientists and volunteers around the world.

Adapted from M. R. Cohen, B. J.Del Giorno, J. D. Harlan, A. J. McCormack, and J. R. Staver, *Scott, Foresman Science, Grade 4* (Glenview, Ill.: Scott, Foresman and Co., 1984), p. 99.

Ultrasound

Some medical research uses sounds that you cannot hear. The word ultrasonic is used to describe sounds with very high frequencies. Ultrasonic sounds range from twenty thousand to more than a billion vibrations per second. These sounds are too high for humans to hear. But dogs and other animals can hear them.

Scientists have found many uses for ultrasonic sounds. For example, doctors use ultrasound to study the health of babies before they are born. Ultrasonic sounds can be sent through the mother's abdomen. The waves reflect off the baby's body into a microphone that picks up these waves. The reflected sounds can be made into a picture and shown on a television screen.

The ultrasonic wave patterns show some of the health problems a baby might have. Heart problems and slow growth can be detected. The doctors can use this information to plan ahead for what the baby might need as soon as it is born. Doctors can also use this method to tell the mother if she is expecting twins or triplets.

Many industrial uses of ultrasonics have also been found. Some factories use ultrasonic waves to look for hidden cracks in metals. Such waves can be used to find gas and oil deposits underground. Paint and homogenized milk can be mixed by ultrasonic waves. Dentists can even clean your teeth with these waves. This unheard sound has become a useful tool in many areas of medicine, industry, and science research.

Adapted from M. R. Cohen, B. J. Del Giorno, J. D. Harlan, A. J. McCormack, and J. R. Staver, *Scott, Foresman Science, Grade 5* (Glenview, Ill.: Scott, Foresman and Co., 1984), p. 239.

Level: Six

Narrative

Concept Questions:

Who is Pele?

_____

_____

_____ (3-2-1-0)

What is soccer?

_____

_____

_____ (3-2-1-0)

What are professional athletes?

_____

_____

_____ (3-2-1-0)

Why do some sports become popular?

_____

_____

_____ (3-2-1-0)

Score: _____ /12 = _____ %

_____ FAM _____ UNFAM

Prediction:

_____

_____

Pele

Pele was born in the South American country of Brazil. He lived in a small village and his family was very poor. But Pele had a dream. He wanted to become a professional soccer player. He could not afford a soccer ball so he fashioned one. He took an old sock, stuffed it with newspapers and sewed it together with string. It was a poor substitute, but it was better than nothing. Pele and his friends formed their own team. They did not have enough money to purchase shoes but that did not stop them. They played barefoot and became known as the "barefoot team."

Pele and his friends saved their money, and eventually the team was able to get a regular ball and shoes. Pele discovered that the ball could be better controlled when he wore shoes. Pele and his team practiced continuously. They soon began playing older and more established teams from the big cities. The team began to win most of its games. Pele was the star of the team. People thought this was amazing because he was only eleven years old!

Pele's skill at soccer came to the attention of influential people and when he was fifteen, he was signed by the Santos team. Pele led the Santos team to many championships. He also led the Brazilian national team to three world championships. Pele also holds many

Level: Six

records and has scored over twelve hundred goals in his career as a professional player.

Pele decided to retire in 1974. Then he changed his mind and came to the United States where he joined the New York Cosmos. Soccer had not been very popular in the United States up to this point, but Pele's presence had a dramatic effect. Crowds at games doubled and tripled as people came to see the famous and exciting Pele. Games began to be shown on television. Soccer gained in popularity and many children in the United States began to play soccer. Soccer is now one of the most popular sports in the United States, due in part to the dream of a young boy in Brazil. (351 words)

From *Holt Social Studies, Our World, Our Regions, and Our History,* edited by JoAnn Cangemi, copyright © 1983 by Holt, Rinehart and Winston, Inc. Reprinted by permission of the publisher.

Number of Total Miscues
(Total Accuracy): _____

Number of Meaning Change Miscues
(Total Acceptability):_____

Total Accuracy		Total Acceptability
0–8 miscues _____	Independent _____	0–8 miscues
9–36 miscues _____	Instructional _____	9–19 miscues
37+ miscues _____	Frustration _____	20+ miscues

Rate: 351 x 60/_____ seconds = _____ WPM

Retelling Scoring Sheet for Pele

Setting/Background
____ Pele was born
____ in Brazil.
____ Pele's family was poor.

Goal
____ Pele had a dream.
____ He wanted
____ to become a soccer player
____ a professional player.

Events
____ He could not afford a ball.
____ He fashioned a ball.
____ He took a sock
____ and stuffed it
____ with newspapers
____ and sewed it together
____ with string.
____ Pele
____ and his friends formed a team
____ their own team.
____ They did not have enough money
____ to purchase shoes.
____ They played barefoot
____ and became known
____ as the "barefoot team."
____ Pele
____ and his friends saved their money
____ and eventually
____ the team was able
____ to get a ball
____ a regular ball
____ and shoes.
____ Pele discovered
____ that the ball could be controlled
____ better
____ when he wore shoes.
____ They began
____ to play teams
____ from big cities
____ and to win games
____ most of their games.

Level: Six

____ Pele was the star.
____ He was only eleven.
____ He was signed
____ by the Santos team.

Resolution

____ Pele led the team
____ to championships.
____ He led the team
____ the Brazilian team
____ to championships
____ world championships.
____ Pele held many records.
____ Pele decided
____ to retire
____ in 1974.
____ Then he changed his mind
____ and came to the U.S.
____ where he joined the Cosmos
____ New York Cosmos.
____ Pele's presence had an effect.
____ Crowds doubled
____ and tripled
____ and people came
____ to see Pele.
____ Soccer gained
____ in popularity.
____ Soccer is now one
____ of the most popular sports
____ in the U.S.

Other ideas recalled, including inferences

_____

Questions for Pele

1. What was Pele's main goal?
   Implicit: to become a professional soccer player

2. What did Pele use to make a soccer ball?
   Explicit: an old sock, string, and newspaper

3. Why was Pele's team known as the "barefoot team?"
   Explicit: they had no shoes and played barefoot

4. Why would the purchase of shoes affect the number of games won by Pele's team?
   Implicit: they played better because they could control the ball more effectively

5. Why was it amazing that Pele became a star at the age of eleven?
Implicit: he was very young to be playing so well against older and more established teams from the big cities

6. How old was Pele when he was signed by a professional soccer team?
Explicit: fifteen

7. What American team did Pele join?
Explicit: New York Cosmos

8. How did Pele's presence help to make soccer popular in the United States?
Implicit: people came to see Pele and grew to like the game itself

Number Correct Explicit: _____

Number Correct Implicit: _____

Total: _____

_____ Independent: 8 correct

_____ Instructional: 6–7 correct

_____ Frustration: 0–5 correct

Level: Six

Narrative

Abraham Lincoln

When Abraham Lincoln was nineteen years old, he visited the city of New Orleans. He saw things he would never forget. He saw black people being sold in slave markets. They were chained together and treated like animals. Lincoln watched little children being sold to strangers and taken away from their parents. Lincoln was heartbroken and these memories stayed with him for the rest of his life. Although slavery was allowed in many states of the Union, Lincoln believed that it was wrong and he was not afraid to say so.

In 1858, Lincoln ran for the United States Senate against Stephen Douglas. There was much talk about slavery. Should the owning of slaves be allowed in new states that were just coming into the Union? Douglas said that the decision to own slaves was up to each individual person. Lincoln said that slavery must not be allowed to spread because it was wrong. But he knew that it would not be easy to end slavery in those states which had allowed it for so many years. Lincoln believed that it was important to keep the United States strong. He felt that slavery weakened the country. In one speech, he said the country could not last half slave and half free. He said, "A house divided against itself cannot stand." Lincoln lost the election to the Senate, but he became well known for his views. In 1860 he ran for president of the United States.

Level: Six

The slave states opposed Lincoln as president. They did not want to abolish slavery. They threatened to leave the Union if Lincoln was elected. When he became president, the slave states carried out their threat. A terrible war broke out between the northern and southern states. At times, members of the same family were fighting against one another.

In 1863, Lincoln gave an order called the Emancipation Proclamation which ended slavery. The war finally ended two years later. The southern states once more became part of the Union, but slavery was no longer allowed. No more would little children be torn from their parents and sold to strangers. Abraham Lincoln had achieved his goal. (358 words)

Number of Total Miscues
(Total Accuracy): _____

Number of Meaning Change Miscues
(Total Acceptability): _____

Total Accuracy			Total Acceptability
0–8 miscues	_____ Independent	_____	0–8 miscues
9–37 miscues	_____ Instructional	_____	9–19 miscues
38+ miscues	_____ Frustration	_____	20+ miscues

Rate: 358 x 60/_____ seconds = _____ WPM

Retelling Scoring Sheet for Abraham Lincoln

Setting/Background
____ When Abraham Lincoln was nineteen,
____ he visited the city
____ of New Orleans.
____ He saw things
____ he would never forget.
____ He saw black people
____ being sold
____ in slave markets.
____ They were chained together
____ and treated like animals.
____ Lincoln watched children
____ being sold
____ to strangers
____ and taken away
____ from their parents.

Goal
____ Lincoln believed
____ that slavery was wrong.
____ He was not afraid
____ to say so.

Events
____ Lincoln ran
____ for the Senate
____ against Stephen Douglas.
____ Lincoln said
____ that slavery must not spread.
____ He felt
____ that slavery weakened the country.
____ Lincoln lost the election
____ to the Senate.
____ He ran
____ for president.
____ The slave states opposed Lincoln.
____ They did not want
____ to abolish slavery.
____ They threatened
____ to leave the union
____ if Lincoln was elected.
____ When Lincoln became president,

Level: Six

____ a war broke out
____ a war between the states.

Resolution

____ Lincoln gave an order
____ called the Emancipation Proclamation
____ which ended slavery.
____ The war ended.
____ The southern states became part
____ of the Union
____ but slavery was not allowed.
____ Abraham Lincoln had achieved his goal.

Other ideas recalled, including inferences

_____

Questions for Abraham Lincoln

1. What was Abraham Lincoln's main goal?
   Implicit: to end slavery in the United States

2. Name one thing that Abraham Lincoln saw in the slave markets of New Orleans.
   Explicit: blacks chained together; blacks treated like animals; blacks being sold; children being separated from parents; children being sold to strangers

3. How did the sights of the slave market influence Abraham Lincoln's later life?
   Implicit: he was against slavery and fought to end it; it made him sick and he wanted to stop it

4. What office did Abraham Lincoln run for against Douglas?
   Explicit: he ran for the U.S. Senate

5. What did the southern states threaten to do if Abraham Lincoln was elected president?
   Explicit: leave the Union

6. Why did the southern states oppose Abraham Lincoln as president?
   Implicit: he was against slavery and he would fight to end it in their states

7. How did Abraham Lincoln's prediction that "A house divided against itself cannot stand" come true?
   Implicit: the war between the states broke out

8. What did the Emancipation Proclamation do?
   Explicit: it ended slavery

Number Correct Explicit: _____

Number Correct Implicit: _____

Total: _____

_____ Independent: 8 correct

_____ Instructional: 6–7 correct

_____ Frustration: 0–5 correct

Level: Six

Narrative

Andrew Carnegie

Andrew Carnegie was the son of Scottish immigrants. One of his first jobs was a messenger boy. He earned $2.50 a week! At the age of eighteen, Carnegie got a job on the Pennsylvania Railroad. He soon realized that iron was not a good construction material for the railroad. Iron rails tended to crack and often had to be replaced. The weight of a train weakened iron bridges. Carnegie felt that steel would be a stronger building material. He decided to find ways to increase the production of steel.

Carnegie carefully saved his money and used it to become part owner of a small iron company. Eventually he acquired the owner-ship of several more companies. But making steel was slow and costly. Then Carnegie learned about the Bessemer process. Using this method, steel could be made quickly and on a large scale. Carnegie decided to risk all. He built a huge steel mill. He bought iron and coal mines as well as ships and trains for transport. By 1900, three million tons of steel were produced by Carnegie's mills each year, and his fortune was worth two hundred and fifty million.

Carnegie accomplished his dream, that of increasing steel production, and, in doing so, he developed and shaped the United States steel industry. In 1901, at the peak of his career, Carnegie sold his business and retired.

Level: Six

He then spent much of his time and money in helping others and started more than two thousand libraries in the United States and around the world. Carnegie can truly be called the Man of Steel. (264 words)

From *Holt Social Studies, Our World, Our Regions,* and *Our History,* edited by JoAnn Cangemi, copyright © 1983 by Holt, Rinehart and Winston, Inc. Reprinted by permission of the publisher.

Number of Total Miscues
(Total Accuracy): _____

Number of Meaning Change Miscues
(Total Acceptability):_____

Total Accuracy				Total Acceptability
0–6 miscues	_____	Independent	_____	0–6 miscues
7–27 miscues	_____	Instructional	_____	7–14 miscues
28+ miscues	_____	Frustration	_____	15+ miscues

Rate: 264 x 60/_____ seconds = _____ WPM

Retelling Scoring Sheet for Andrew Carnegie

Setting/Background
____ Andrew Carnegie was the son
____ of immigrants
____ Scottish immigrants.
____ One of his jobs
____ first jobs
____ was a messenger boy.
____ He earned $2.50
____ a week.
____ At the age of eighteen
____ Carnegie got a job

____ on the railroad.
____ He realized
____ that iron was not a good material
____ for the railroad.
____ Rails cracked.
____ iron rails
____ The weight of the train
____ weakened bridges.
____ iron bridges.

Goal
____ Carnegie felt
____ steel would be stronger.
____ He decided
____ to find ways
____ to increase steel production.

Events
____ Carnegie saved his money.
____ He became the owner
____ of a company
____ iron company.
____ He acquired the ownership
____ of more companies.
____ Making steel was
____ slow
____ and costly.
____ Carnegie learned
____ about the Bessemer process.
____ Steel could be made
____ quickly
____ Carnegie decided
____ to risk all.
____ He built a steel mill.
____ He bought mines,
____ ships,
____ and trains.
____ By 1900
____ his fortune was worth millions.

Resolution
____ Carnegie accomplished his dream
____ of increasing steel production.
____ He developed the steel industry
____ in the United States.

____ He sold his business
____ and retired.
____ He helped others
____ and started libraries.
____ He can be called the Man of Steel.

Other ideas recalled, including references

_____

Questions for Andrew Carnegie

1. What was Carnegie's main goal?
   Implicit: to make steel faster and cheaper

2. What was one of Andrew Carnegie's first jobs?
   Explicit: messenger boy

3. Why would using steel as construction material make railroads safer?
   Implicit: bridges and rails would be stronger

4. What was the first business that Andrew Carnegie bought?
   Explicit: an iron company

5. Why wasn't steel used a lot for construction?
   Implicit: it was slow to make and cost a lot

6. Why did Andrew Carnegie buy ships and trains?
   Explicit: to transport iron and coal

7. Why did the Bessemer process of making steel make Andrew Carnegie's fortune?
   Implicit: he could make more steel with less cost

8. During his retirement, what did Andrew Carnegie start?
   Explicit: libraries

Number Correct Explicit: _____

Number Correct Implicit: _____

Total: _____

_____ Independent: 8 correct

_____ Instructional: 6–7 correct

_____ Frustration: 0–5 correct

Level: Six

Expository

Computers

Computers are <u>machines</u> that help solve problems, but they can't do anything without directions from humans. People give computers information. Then they tell them what to do with it. Computers cannot come up with any new information, but they can save much work and time.

For example, you could store all the information in the phone book in a computer's memory. Then you could ask the computer to tell you all the names of people living on one single street. If you lived in a big city, it might take days or even weeks for you to come up with all the names. But the computer could do it in seconds!

The first computers were huge. One filled up the floor of a large office building. The <u>machines</u> were very costly. Only big industries could buy them. But because computers could save so much time, other <u>businesses</u> wanted them. So scientists found a way to make computers smaller and cheaper by inventing chips. Chips made it possible to store more information in less space.

Today a computer can fit on the top of a table. They are still <u>shrinking</u> in size and price. More <u>businesses</u> use them. Hospitals use them to keep track of billing. Stores use them to make check-outs easier and faster. Families use computers too. Many students have computers at home that help them with

Level: Six

their homework. Computer games are very popular. A computer can help to keep track of a family's expenses. Someday every family may have a home computer. (254 words)

Adapted from M. R. Cohen, B. J. Del Giorno, J. D. Harlan, A. J. McCormack, and J. R. Straver, *Scott, Foresman Science, Grade 5* (Glenview, Ill.: Scott, Foresman and Co., 1984), pp. 348–349.

Number of Total Miscues
(Total Accuracy): _____

Number of Meaning Change Miscues
(Total Acceptability):_____

Total Accuracy			**Total Acceptability**
0–6 miscues	_____ Independent	_____	0–6 miscues
7–26 miscues	_____ Instructional	_____	7–13 miscues
27+ miscues	_____ Frustration	_____	14+ miscues

Rate: 254 x 60/_____ seconds = _____ WPM

Retelling Scoring Sheet for Computers

Main Idea

____ Computers are machines
____ that solve problems
____ and save work
____ and time.

Details

____ Computers can't do anything
____ without directions
____ from humans.
____ You can store the information
____ in the phone book
____ in the computer.

____ The computer could tell you
____ the names
____ of people living
____ on one street.
____ It might take days
____ for you to come up
____ with the names.
____ A computer can do it
____ in seconds.

Main Idea

____ The first computers were huge.

Details

____ One filled the floor
____ of a building.
____ The machines were costly.
____ Only industries
____ big industries
____ could buy them.
____ But because computers could save so much time,
____ other businesses wanted them.
____ Scientists found a way
____ to make computers
____ smaller
____ and cheaper
____ by inventing chips.
____ Chips made it possible
____ to store information
____ in less space.

Main Idea

____ Computers are shrinking
____ in size
____ and price.

Details

____ Computers can fit
____ on the top
____ of a table.
____ More businesses use them.
____ Hospitals use them.
____ Stores use them.
____ Families use computers

Level: Six

____ to help
____ with homework.
____ Computer games
____ are popular.
____ Someday
____ every family may have a computer.

Other ideas recalled, including inferences

_____

Questions for Computers

1. What is this passage mainly about?
   Implicit: how computers have changed

2. Why might a computer arrive at a wrong answer to a problem?
   Implicit: it was given the wrong information

3. Why were big businesses the only ones who could afford the first computers?
   Explicit: they cost so much

4. What did scientists invent that made computers smaller?
   Explicit: the computer chip

5. Why would businesses want a smaller computer?
   Implicit: it would take less space and/or cost less

6. Why are computers still getting smaller and cheaper?
   Implicit: the chips are more efficient; the chips store more information

7. According to the passage, how do stores use computers?
   Explicit: they help with check-out

8. According to the passage, what is one way that a family might use a computer?
   Explicit: homework; games; to keep track of expenses

Number Correct Explicit: _____

Number Correct Implicit: _____

Total: _____

_____ Independent: 8 correct

_____ Instructional: 6–7 correct

_____ Frustration: 0–5 correct

Level: Six

Expository

Concept Questions:

What are earthquakes?

_____

_____

_____ (3-2-1-0)

What do "sizes of earthquakes" mean to you?

_____

_____

_____ (3-2-1-0)

Where are places where earthquakes happen?

_____

_____

_____ (3-2-1-0)

What are things that animals can sense but humans can't?

_____

_____

_____ (3-2-1-0)

Score: _____ /12 = _____ %

_____ FAM _____ UNFAM

Prediction:

_____

_____

Predicting Earthquakes

Some scientists think that certain animals know when an earthquake is coming. They sense the earthquake days or hours before it happens. In some cases, animal behavior has predicted a coming earthquake.

Before the Chinese earthquake in February of 1975, people noted animals doing strange things. Birds suddenly flew away. They would not return to their nests. Chickens refused to enter their coops. Rats ran around bumping into things. Well-trained police dogs howled and would not obey their masters. They kept sniffing the ground.

What might these animals know that we do not? Perhaps they can sense some of the changes that happen in the earth before an earthquake. Certain animals might hear low booms that come before an earthquake. Perhaps they can smell certain gases that escape from the earth.

Scientists wanted to study the possible connection between animal behavior and earthquakes. They set up a project in California. It ran for three years. Over a thousand volunteers took part. The volunteers watched animals and called the project every day to report on their actions. During the project at least thirteen earthquakes were recorded. Some were

Level: Six

bigger than others. The <u>volunteers</u> saw an unusually high amount of strange <u>behavior</u> before seven of the <u>earthquakes</u>. Someday we may use animals to warn people of an <u>earthquake</u>. If this happens, we can thank the efforts of scientists and <u>volunteers</u> around the world. (231 words)

Adapted from M. R. Cohen, B. J. Del Giorno, J. D. Harlan, A. J. McCormack, and J. R. Staver, *Scott, Foresman Science, Grade 4* (Glenview, Ill.: Scott, Foresman and Co., 1984), p. 99.

Number of Total Miscues
(Total Accuracy): _____

Number of Meaning Change Miscues
(Total Acceptability): _____

Total Accuracy			Total Acceptability
0–5 miscues	_____ Independent	_____	0–5 miscues
6–24 miscues	_____ Instructional	_____	6–12 miscues
25+ miscues	_____ Frustration	_____	13+ miscues

Rate: 231 x 60/_____ seconds = _____ WPM

Retelling Scoring Sheet for Predicting Earthquakes

Main Idea

____ Scientists think
____ that animals know
____ when an earthquake is coming.

Details

____ Animal behavior
____ has predicted an earthquake.
____ Before the earthquake

____ the Chinese earthquake
____ of 1975,
____ people noted animals
____ doing strange things.
____ Birds flew away
____ and would not return
____ to their nests.
____ Chickens would not enter their coops.
____ Rats ran around
____ bumping into things.
____ Dogs howled
____ police dogs
____ and would not obey their masters.
____ They kept sniffing
____ the ground.

Main Idea

____ What might these animals know?

Details

____ They might sense changes
____ that happen
____ in the earth.
____ They might hear booms
____ low booms.
____ They might smell certain gases
____ that escape
____ from the earth.

Main Idea

____ Scientists wanted
____ to study the connection
____ between animal behavior
____ and earthquakes.

Details

____ They set up a project
____ in California.
____ It ran
____ for years
____ three years.
____ They watched animals
____ and reported their actions.
____ Earthquakes

____ thirteen earthquakes
____ were recorded.
____ Volunteers saw
____ strange behavior
____ before seven
____ of the earthquakes.
____ Someday
____ we may use animals
____ to warn people
____ of an earthquake.
____ If this happens
____ we can thank the efforts
____ of scientists
____ and volunteers.

Other ideas recalled, including inferences

_____

Questions for Predicting Earthquakes

1. What is this passage mainly about?
   Implicit: how animals may be able to predict earthquakes

2. How did chickens behave before the Chinese earthquake?
   Explicit: they wouldn't enter their coops

3. What might animals hear before an earthquake?
   Explicit: low booms

4. Why might dogs sniff the ground before an earthquake?
   Implicit: they may smell escaping gases

5. What did the California project volunteers observe?
   Explicit: animals; animal actions; animal behaviors

6. How many earthquakes were predicted by the animals during the California project?
   Explicit: seven

7. Why didn't the animals in the California project show strange behavior before all the earthquakes?
   Implicit: some earthquakes were not big enough

8. Why was California a good state for an earthquake project?
   Implicit: they have a lot of earthquakes

Number Correct Explicit: _____

Number Correct Implicit: _____

Total: _____

_____ Independent: 8 correct

_____ Instructional: 6–7 correct

_____ Frustration: 0–5 correct

Level: Six

Expository

Ultrasound

Some medical research uses sounds that you cannot hear. The word ultrasonic is used to describe sounds with very high frequencies.

Ultrasonic sounds range from twenty thousand to more than a billion vibrations per second. These sounds are too high for humans to hear. But dogs and other animals can hear them.

Scientists have found many uses for ultrasonic sounds. For example, doctors use ultrasound to study the health of babies before they are born. Ultrasonic sounds can be sent through the mother's abdomen. The waves reflect off the baby's body into a microphone that picks up these waves. The reflected sounds can be made into a picture and shown on a television screen.

The ultrasonic wave patterns show some of the health problems a baby might have. Heart problems and slow growth can be detected. The doctors can use this information to plan ahead for what the baby might need as soon as it is born. Doctors can also use this method to tell the mother if she is expecting twins or triplets.

Many industrial uses of ultrasonics have also been found. Some factories use ultrasonic waves to look for hidden cracks in metals. Such waves can be used to find gas and oil deposits underground. Paint and homogenized milk can be mixed by ultrasonic waves. Dentists can even clean your teeth with

Level: Six

these waves. This unheard sound has become a useful tool in many areas of medicine, industry, and science research. (242 words)

Adapted from M. R. Cohen, B. J. Del Giorno, J. D. Harlan, A. J. McCormack, and J. R. Staver, *Scott, Foresman Science, Grade 5* (Glenview, Ill.: Scott, Foresman and Co., 1984), p. 239.

Number of Total Miscues
(Total Accuracy): _____

Number of Meaning Change Miscues
(Total Acceptability): _____

Total Accuracy				Total Acceptability
0–6 miscues	_____	Independent	_____	0–6 miscues
7–25 miscues	_____	Instructional	_____	7–13 miscues
26+ miscues	_____	Frustration	_____	14+ miscues

Rate: 242 x 60/_____ seconds =   _____ WPM

Retelling Scoring Sheet for Ultrasound

Main Idea
____ Ultrasonic is used to describe sounds
____ with very high frequencies.

Details
____ These sounds are too high
____ for humans to hear.
____ But dogs
____ and other animals can hear them.

Main Idea
____ Scientists have found many uses
____ for ultrasonic sounds.

Details
____ Doctors use ultrasound
____ to study the health

____ of babies
____ before they are born.
____ Ultrasonic sounds can be sent
____ through the abdomen
____ the mother's abdomen.
____ The ultrasonic patterns show some of the problems
____ a baby might have.
____ Heart problems
____ and slow growth can be detected.
____ Doctors can use this method
____ to tell the mother
____ if she is expecting twins
____ or triplets.

Main Idea
____ Industrial uses of ultrasonics have been found.

Details
____ Factories use ultrasonic waves
____ to look for cracks
____ in metals.
____ Such waves can be used
____ to find gas
____ and oil
____ underground.
____ Paint
____ and milk
____ can be mixed
____ by ultrasound.
____ Dentists can clean your teeth
____ with these waves.
____ This sound has become a tool
____ this unheard sound
____ a useful tool
____ in many areas
____ of medicine,
____ industry,
____ and science.

Other ideas recalled, including inferences

_____

Level: Six

Questions for Ultrasound

1. What is this passage mainly about?
   Implicit: how ultrasound is used

2. What kinds of frequencies do ultrasounds have?
   Explicit: very high ones

3. Why can't humans hear ultrasounds?
   Explicit: they are too high

4. How is animal hearing different than human hearing?
   Implicit: animals can hear higher frequencies

5. What possible health problems of an unborn baby can a doctor see by using ultrasound?
   Explicit: heart problems or slow growth

6. Why is it important for doctors to use ultrasound with unborn babies?
   Implicit: the doctors can plan ahead

7. How does the paint industry use ultrasounds?
   Explicit: to mix paint

8. How could ultrasound be used to discover if a bridge is sound?
   Implicit: it could locate hidden cracks

Number Correct Explicit: _____

Number Correct Implicit: _____

Total: _____

_____ Independent: 8 correct

_____ Instructional: 6–7 correct

_____ Frustration: 0–5 correct

Lewis and Clark

In April 1803, President Thomas Jefferson purchased the entire area of Louisiana from France. The territory stretched from the Mississippi River to the middle of the Rocky Mountains, but no one was really sure where the Mississippi River started or where exactly the Rocky Mountains were located. Meriwether Lewis and William Clark were commissioned by Jefferson to find answers to some of the many questions that people had regarding the new purchase. They were to explore the area and describe the land and its human and animal inhabitants.

Lewis and Clark departed in May 1804 with forty-three men and sufficient supplies for two years. They paddled up the Missouri River in canoes and halted with the coming of winter. They became acquainted with a sixteen-year-old Indian woman and adopted her as their primary guide. Her name was Sacajawea which means Bird Woman. When the ice melted, they continued on their journey. All along the way, Lewis and Clark drew maps and diagrams and recorded what they observed in meticulous detail. They encountered Indian leaders, told them about the United States and presented them with medals and American flags from the President. They acquired knowledge about soil and weather conditions and investigated fur trading possibilities. After seven months of difficult travel, they reached the Rocky Mountains.

Due to Sacajawea's influence, Lewis and Clark obtained horses from the Indians. Their intention was to cross the Rockies with the Pacific Ocean as their final destination. The weather grew cold, the food became scarce, and the mountains seemed endless. When they finally arrived at the ocean, Clark wrote in his journal, "The ocean is in view! Oh what joy!" When the expedition finally returned home over two years after they began their journey, they were awarded a tumultuous welcome. People had long since given them up for dead. That welcome was well deserved. During the long and arduous voyage, Lewis and Clark had accomplished an outstanding feat in describing the land, the rivers, and the Indian inhabitants. They had proven that there was a way to reach the Pacific and had opened a huge new area for settlement and trade. Many other Americans would soon follow in their footsteps.

Adapted from L. J. Buggey, G. A. Danzer, C. L. Mitsakos, and C. F. Risinger, *America! America!* (Glenview, Ill.: Scott, Foresman and Co., 1982), pp. 267–269.

Ferdinand Magellan

In the early sixteenth century, a Portuguese noble, soldier, and sailor named Ferdinand Magellan performed what has been designated the greatest single human achievement on the sea. Magellan had spent long years in Asia, and he often gazed across the wide expanse of the Pacific Ocean and asked himself a question. "How far away from here are the lands discovered by Columbus? If I sailed to the New World, could I find a passage to the Pacific Ocean and the rich Spice Islands?" Magellan hoped to find answers to his questions as well as obtain a large cargo of rare and costly spices. When the Portuguese king refused to assist him, he turned to Spain for help.

In 1519, Magellan sailed from Spain with five ships and a crew of almost three hundred sailors. He navigated the Atlantic and when he reached the New World, he followed the coast of South America until he found the straits that connected the two oceans. It took Magellan thirty-eight days to sail through the stormy straits to the Pacific Ocean and during that difficult time, one ship was wrecked and one headed back to Spain. Once in the Pacific Ocean, Magellan turned north and traveled for months without sighting land.

The voyage was filled with extreme hardship. At one point several resentful Spanish captains initiated a rebellion against their Portuguese admiral. Magellan defeated the rebels and left two of them on shore to die. Several times the ships ran low on supplies, and with little food and water, the sailors begged to turn back but Magellan would not allow this. At one point he declared that they would continue the voyage even if they had to eat the leather rigging of the ships. Disease and starvation claimed many of the crew but, mindful of the fate of the earlier rebels, no one opposed Magellan's will.

Magellan finally reached the islands of the Pacific, but he was unfortunately killed in a skirmish with some natives. One of his ships became unseaworthy and the other was wrecked. The remaining vessel with only seventeen of the original crew members sailed west through the Indian Ocean and around the southern tip of Africa. When they limped into a Spanish port, they had been gone three years! Although Magellan did not live to see the conclusion of the voyage, he and his crew accomplished what no one had ever done before. They had circumnavigated or sailed around the world. Magellan would never know that he had proved what Columbus had correctly predicted, that the lands of the East could be reached by sailing west.

Adapted from L. J. Buggey, G. A. Danzer, C. L. Mitsakos, and C. F. Risinger, *America! America!* (Glenview, Ill.: Scott, Foresman and Co., 1982), pp. 83–86.

Peter the Great

A young tsar named Peter, later called Peter the Great, was responsible for changing Russia. He brought western ways to that nation. As a boy, Peter was interested in western countries. He spent many hours talking with foreign merchants and visitors about their homelands. He eventually decided to visit some Western European countries. He hoped to tour factories and learn how ships were built that could actually sail against the wind as well as with it. The young tsar worked in the shipyards of the Netherlands. He visited the English houses of Parliament. He collected a variety of things such as compasses, anchors, sailcloth, pistols, and tools of all kinds.

Peter returned to Russia determined to establish a powerful and modern government based upon western ways of doing things. He strengthened and developed his armed forces and was responsible for building Russia's first navy. Peter tried to establish modern industries although he was not very successful in doing this. It was difficult for the Russian people to work with the new and often confusing machines when before all goods had been laboriously produced by hand.

Peter recognized the need to change Russian ways of thinking. He established schools and ordered all young men of the upper classes to learn other languages so they would be able to read books from the Western European countries. To emphasize his admiration for western ways, he shaved his beard and ordered all Russian men to do likewise. Peter also insisted that they adopt western ways of dress.

However, Peter did not bring back from England any ideas about allowing the people to govern themselves. He did not desire a Russian parliament which would limit the powers of the tsar but continued to rule according to his will. Like the tsars before him, Peter was an autocrat who believed that the people did not always know what was good for them and therefore should have little say in their own lives. He believed that every Russian should serve his country "by labor of hand or brain," and he had no hesitation in forcing thousands of people to work at building a new capital. The new capital was situated in a marshy area and disease was common during the summer months. The workers also labored in the bitter cold of the Russian winter and many died. Peter called this city Saint Petersburg in honor of the saint for whom he was named.

Adapted from *Europe, Africa, Asia and Australia* by K. S. Cooper, Copyright © 1984, by Silver, Burdett and Ginn, Inc. Used with permission.

Fireworks

Most of us have seen beautiful fireworks. They are often used on the Fourth of July, Labor Day, or other holidays. Around the world, firecrackers, Roman candles, cherry bombs, and rockets are used to celebrate many important events. Royal weddings, military victories, important births, peace treaties, and religious holidays have all been causes for setting off fireworks. Fireworks are also used just for fun. Their sound, color, and sparkle have charmed people for centuries.

Fireworks were probably invented in China about seven hundred years ago. A mixture of saltpeter, sulfur, and carbon was found to be useful for two quite different purposes: gunpowder and fireworks. Since then, these two uses of explosives have developed at the same time. A Roman candle is not much different than a small bomb. An explosion sends the rocket into the air and then makes it blow apart. Powdered metals catch fire and cause the sparks and flames. Metallic compounds add color to the sparks. Sodium compounds produce a yellow color. Calcium compounds make red. Green comes from barium and blue-green from copper. Ammonium compounds change the shades of these colors while sulfur makes the colors more brilliant.

Because fireworks are so dangerous, they are not allowed in many parts of the United States. Every year fireworks used without careful supervision hurt both children and adults, some very seriously. People do not understand how fast fireworks explode after the fuse is lit. They also do not realize the force of the explosion. Putting on a huge fireworks display is a dangerous job even for those who know what they are doing. Timing is crucial as is knowing how far apart to place the various kinds of fireworks used. A rocket may not explode when it is expected to, or it may not shoot as far into the sky as it should. Fireworks may be fun but they are a dangerous kind of fun.

Adapted from T. Cooney, J. Pasachoff, and N. Pasachoff, *Physical Science* (Glenview, Ill.: Scott, Foresman and Co., 1984), p. 269.

There is an episode on an old Superman television show in which the Man of Steel crushes a piece of coal in his hand and makes a diamond. This story is not as farfetched as you might think because, like coal, diamonds are made from carbon. The carbon in a diamond comes from deep inside the earth. It was never part of a life process. On the other hand, the carbon in coal is what is left of ancient plants so coal is considered a mineral but diamonds are not.

Diamonds form deep within the mantle of the earth where the temperature and pressure are so great that even rocks are melted. Tremendous explosions drive the diamonds and other hard materials up through the mantle and out of the crust from passages in volcanoes. In Africa, most diamonds are mined directly from ancient volcanic passages. If the passages have been worn away by running water, the diamonds can be found in nearby river beds. Most diamonds from India were recovered from river beds.

The history of certain large diamonds is characterized by mystery and adventure. Perhaps no gem has had as colorful a history as the Koh-i-noor diamond. This diamond originally weighed 186 carats, which is about two hundred times bigger than the diamonds in most engagement rings. It originally belonged to a prince in India in the fourteenth century but was captured and held by a variety of rulers from that time on. In the eighteenth century, a Persian ruler, Nadir Shah, found the diamond concealed in the turban of another sovereign. He took the stone and gave it the name of Koh-i-noor which means Mountain of Light.

Eventually the diamond passed to Queen Victoria in England in 1849. Victoria thought the diamond looked dull and she had it cut and polished. The cutting did not improve the brilliance of the stone but it did reduce its size to 109 carats. The Koh-i-noor can now be found with the crown jewels of England in the Tower of London.

Adapted from T. Cooney, J. Pasachoff, and N. Pasachoff, *Earth Science* (Glenview, Ill.: Scott, Foresman and Co., 1984), p. 131.

The City of Constantine

One of Rome's most extraordinary emperors was Constantine. He rose to power nearly three centuries after the reign of Augustus. Constantine decided to construct a new capital for the Roman Empire. This capital would be situated in the East. The eastern part of the empire contained more people and represented greater wealth than the western part. The ancient Greek city of Byzantium was chosen by Constantine as the site of his capital. He rebuilt Byzantium into an immense and majestic city. Constantine called his capital New Rome. It became known as Constantinople, the city of Constantine.

Romans were needed to fill Constantine's New Rome. Many western Romans were reluctant to leave their homes. The emperor ordered certain Roman families of importance to move to the East. Each family brought with them a handful of soil from the old capital. The emperor also transported statues and monuments from Old Rome. Palaces, public baths, stadiums, and government buildings were formed like those in the old capital. Constantine also built a Senate House even though Senators no longer played any role in government affairs.

There was one big difference between Old and New Rome. There were no temples to the Roman gods in the new capital. Constantine built Christian churches instead. He was the first Roman emperor to accept that religion as his own. The greatest of Constantine's churches was called Hagia Sophia which means the Church of the Holy Wisdom. Fire eventually destroyed Hagia Sophia, but a later emperor replaced it on an even grander scale. It still stands today although it is no longer a church. It is a museum instead. It is probably the best known building in the modern city of Istanbul, the name by which Constantinople is now called.

Adapted from *Europe, Africa, Asia and Australia* By K. S. Cooper, Copyright © 1984, by Silver, Burdett and Ginn, Inc. Used with permission.

Level: Junior High

Narrative

Lewis and Clark

In April 1803, President Thomas Jefferson purchased the entire area of Louisiana from France. The territory stretched from the Mississippi River to the middle of the Rocky Mountains, but no one was really sure where the Mississippi River started or where exactly the Rocky Mountains were located. Meriwether Lewis and William Clark were commissioned by Jefferson to find answers to some of the many questions that people had regarding the new purchase. They were to explore the area and describe the land and its human and animal inhabitants.

Lewis and Clark departed in May 1804 with forty-three men and sufficient supplies for two years. They paddled up the Missouri River in canoes and halted with the coming of winter. They became acquainted with a sixteen-year-old Indian woman and adopted her as their primary guide. Her name was Sacajawea which means Bird Woman. When the ice melted, they continued on their journey. All along the way, Lewis and Clark drew maps and diagrams and recorded what they observed in meticulous detail. They encountered Indian leaders, told them about the United States and presented them with medals and American flags from the President. They acquired knowledge about soil and weather conditions and investigated fur trading possibilities. After seven months of difficult travel, they reached the Rocky Mountains.

Due to Sacajawea's influence, Lewis and Clark obtained horses from the Indians. Their intention was to cross the Rockies with the Pacific Ocean as their final destination. The weather grew cold, the food became scarce and the mountains seemed endless. When they finally arrived at the ocean, Clark wrote in his journal, "The ocean is in view! Oh what joy!" When the expedition finally returned home over two years after they began their journey, they were awarded a tumultuous welcome. People had long since given them up for dead. That welcome was well deserved. During the long and arduous voyage, Lewis and Clark had accomplished an outstanding feat in describing the land, the rivers and the Indian inhabitants. They had proven that there was a way to reach the Pacific and had opened a huge new area for settlement and trade. Many other Americans would soon follow in their footsteps. (368 words)

Adapted from L. J. Buggey, G. A. Danzer, C. L. Mitsakos, and C. F. Risinger, *America! America!* (Glenview, Ill.: Scott, Foresman and Co., 1982), pp. 267–269.

Number of Total Miscues
(Total Accuracy): _____

Number of Meaning Change Miscues
(Total Acceptability): _____

Total Accuracy		**Total Acceptability**
0–9 miscues _____	Independent _____	0–9 miscues
10–38 miscues _____	Instructional _____	10–20 miscues
39+ miscues _____	Frustration _____	21+ miscues

Rate: 368 x 60/_____ seconds = _____ WPM

Retelling Scoring Sheet for Lewis and Clark

Background/Setting

_____ In 1803,
_____ Thomas Jefferson purchased Louisiana
_____ from France.
_____ The territory stretched
_____ from the Mississippi River
_____ to the middle
_____ of the Rocky Mountains.
_____ No one knew
_____ where the Mississippi River started or
_____ where the Rocky Mountains were.
_____ Jefferson commissioned Meriwether Lewis
_____ and William Clark
_____ to find answers to questions
_____ about the new purchase.

Goal

_____ They were to explore the area
_____ and describe the land
_____ and its human inhabitants
_____ and animal inhabitants.

Events

_____ Lewis
_____ and Clark departed

____ with men
____ forty-three men
____ and supplies
____ for years
____ two years.
____ They paddled
____ up the Missouri River.
____ They became acquainted
____ with a woman
____ a sixteen-year-old woman
____ an Indian woman
____ and adopted her
____ as their guide
____ primary guide.
____ Her name was Sacajawea
____ which means Bird Woman.
____ They drew maps.
____ They encountered leaders
____ Indian leaders
____ and presented them with medals.
____ They acquired knowledge
____ about soil,
____ weather,
____ and trading
____ fur trading.
____ They reached the Rocky Mountains.
____ They obtained horses
____ from the Indians.
____ Their intention was to cross the Rockies.
____ The Pacific Ocean was their destination.
____ The weather grew cold.
____ Food became scarce
____ and the mountains seemed endless.
____ They finally arrived at the ocean.
____ Clark wrote,
____ in his journal,
____ "The ocean is in view!
____ Oh, what joy."

Resolution

____ When the expedition returned,
____ they were awarded a welcome
____ a tumultuous welcome.
____ People had given them up
____ for dead.

____ They had accomplished a feat
____ an outstanding feat.
____ They had opened an area
____ a huge area
____ for settlement
____ and trade.
____ Americans
____ would follow
____ in their footsteps.

Other ideas recalled, including inferences

_____

Questions for Lewis and Clark

1. What was the main goal of Meriwether Lewis and William Clark?
   Implicit: to explore the new territory

2. Name one of the boundaries of the new Louisiana territory.
   Explicit: Mississippi River and/or Rocky Mountains

3. In this selection, what tells us that Lewis and Clark expected to be gone a long time?
   Implicit: they carried supplies for two years

4. Who did Lewis and Clark adopt as their primary guide?
   Explicit: an Indian woman, Sacajawea; Bird Woman

5. What did Lewis and Clark give to the Indians they met?
   Explicit: American flags and/or medals from the President

6. Why would the President of the U.S. want Lewis and Clark to give these special items to the Indians?
   Implicit: the Indians now lived in territory owned by the United States; he wanted friendly relations with the Indians

7. What body of water was their final destination?
   Explicit: Pacific Ocean

8. What hardships did they suffer crossing the Rocky Mountains?
   Explicit: cold and scarce food

9. Why would Clark be so happy to see the Pacific Ocean?
   Implicit: it represented the end of the journey; they had suffered so many hardships crossing the Rockies

10. How did the journey of Lewis and Clark make it easier for the settlers who would follow?
    Implicit: there were maps to follow; they knew what to expect

Number Correct Explicit: _____

Number Correct Implicit: _____

Total: _____

_____ Independent: 9–10 correct

_____ Instructional: 7–8 correct

_____ Frustration: 0–6 correct

Level: Junior High

Narrative

Ferdinand Magellan

In the early sixteenth century, a Portuguese noble, soldier, and sailor named Ferdinand Magellan performed what has been designated the greatest single human achievement on the sea. Magellan had spent long years in Asia and he often gazed across the wide expanse of the Pacific Ocean and asked himself a question. "How far away from here are the lands discovered by Columbus? If I sailed to the New World, could I find a passage to the Pacific Ocean and the rich Spice Islands?" Magellan hoped to find answers to his questions as well as obtain a large cargo of rare and costly spices. When the Portuguese king refused to assist him, he turned to Spain for help.

In 1519, Magellan sailed from Spain with five ships and a crew of almost three hundred sailors. He navigated the Atlantic and when he reached the New World, he followed the coast of South America until he found the straits that connected the two oceans. It took Magellan thirty-eight days to sail through the stormy straits to the Pacific Ocean and during that difficult time, one ship was wrecked and one headed back to Spain. Once in the Pacific Ocean, Magellan turned north and traveled for months without sighting land.

Level: Junior High

The voyage was filled with extreme hardship. At one point several resentful Spanish captains initiated a rebellion against their Portuguese admiral. Magellan defeated the rebels and left two of them on shore to die. Several times the ships ran low on supplies and with little food and water, the sailors begged to turn back but Magellan would not allow this. At one point he declared that they would continue the voyage even if they had to eat the leather rigging of the ships. Disease and starvation claimed many of the crew but, mindful of the fate of the earlier rebels, no one opposed Magellan's will.

Magellan finally reached the islands of the Pacific, but he was unfortunately killed in a skirmish with some natives. One of his ships became unseaworthy and the other was wrecked. The remaining vessel with only seventeen of the original crew members sailed west through the Indian Ocean and around the southern tip of Africa. When they limped into a Spanish port, they had been gone three years! Although Magellan did not live to see the conclusion of the voyage, he and his crew accomplished what no one had ever done before. They had circumnavigated or sailed around the world. Magellan would never know that he had proved what Columbus had correctly predicted, that the lands of the East could be reached by sailing west. (436 words)

Adapted from L. J. Buggey, G. A. Danzer, C. L. Mitsakos, and C. F. Risinger, *America! America!* (Glenview, Ill.: Scott, Foresman and Co., 1982), pp. 83–86.

Number of Total Miscues
(Total Accuracy): _____

Number of Meaning Change Miscues
(Total Acceptability): _____

Total Accuracy		Total Acceptability
0–10 miscues ____	Independent	0–10 miscues
11–45 miscues ____	Instructional	11–23 miscues
46+ miscues ____	Frustration	24+ miscues
Rate: 436 x 60/____ seconds =		____ WPM

Retelling Scoring Sheet for Ferdinand Magellan

Setting/Background

____ In the sixteenth century
____ a Portuguese sailor
____ named Ferdinand Magellan
____ performed a great achievement
____ on the sea.

Goal

____ Magellan asked,
____ "If I sailed
____ to the New World

____ could I find a passage
____ to the Pacific Ocean
____ and the Spice Islands?"

Events

____ When the Portuguese king refused
____ to help him,
____ he turned to Spain
____ for help.
____ Magellan sailed
____ from Spain
____ with ships
____ five ships
____ and a crew
____ of sailors
____ three hundred sailors.
____ He navigated the Atlantic
____ and followed the coast
____ of South America
____ until he found the straits
____ that connected the two oceans.
____ It took days
____ thirty-eight days
____ to sail through the straits
____ to the Pacific Ocean.
____ One ship was wrecked
____ and one headed back.
____ The voyage was filled
____ with hardship.
____ Several captains initiated a rebellion
____ against their admiral.
____ Magellan defeated the rebels
____ and left two
____ on shore
____ to die.
____ The ships ran low
____ on supplies
____ with little food
____ and water.
____ The sailors begged
____ to turn back
____ but Magellan would not allow this.
____ He said
____ they would continue the voyage

____ if they had to eat the rigging
____ the leather rigging.
____ Disease
____ and starvation claimed many.

Resolution

____ Magellan reached islands
____ in the Pacific
____ but he was killed
____ in a skirmish
____ with natives.
____ One ship became unseaworthy
____ and the other was wrecked.
____ The remaining ship sailed
____ around the tip
____ of Africa
____ with seventeen
____ of the original crew.
____ When they limped
____ into port
____ Spanish port
____ they had been gone
____ for years
____ three years.
____ Magellan had sailed around the world.
____ He had proven
____ that the East could be reached
____ by sailing west.

Other ideas recalled, including inferences

_____

Questions for Ferdinand Magellan

1. What was Ferdinand Magellan's main goal?
   Implicit: to reach the Pacific by sailing west through the Atlantic

2. What kind of cargo did Ferdinand Magellan hope to find on his journey?
   Explicit: rich spices

3. Why do you think Spain was interested in helping Magellan with his venture?
   Implicit: they wanted a route to the Spice Islands; they wanted the cargo of spices

4. How long did it take Ferdinand Magellan to sail through the straits connecting the Atlantic and Pacific?
   Explicit: thirty-eight days

5. Why did the Spanish captains rebel against Ferdinand Magellan?
   Implicit: the hardship; they resented him; he was not Spanish

6. What did Ferdinand Magellan do to the rebels?
   Explicit: defeated them and left two to die

7. What did Ferdinand Magellan say they would eat before they would turn back?
   Explicit: the leather rigging

8. Why did Ferdinand Magellan's crew continue on the journey despite all of the past problems and hardships?
   Implicit: they knew what had happened to the rebels; they hoped to get rich

9. How did Ferdinand Magellan die?
   Explicit: he was killed in a battle with some natives

10. How did Ferdinand Magellan prove beyond a doubt that the earth was round?
    Implicit: he and his crew circumnavigated or sailed around it

Number Correct Explicit: _____

Number Correct Implicit: _____

Total: _____

_____ Independent: 9–10 correct

_____ Instructional: 7–8 correct

_____ Frustration: 0–6 correct

Level: Junior High

Narrative

Peter the Great

A young tsar named Peter, later called Peter the Great, was responsible for changing Russia. He brought western ways to that nation. As a boy, Peter was interested in western countries. He spent many hours talking with foreign merchants and visitors about their homelands. He eventually decided to visit some Western European countries. He hoped to tour factories and learn how ships were built that could actually sail against the wind as well as with it. The young tsar worked in the shipyards of the Netherlands. He visited the English houses of Parliament. He collected a variety of things such as compasses, anchors, sailcloth, pistols, and tools of all kinds.

Peter returned to Russia determined to establish a powerful and modern government based upon western ways of doing things. He strengthened and developed his armed forces and was responsible for building Russia's first navy. Peter tried to establish modern industries although he was not very successful in doing this. It was difficult for the Russian people to work with the new and often confusing machines when before all goods had been laboriously produced by hand.

Peter recognized the need to change Russian ways of thinking. He established schools and ordered all young men of the upper classes to learn other languages so they would be able to read books from the

Level: Junior High

Western European countries. To emphasize his admiration for western ways, he shaved his beard and ordered all Russian men to do likewise. Peter also insisted that they adopt western ways of dress.

However, Peter did not bring back from England any ideas about allowing the people to govern themselves. He did not desire a Russian <u>parliament</u> which would limit the powers of the <u>tsar</u> but continued to rule according to his will. Like the <u>tsars</u> before him, Peter was an autocrat who believed that the people did not always know what was good for them and therefore should have little say in their own lives. He believed that every Russian should serve his country "by labor of hand or brain," and he had no hesitation in forcing thousands of people to work at building a new capital. The new capital was situated in a marshy area and disease was common during the summer months. The workers also labored in the bitter cold of the Russian winter and many died. Peter called this city Saint Petersburg in honor of the saint for whom he was named. (404 words)

Adapted from *Europe, Africa, Asia and Australia* by K. S. Cooper, © Copyright 1984, by Silver, Burdett and Ginn, Inc. Used with permission.

Number of Total Miscues
(Total Accuracy): _____

Number of Meaning Change Miscues
(Total Acceptability): _____

Total Accuracy		Total Acceptability
0–10 miscues ____	Independent ____	0–10 miscues
11–42 miscues ____	Instructional ____	11–22 miscues
43+ miscues ____	Frustration ____	23+ miscues
Rate: 404 x 60/____ seconds =		____ WPM

Retelling Scoring Sheet for Peter the Great

Setting/Background

____ A young tsar
____ called Peter the Great
____ was responsible
____ for changing Russia.
____ He brought western ways
____ to that nation.
____ As a boy Peter was interested in western countries.
____ He decided
____ to visit some countries
____ Western European countries.
____ He hoped
____ to learn how ships were built.
____ The tsar worked
____ in the shipyards.
____ He visited the Houses of Parliament.
____ He collected things
____ such as compasses,
____ anchors,
____ sailcloth,
____ pistols,
____ and tools.

Level: Junior High

Goal

____ Peter returned
____ to Russia
____ determined
____ to establish a government
____ modern government
____ based upon western ways.

Events

____ He built Russia's navy
____ first navy.
____ Peter tried
____ to establish industries
____ modern industries.

Resolution

____ He was not successful,
____ it was difficult for the Russian people
____ to work with machines
____ when goods had been produced
____ by hand.

Goal

____ He recognized the need
____ to change ways
____ of thinking.

Events

____ He established schools
____ and ordered all men
____ of the upper classes
____ to learn other languages
____ so they could read books
____ from the western countries.
____ He shaved his beard
____ and ordered all Russian men
____ to do likewise.
____ He insisted
____ they adopt western ways
____ of dress.

Resolution

____ Peter did not bring back ideas
____ about allowing people
____ to govern themselves.

____ He did not desire a Parliament
____ that would limit his powers
____ but continued to rule
____ according to his will.
____ Peter was an autocrat
____ who believed
____ the people did not know
____ what was good for them.
____ He believed
____ that every Russian should serve his
      country.
____ He forced thousands
____ to build a new capital.
____ Many died.
____ Peter called this city
____ St. Petersburg.

Other ideas recalled, including inferences

_____

Questions for Peter the Great

1. What was Peter's main goal?
   Implicit: to bring modern, western
   European ways to Russia

2. Name one thing that Peter collected on his
   trip.
   Explicit: anchors, compasses, pistols,
   sailcloth; or tools of all kinds

3. For what reason would Peter collect
   compasses, anchors, and sailcloth?
   Implicit: he wanted to build a Russian navy

4. Why did Peter establish schools and order upper-class Russian men to attend and learn other languages?
Explicit: so they could read western books

5. What did Peter do to show his admiration for western ways?
Explicit: he shaved off his beard

6. As an autocrat, what did Peter believe about the Russian people?
Explicit: the people do not know what is good for them and should have little say in their own lives

7. How do we know that Peter was less impressed with his visit to Parliament than with his visit to the shipyards?
Implicit: he built a navy but he did not establish a Parliament or change his way of ruling

8. What did Peter do that showed he was a religious man?
Implicit: he named his capital for a saint

9. How was Peter able to build his new capital?
Explicit: he forced thousands to work on it

10. Which actions of Peter's would not have been allowed in the western countries he so admired?
Implicit: forcing people to shave and dress as he did; forcing people to build a city

Number Correct Explicit: _____

Number Correct Implicit: _____

Total: _____

_____ Independent: 9–10 correct

_____ Instructional: 7–8 correct

_____ Frustration: 0–6 correct

Level: Junior High

Expository

Concept Questions:

What are fireworks?

_____

_____

_____ (3-2-1-0)

What does making fireworks mean?

_____

_____

_____ (3-2-1-0)

What makes colors in fireworks?

_____

_____

_____ (3-2-1-0)

What are dangers of fireworks?

_____

_____

_____ (3-2-1-0)

Score: _____ /12 = _____ %

_____ FAM _____ UNFAM

Prediction:

_____

_____

Fireworks

Most of us have seen beautiful fireworks. They are often used on the Fourth of July, Labor Day, or other holidays. Around the world, firecrackers, Roman candles, cherry bombs, and rockets are used to celebrate many important events. Royal weddings, military victories, important births, peace treaties, and religious holidays have all been causes for setting off fireworks. Fireworks are also used just for fun. Their sound, color, and sparkle have charmed people for centuries.

Fireworks were probably invented in China about seven hundred years ago. A mixture of saltpeter, sulfur, and carbon was found to be useful for two quite different purposes: gunpowder and fireworks. Since then, these two uses of explosives have developed at the same time. A Roman candle is not much different than a small bomb. An explosion sends the rocket into the air and then makes it blow apart. Powdered metals catch fire and cause the sparks and flames. Metallic compounds add color to the sparks. Sodium compounds produce a yellow color. Calcium compounds make red. Green comes from barium and blue-green from copper. <u>Ammonium</u> compounds change the shades of these colors while sulfur makes the colors more brilliant.

Level: Junior High

Because fireworks are so dangerous, they are not allowed in many parts of the United States. Every year fireworks used without careful supervision hurt both children and adults, some very seriously. People do not understand how fast fireworks explode after the fuse is lit. They also do not realize the force of the explosion. Putting on a huge fireworks display is a dangerous job even for those who know what they are doing. Timing is <u>crucial</u> as is knowing how far apart to place the various kinds of fireworks used. A rocket may not explode when it is expected to, or it may not shoot as far into the sky as it should. Fireworks may be fun but they are a dangerous kind of fun. (318 words)

Adapted from T. Cooney, J. Pasachoff, and N. Pasachoff, *Physical Science* (Glenview, Ill.: Scott, Foresman and Co., 1984), p. 269.

Number of Total Miscues
(Total Accuracy): _____

Number of Meaning Change Miscues
(Total Acceptability): _____

Total Accuracy		Total Acceptability
0–7 miscues _____	Independent _____	0–7 miscues
8–33 miscues _____	Instructional _____	8–17 miscues
34+ miscues _____	Frustration _____	18+ miscues

Rate: 318 x 60/_____ seconds = _____ WPM

Retelling Scoring Sheet for Fireworks

Main Idea

____ Fireworks are used to celebrate events
____ important events.

Details

____ They are used
____ on the Fourth of July
____ and Labor Day.
____ Weddings,
____ military victories,
____ births,
____ peace treaties,
____ and holidays
____ have been causes
____ for fireworks.

Main Idea

____ Fireworks were invented
____ in China
____ 700
____ years ago.

Details

____ A mixture
____ of saltpeter,
____ sulfur,
____ and carbon
____ was used for gunpowder
____ and fireworks.
____ A Roman candle
____ is like a bomb.
____ a small bomb
____ An explosion sends the rocket
____ into the air
____ and blows it apart.
____ Powdered
____ metals cause sparks.
____ Metallic
____ compounds add color.
____ Sodium
____ compounds produce color
____ yellow color.

Level: Junior High

____ Calcium
____ compounds make red.
____ Green comes from barium
____ and blue-green from copper.

Main Idea

____ Fireworks are dangerous.

Details

____ They are not allowed
____ in parts of the U.S.
____ Fireworks hurt children
____ and adults
____ some very seriously.
____ People do not understand
____ how fast
____ fireworks explode.
____ Putting on a display
____ is a dangerous job
____ even for those who know
____ what they are doing.
____ Timing is crucial.
____ Fireworks may be fun
____ but they are dangerous.

Other ideas recalled, including inferences

_____

Questions for Fireworks

1. What is this selection mainly about?
   Implicit: how fireworks are made; what they are used for; their dangers

2. What is one kind of firework mentioned in the selection?
   Explicit: firecrackets; Roman candles; cherry bombs; rockets

3. What is one special event mentioned in the article that is celebrated by fireworks?
   Explicit: holidays (July 4th, Labor Day); royal weddings; military victories; peace treaties; important births; religious holidays

4. How are gunpowder and fireworks alike?
   Implicit: share the same ingredients; can injure people; both are explosives

5. Name one ingredient shared by gunpowder and fireworks.
   Explicit: saltpeter; sulfur; carbon

9. Why do you think many fireworks injuries occur to the hands?
   Implicit: people hold them too long because they don't realize how fast they can explode

6. Why would the color of calcium compounds be especially useful for Fourth of July fireworks?
   Implicit: they make the color red; red is a color in our flag

10. What specific dangers might be faced by those who design and set off holiday fireworks displays?
    Implicit: one may ignite those nearby and too many may explode at one time

7. What do ammonium compounds do to the color of fireworks?
   Explicit: change the shades of the colors

8. Why are fireworks not allowed in some parts of the United States?
   Explicit: they are so dangerous

Number Correct Explicit: _____

Number Correct Implicit: _____

Total: _____

_____ Independent: 9–10 correct

_____ Instructional: 7–8 correct

_____ Frustration: 0–6 correct

Level: Junior High

Expository

Diamonds

There is an episode on an old Superman television show in which the Man of Steel crushes a piece of coal in his hand and makes a diamond. This story is not as farfetched as you might think because, like coal, diamonds are made from carbon. The carbon in a diamond comes from deep inside the earth. It was never part of a life process. On the other hand, the carbon in coal is what is left of ancient plants so coal is considered a mineral but diamonds are not.

Diamonds form deep within the mantle of the earth where the temperature and pressure are so great that even rocks are melted. Tremendous explosions drive the diamonds and other hard materials up through the mantle and out of the crust from passages in volcanoes. In Africa, most diamonds are mined directly from ancient volcanic passages. If the passages have been worn away by running water, the diamonds can be found in nearby river beds. Most diamonds from India were recovered from river beds.

The history of certain large diamonds is characterized by mystery and adventure. Perhaps no gem has had as colorful a history as the Koh-i-noor diamond. This diamond originally weighed 186 carats, which is about two hundred times bigger than the diamonds in most engagement rings. It originally belonged to a prince in India in the fourteenth century but was captured and held by a variety of rulers from that time on. In the eighteenth century, a Persian ruler, Nadir Shah, found the diamond concealed in the turban of another <u>sovereign</u>. He took the stone and gave it the name of Koh-i-noor which means Mountain of Light.

Eventually the diamond passed to Queen Victoria in England in 1849. Victoria thought the diamond looked dull and she had it cut and polished. The cutting did not improve the brilliance of the stone but it did reduce its size to 109 carats. The Koh-i-noor can now be found with the crown jewels of England in the Tower of London. (339 words)

Adapted from T. Cooney, J. Pasachoff, and N. Pasachoff, *Earth Science* (Glenview, Ill.: Scott, Foresman and Co., 1984), p. 131.

Number of Total Miscues
(Total Accuracy): _____

Number of Meaning Change Miscues
(Total Acceptability): _____

Total Accuracy		Total Acceptability
0–8 miscues	Independent	0–8 miscues
9–35 miscues	Instructional	9–18 miscues
36+ miscues	Frustration	19+ miscues

Rate: 339 x 60/_____ seconds = _____ WPM

Retelling Scoring Sheet for Diamonds

Main Idea

____ Like coal,
____ diamonds are made
____ from carbon.

Details

____ On a television show,
____ Superman crushes a piece of coal
____ and makes a diamond.
____ The carbon in a diamond
____ comes from inside the earth.
____ Carbon in coal
____ is what is left of plants.
____ Coal is a mineral
____ but diamonds are not.
____ Diamonds form deep
____ within the mantle
____ of the earth
____ where temperature
____ and pressure are so great
____ that rocks are melted.
____ Explosions drive the diamonds
____ up through the mantle
____ and out of the crust
____ from passages
____ in volcanoes.
____ In Africa,
____ diamonds are mined
____ from volcanic passages.
____ If the passages have been worn away
____ by water,
____ the diamonds can be found
____ in river beds.
____ Most diamonds were recovered
____ from India
____ from river beds.

Main Idea

____ The history of large diamonds is characterized
____ by mystery
____ and adventure.

Details

____ The Koh-i-noor diamond is bigger
____ two hundred times bigger
____ than diamonds in most rings
____ engagement rings.
____ It belonged to a prince
____ in India
____ in the fourteenth century
____ but was captured
____ and held
____ by a variety of rulers
____ in the eighteenth century.
____ A ruler found the diamond
____ and gave it the name
____ of Koh-i-noor,
____ which means Mountain of Light.
____ The diamond passed to Queen Victoria
____ in 1849.
____ Victoria thought
____ the diamond looked dull.
____ She had it
____ cut
____ and polished.
____ The cutting did not improve the brilliance
____ but it did reduce the size
____ to carats.
____ 109 carats
____ The Koh-i-noor can be found
____ with the crown jewels
____ of England
____ in the Tower of London.

Other ideas recalled, including inferences

_____

Questions for Diamonds

1. What is this selection mainly about?
   Implicit: how diamonds are formed; the history of the Koh-i-noor diamond

2. What are both coal and diamonds made of?
   Explicit: carbon

3. Where does the carbon in a diamond come from?
   Explicit: deep within the earth

4. What is a characteristic of all minerals?
   Implicit: they were once part of a life process

5. Where are most diamonds found in Africa?
   Explicit: ancient volcanic passages

6. Where might you look for diamonds in this country?
   Implicit: where volcanoes are or by rivers

7. Why would Nadir Shah call the Koh-i-noor diamond "Mountain of Light?"
   Implicit: because it was so very big

8. Why did Victoria have the Koh-i-noor cut and polished?
   Explicit: she thought it looked dull

9. Why didn't Victoria use the Koh-i-noor in a ring?
   Implicit: it was much too big; it was dull

10. Where is the Koh-i-noor now?
    Explicit: in the Tower of London; with the crown jewels of England

Number Correct Explicit: _____

Number Correct Implicit: _____

Total: _____

_____ Independent: 9–10 correct

_____ Instructional: 7–8 correct

_____ Frustration: 0–6 correct

Expository

Concept Questions:

Who was Constantine?

_____

_____

_____ (3-2-1-0)

What does "power of emperors" mean to you?

_____

_____

_____ (3-2-1-0)

What are historical landmarks?

_____

_____

_____ (3-2-1-0)

What do people do to feel comfortable in a new place?

_____

_____

_____ (3-2-1-0)

Score: _____ /12 = _____ %

_____ FAM _____ UNFAM

Prediction:

_____

_____

The City of Constantine

One of Rome's most extraordinary emperors was Constantine. He rose to power nearly three centuries after the reign of Augustus. Constantine decided to construct a new capital for the Roman Empire. This capital would be situated in the East. The eastern part of the empire contained more people and represented greater wealth than the western part. The ancient Greek city of Byzantium was chosen by Constantine as the site of his capital. He rebuilt Byzantium into an immense and majestic city. Constantine called his capital New Rome. It became known as Constantinople, the city of Constantine.

Romans were needed to fill Constantine's New Rome. Many western Romans were reluctant to leave their homes. The emperor ordered certain Roman families of importance to move to the East. Each family brought with them a handful of soil from the old capital. The emperor also transported statues and monuments from Old Rome. Palaces, public baths, stadiums, and government buildings were formed like those in the old capital. Constantine also built a Senate House even though Senators no longer played any role in government affairs.

Level: Junior High

There was one big difference between Old and New Rome. There were no temples to the Roman gods in the new capital. Constantine built Christian churches instead. He was the first Roman emperor to accept that religion as his own. The greatest of Constantine's churches was called Hagia Sophia which means the Church of the Holy Wisdom. Fire eventually destroyed Hagia Sophia, but a later emperor replaced it on an even grander scale. It still stands today although it is no longer a church. It is a museum instead. It is probably the best known building in the modern city of Istanbul, the name by which Constantinople is now called. (291 words)

Adapted from *Europe, Africa, Asia and Australia* by K. S. Cooper, © Copyright 1984, by Silver, Burdett and Ginn, Inc. Used with permission.

Number of Total Miscues
(Total Accuracy): _____

Number of Meaning Change Miscues
(Total Acceptability): _____

Total Accuracy			Total Acceptability
0–7 miscues	_____	Independent	0–7 miscues _____
8–30 miscues	_____	Instructional	8–16 miscues _____
31+ miscues	_____	Frustration	17+ miscues _____

Rate: 291 x 60/_____ seconds = _____ WPM

Retelling Scoring Sheet for The City of Constantine

Main Idea
____ Constantine decided
____ to construct a capital
____ a new capital
____ for the Roman Empire.

Details
____ Constantine was an emperor
____ of Rome.
____ The capital would be situated
____ in the East.
____ This part contained more people
____ and represented wealth
____ greater wealth.
____ Constantine called his capital
____ New Rome.
____ It became known as Constantinople.

Main Idea
____ Romans were needed
____ to fill New Rome.

Details
____ Western
____ Romans were reluctant
____ to leave their homes.
____ The emperor ordered families
____ Roman families
____ of importance
____ to move
____ to the East.
____ Each family brought a handful
____ of soil
____ from the old capital.
____ The emperor transported statues
____ from Old Rome.
____ Palaces,
____ baths,
____ stadiums,
____ and buildings were formed
____ like those in the old capital.

Level: Junior High

Main Idea

____ There was a difference
____ big difference
____ between Old and New Rome.

Details

____ There were no temples
____ to the gods
____ Roman gods
____ in the new capital.
____ Constantine built churches
____ Christian churches.
____ He was the first emperor
____ to accept that religion.
____ The greatest was called Hagia Sophia
____ which means the Church of Holy Wisdom.
____ Fire destroyed Hagia Sophia
____ but an emperor replaced it.
____ It still stands
____ today.
____ It is a museum.

Other ideas recalled, including inferences

_____

Questions for The City of Constantine

1. What is this passage mainly about?
   Implicit: how Constantine built
   Constantinople

2. Why did Constantine decide to build a new
   capital in the East?
   Implicit: it had more people *or* there was
   more money.

3. What did each family who moved to
   Constantinople take with them?
   Explicit: a handful of soil from the old
   capital

4. What things did Constantine move from
   Rome to the new capital?
   Explicit: statues *or* monuments

5. Why did Constantine make the new capital similar to old Rome?
Implicit: to make the people who moved there from Rome feel more comfortable

6. How do we know that Constantine completely controlled the government?
Implicit: he could move a capital at will and order people to move there; it said that the senators had no part in the government

7. What was one big difference between Old and New Rome?
Explicit: there were no temples to Roman gods in the new city

8. What did Constantine build instead of temples to the gods?
Explicit: Christian churches

9. What is the modern name of Constantinople?
Explicit: Istanbul

10. Why do you think Hagia Sophia is the best known building in Istanbul?
Implicit: it is so old; it was the greatest of Constantine's churches; it must be very large

Number Correct Explicit: _____

Number Correct Implicit: _____

Total: _____

_____ Independent: 9–10 correct

_____ Instructional: 7–8 correct

_____ Frustration: 0–6 correct

16 Technical Development of the *Qualitative Reading Inventory–II*

The Pilot

Development of the Word-Identification Tests
Analysis of the Word-List Data

Development of the Prior-Knowledge Assessment Tasks
Identification of Concepts
Instructions

Development of the Measures of Comprehension

Development of the Passages
Development of the Pre-primer Passages
Development of the Primer Through Junior High Passages
Development of Pictured Passages at the Primer, First, and Second Levels
Empirical Validation

Rationale for Scoring Oral-Reading Miscues

Reliability and Validity
Issues of Reliability of an Informal Reading Inventory
Issues of Validity of an Informal Reading Inventory

Using the *QRI*–II to Guide Instruction

This section describes our rationale for the development of the *QRI*–II. The rationale includes our initial decisions in designing the instrument, as well as information we obtained from piloting, and decisions made as a result of pilot data. This section is divided into three parts. The first part includes the purposes for the pilot and a description of the children who formed our pilot sample. The second part describes a rationale for the development of each part of the *QRI*–II and presents the results of data analyses supporting our decisions. This section provides validity data for sections of the test. The third part discusses the reliability and validity data for the overall test.

The Pilot

The piloting for the second edition of the *QRI* was focused on four objectives. First was to try out our new measures of prior knowledge to see how the questions and prediction tasks worked and to determine if the scores were correlated with retelling or comprehension. Second, we examined whether interest in the topic correlated with comprehension. Third, we examined whether children could engage in look-backs to assist their comprehension. In addition to these major objectives, we rephrased or rewrote some of the questions with which children had continued to have difficulty. Finally, we reassessed the reliability and validity of passages.

Research for the *QRI*–II was conducted over two years. In the first year (1991–92), Leslie and Cooper (1993) examined the effects of directions for the free-association task on prior-knowledge scores and comprehension, and also examined whether predictions correlated with comprehension. As described in Section 8, Leslie and Cooper's study of 57 sixth-graders found that more precise directions resulted in somewhat high knowledge scores, but more importantly, these scores were more highly correlated with retelling and comprehension. We also found that prediction was correlated with sixth-graders' retelling and comprehension of expository text. In an unpublished aspect of the Leslie and Cooper study, we examined how look-backs influenced comprehension, and whether interest was correlated with comprehension. Details will be presented later in this section.

The next year (1992–93), we chose concepts as described in Section 8, wrote all the concepts into question form, rewrote questions on any passage on which the proportion correct on the original *QRI* was below .25, and continued the research on interest and look-backs. The sample reported here are those children who received the new concepts and questions. Where pertinent, we will also make specific reference to Leslie and Cooper's study of sixth-graders. The analyses reported throughout this section are based on the sample described here unless otherwise noted. We felt it unnecessary to redo all of the statistical analyses presented in the original version of the *QRI*. However, we report new data whenever we had at least ten students read a particular selection. To make this section as concise as possible, we are not repeating the original *QRI* piloting information.

The current sample comprised 213 children from kindergarten through eighth grade from four schools. Three schools were private: two inner city (Milwaukee) and one small town, and one was a suburban public school. One of the inner-city private schools is a parent-owned-and-operated Montessori school enrolling children ages three to nine years from approximately 70 families. The other inner-city K–8 private school enrolls 265 and is composed exclusively of African-American or Hispanic children. Families either pay tuition or choose the schools through Milwaukee's Choice Program. This program allows families to use tax money to send their children to private schools. Both of these inner-city schools were involved in Marquette University's Family Literacy Project, directed by Lauren Leslie and Linda Allen. The small town (population 8,550) private school enrolled 430 students. All students in grades 1, 2 and 4 were assessed if parent permission was granted. The suburban school enrolls 288 from a community of 51,000 and participates in Milwaukee's desegregation program (Chapter 220) where students from the city may be bussed to neighboring suburban schools. All end-of-year kindergarteners recommended by their teacher as potential readers and three first-grade children in an intervention program were assessed as part of an end-of-year assessment program. Of the total sample, 50% were males and 50% females. There were 38% minority children, of whom 91% were African American. Table 16.1 presents the number of children in each grade, their sex and the percent who scored below the 50% percentile on national standardized tests.

TABLE 16.1 Subjects in the Pilot Sample According to Grade, Sex, and National Curve Equivalent Score on Standardized Tests

Grade	Number	% male	% female	% below 50 NCE
K	21	50%	50%	na
1	64	63%	37%	47%
2	50	44%	56%	60%
3	11	55%	45%	100%
4	44	48%	52%	66%
5	7	43%	57%	100%
6	6	50%	50%	50%
7	9	29%	71%	33%
8	3	33%	67%	33%

As Table 16.1 illustrates, students in the pilot sample varied in their overall reading achievement on standardized tests (California Achievement Test and Iowa Test of Basic Skills). We did not have achievement test data on the kindergartners who were assessed at the end of the school year and the first-graders who were assessed at the beginning of the year because their schools did not administer a standardized test to these young children. The NCE first-grade data comes from first graders assessed at the end of the first-grade year. Overall, our sample is more heavily weighted with children of below-average reading ability. This is the sample on which the *QRI*–II is most frequently used, so it seems appropriate.

We have conducted a variety of analyses, and we have used the results to document our decisions in scoring and interpreting the *QRI*–II. The results of these analyses are presented within each section below describing the development of the instrument.

Development of the Word-Identification Tests

The words on the word-identification test came from the 45 passages on the *QRI*–II. We used this procedure to facilitate direct comparison between words read in isolation and in context. This is particularly valuable for beginning readers who may "recognize" words in context that they are unable to recognize on word lists.

We chose words from each passage that were representative of the difficulty of words at that readability level. We estimated word frequency from the Standard Frequency Index in the Carroll, Davies, and Richman *Word Frequency Book* (1971). The average frequency of the lists was determined using the Standard Frequency Index (SFI). The average SFI of each word list is presented in Table 16.2.

In addition to these measures, we took care that the words on the pre-primer, primer and first-grade lists appeared in reading series frequently used

TABLE 16.2 Mean Standard Frequency Index for Word Lists

Pre-primer	Primer	First	Second	Third	Fourth	Fifth	Sixth	JH
74.78	70.01	66.08	59.72	56.67	54.16	50.43	47.08	40.28

at those levels. Thus, the words composing our pre-primer, primer and first-grade lists appear at those levels in recent editions of several reading series: Silver Burdett-Ginn Reading Program (Ginn, 1991), Heath Reading (D.C. Heath, 1991) and Houghton-Mifflin Reading (Houghton-Mifflin, 1991). On our pre-primer list, 12 words occurred in all three pre-primer or readiness materials published by the companies listed above. Four other words occurred in two out of three series, and the other four occurred only in one. Two of these four words were heavily cued by pictures (e.g., write, work). The other words not appearing as often were "other" and "many." On the primer list, 14 words were at that level or earlier in all three series, four occurred at that level or earlier in two out of the three series, and two words only occurred in one series (i.e., the words "children" and "take"). On the first-grade list, all words except "song" occurred somewhere in the first-grade material of all three publishers.

Analysis of the Word-List Data

1. Which is more predictive of contextual reading: words correct or words correct and automatic?   We compared the total number of words on each word list that subjects read correctly to the total number that they read correctly and within one second (automatic). Students at all levels read an average of one or two more words correct than automatic. For children reading at less than a third-grade level, we found that the number words read *correctly and automatically* was more highly correlated with word-recognition accuracy and reading rate in context than total words read correctly. It should be recognized that the number of words read correctly and automatically and the total read correctly are highly correlated (significant at all levels, and $r = .73+$ at all levels). Thus, although we find automaticity of word recognition in isolation to be more highly correlated with word recognition accuracy and reading rate, persons using simple number correct will certainly see a relationship between performance on the word lists and word recognition and reading rate in context.

2. What is the relationship between word identification in isolation and word identification in context?   An examination of the correlations between word identification on the word lists and in the context of the passages indicated significant correlations for seven out of the eleven pre-primer, through first-grade passages. Thus, word identification on word lists predicted word identification in context at these levels. However, there were several first-graders who could read most of the words on the primer word list and who could read the pre-primer passages with above 90% accuracy, but whose oral reading accuracy scores on the primer passages were around 80%. Remember that the words on the lists are a high-frequency sample of those found in the passages. Thus, beyond these high-frequency words, these first-graders did not have a large enough word-recognition vocabulary to read very accurately in context. Although they could read the pre-primer passages, which were short and predictable texts, (some with picture support), they were unable to read the longer primer passages with or without picture support. These observations provide support for the inclusion of the pre-primer passages.

At second-grade level and above, the relationship between word identification and oral-reading accuracy in context was not significant. This was likely because of a high word-identification ability in context on the part of most of the children reading those passages and also because as the readability level of the passage increased, fewer students read the passages orally, reducing the number upon which the correlations were based.

It appears that when students are beginning readers, defined as reading at instruction levels from pre-primer through first grade, word identification in isolation is significantly correlated with accuracy in oral reading. Thus for users assessing children within these ranges, the word lists provide useful information about the level of passages with which to begin assessment. If the examiner is unaware of the approximate range of the student's reading ability, the word lists provide a quick estimation. (See Section 7 for our recommendations of where to start depending upon the grade level of the student.)

3. Are the word lists of increasing difficulty? This question was addressed by examining how students of different instructional levels performed on word lists below, above, or at their instructional levels. For example, the analyses examined performance on first-grade lists by students whose overall instructional levels were primer, first, and second grade. It is important to note that their performance on the word lists is not used to judge their instructional levels. The analyses compared the number of words read *correctly and automatically* with the total correct as a function of the level of the word list. In all analyses, the number of words read decreased on both measures (automatic and total correct) as the level of the list increased, relative to the students' instructional levels. The average number of words read correctly on the word list corresponding to students' instructional levels was 16 (80%). This figure corresponds to figures cited by McCracken (1966).

Development of the Prior-Knowledge Assessment Tasks

Identification of Concepts

We chose the concepts, which were phrased as questions, for the conceptual-question task based upon their relationship to the comprehension questions. Chrystal (1991) examined the predictive validity of concepts, the understanding of which were necessary to answer implicit comprehension questions. She examined the correlation between these concepts and comprehension of two second-grade and two fifth-grade texts. She found that concepts chosen because of their relationship to implicit questions correlated more highly with comprehension than the original *QRI* concepts. Furthermore, concepts scored in relation to information found in the passage predicted as well for Native American as for Caucasian students. Therefore, in developing the *QRI*–II, the authors (Leslie and Caldwell) and two master's degree students in reading independently chose concepts, the understanding of which appeared necessary to answer implicit questions on each passage. For example, consider the first-grade passage, "Bear and the Rabbit." The last question, a difficult one for many young readers, is, "Why did the bear and the rabbit become friends?" We felt that in order to answer that question, using the clues in the passage, children needed to know that one reason that people become friends is because of shared interests (in this particular case because of their love of music). Thus, we chose the concept question "What makes a friend?" After the four of us independently chose concepts, we met to examine the consistency of our selection. We were pleased to discover that in over 90% of the cases we chose the same concepts. Often our wording was different so we negotiated what we thought would be the best wording, and final decisions were determined after piloting.

Instructions

The instructions for the concepts, phrases and questions were examined in piloting and in a study by Leslie and Cooper (1993). The more precise definitional-type instructions (see Section 8) resulted in slightly higher concept scores at all levels studied (i.e., 2nd, 3rd, 4th, and 6th reading levels) although in all cases the differences were not statistically significant at the .05 level. Interestingly, in all cases the p values were between .052 and .07, suggesting a consistent marginal relationship. More importantly, in Leslie and Cooper (1993) the concept scores of sixth-graders who received the more precise definitional-type instructions were significantly correlated with retelling and comprehension of narrative text; whereas, the concept scores of students receiving the standard free-association instructions were not statistically significantly correlated with retelling or comprehension. A follow-up analysis of these correlations found that students who received definition-type instructions gave more 3 point and 0 point responses, whereas students who received the free-association instructions gave more 1 point responses. It appears that the definition-type instructions tapped more directly into what students knew or didn't know about the concepts, phrases, and questions. For this reason the *QRI*–II contains direct, precise questions about the concepts.

1. Does prior knowledge measured by concept questions or prediction predict comprehension? We correlated the total conceptual knowledge question score, with comprehension, as measured by retelling and questions. We also correlated the prediction scores with retelling and answers to comprehension questions. We examined the results on passages at all levels in which the number of students who had read the passages was greater than or equal to 10.

The results support a developmental view of reading acquisition. At the pre-primer and primer levels, prior knowledge measures were not related to retelling or comprehension. At these levels, the children's word-recognition ability and use of picture clues supported comprehension. At the first- and second-grade levels, retelling was predicted by either conceptual knowledge scores or prediction scores. At third-grade, retelling of narrative text was predicted by prediction scores, whereas on expository text, retelling and comprehension was predicted by conceptual-knowledge scores. At fourth-grade level, retelling of narrative text was predicted by conceptual-knowledge scores, as was retelling and comprehension of expository text. Leslie and Cooper (1993) found conceptual-knowledge scores were correlated with retelling and comprehension of narrative text, but prediction scores correlated with retelling and comprehension of expository text.

In summary, at first-grade level and above either conceptual knowledge or prediction was significantly correlated with some form of comprehension, either the retelling or question score.

The results on the prediction task in general indicated that children reading at the third-grade level and higher could use the title of the passage and the concepts, phrases, and questions to make overall predictions of passage content that correlated significantly with retelling or answers to comprehension questions. Specifically, at the third-grade level, prediction correlated significantly (range of correlations was .70–.84) with comprehension, as measured by retelling, on four out of six passages. At sixth grade, prediction was significantly correlated with retelling (.55) and comprehension (.57) of the three expository texts.

2. Do prior knowledge measures predict comprehension better on narrative or expository texts?   In contrast to the results of Valencia and Stallman (1989), we did not consistently find that prior knowledge, measured by either our concept tasks, or predictions, correlated more highly on expository than narrative text. Only at sixth-grade level did we find that prediction consistently correlated with retelling and comprehension of expository text but not narrative text (Leslie & Cooper, 1993).

3. Is knowledge or general reading ability more predictive of comprehension?   We had National Curve Equivalence (NCE) scores from Total Reading Composite score from the California Achievement Test on all first-, second-, and fourth-graders from one private school. An examination of the correlation between NCE, conceptual-knowledge scores and retelling or comprehension found that on all the measures where conceptual knowledge scores were correlated with either retelling or comprehension, NCE never added to the prediction. However, at the fourth-grade level, there were two occasions in which NCE correlated with comprehension while conceptual-knowledge scores did not, and one occasion in which NCE correlated with retelling but conceptual-knowledge scores correlated with comprehension. At no other passage level did NCE correlate with retelling or comprehension.

Prior knowledge of concepts contained in passages more frequently predicted passage comprehension than a general measure of reading achievement. This finding illustrates the value of measuring conceptual knowledge in reading assessment.

4. How much prior knowledge is enough?   We conducted discriminant function analyses on all passages which showed significant correlations between the total-concept scores and the total-comprehension score to determine the concept score that best discriminated instructional level comprehension (70%+) from frustration level comprehension (<70% comprehension). The concept score that best predicted the cut-off score was obtained from the classification function coefficients. The average concept score across the passages was 55% (range 40%–66%, with 70% between 50%–60%) The average score is a bit higher for the *QRI*–II than for the first edition of the *QRI*. This is because our new instructions generate somewhat higher scores on the conceptual-knowledge task.

Development of the Measures of Comprehension

We have three measures of comprehension: a retelling measure where the student is required to retell what s/he remembers from the passage; explicit questions (those where the answer is stated explicitly in the passage); and implicit questions (where an inference must be made in order to answer the question). We have included both a retelling measure of comprehension and a question measure, because research has indicated that the two are not measuring the same aspects of comprehension (Miller & Leslie, unpublished; Taft & Leslie, 1985). A retelling measure allows one to examine how the memory for the text is structured. Although we do not score sequence of retelling, the more the student's retelling sequence conforms to the structure of the narrative, the greater the recall. Retelling indicates how the child organized the information, and it may divulge inferences made during comprehension. Questions, on the other hand, contain information which may drive the inferencing process (Miller & Leslie, unpublished). Despite the information provided by questions, they are the primary vehicle for assessing comprehension in the classroom (Durkin, 1978–79; *Becoming a Nation of Readers,* 1985). We included explicit and implicit questions in order to tap both kinds of comprehension (Pearson & Johnson, 1978). We chose not to include a third type of question, scriptally implicit (Pearson & Johnson, 1978), because we felt that it assessed prior knowledge (Taft & Leslie, 1985), which we measured on the free association test.

The authors designed the questions. Those from narrative texts were designed to tap the most important information in the story. According to story grammars, the goal of the main character (protagonist) is the focus around which all other information is interpreted. Therefore, in all narratives one question asked for the goal of the protagonist. The other questions were designed to tap important information to enable the student to make a coherent representation of the text. That is, a detail was questioned if it was an important detail in the story, but not if it was unimportant. In expository text of third-grade readability and above, the first question always asked for the implicit main idea of the passage. Again, the other questions were written to tap understanding of important information contained in the exposition. In each case the authors read each passage and questions and categorized the questions into explicit/implicit categories. If the authors disagreed as to whether an answer was explicitly or implicitly stated in the passage, it was rewritten or dropped.

The passage dependency of questions on the expositional passages was of concern, particularly at the primer and first-grade levels. In order to determine the percentage of children who could answer the questions correctly without having read the passage, fifteen first- and second-grade poor readers were read the questions from two passages: "Living and Not Living" (primer) and "What You Eat" (first). These passages were chosen because their questions seemed most likely to be passage independent. We chose this sample of children because it comprised the type of children for whom the *QRI*–II was intended. On the basis of the results, we changed three questions on "Living and Not Living." Despite kindergarten instruction on food groups, the children were unable to answer the questions on "What You Eat" without reading the passage. We must acknowledge that high-achieving students are more likely to have knowledge that they can use to answer questions on expositional passages. Thus, if a school used the *QRI*–II to place high-achieving students, the students would more likely be able to answer questions correctly without reading the expository passages. However, a comparison of the ability of these students to retell the passage vs. answer questions might identify what the student was able to recall independently of the information provided by questions.

One author conducted all the propositional analyses (Clark & Clark, 1977) necessary for scoring the retellings. Another judge propositionally analyzed a sample of nine passages. The interjudge reliability of the propositions identified on a passage was .98+ on the passages. After more than twenty subjects had read each passage on the *QRI,* the percent of readers recalling each proposition on a passage was calculated. A map of each text following the story map format for narratives, and a main idea that supported detail structure for exposition, was constructed. Each map was designed from theoretical considerations of importance and empirical evidence from students that these propositions were recalled with some frequency. First, one of the *QRI* authors would design a map based on the elements of a story for the narrative passages (such as setting, goal, events, resolution) and, based on main idea, supporting details for expository passages. Then the frequency with which students recalled these propositions would be examined. Usually, propositions which were recalled by more than 20% of the students were placed on the map. However, there were details that many students recalled that were not important to the overall message of the passage but were interesting to the students. For example, on the Margaret Mead passage, 32% of the students recalled that "in the village in Samoa she lived in a house with no running water or bathroom." Also, there were ideas that were theoretically important which were not recalled by the students. For example, in the passage on Andrew Carnegie, students did not recall that "Carnegie accomplished his dream." This was part of the resolution of the narrative and considered important. Thus, this proposition was placed on the map. Similarly, on the "Ultrasound" passage, one main idea was that industrial uses of ultrasonics have been found, but in recall students omitted the detail that "factories use ultrasonic waves." We also put this proposition on the map. Thus, the maps are our best judgment of important propositions and those recalled by the students. After we designed the maps, a research assistant rescored all the retelling. We added to the map any propositions which were not on it but were recalled frequently by students. Also, this rescoring provided us with estimates of the quantity and quality of recall.

1. Is retelling different in narrative and expository text? The student's retelling is evaluated in comparison to the ideas listed on the passage maps, plus appropriate inferences. Our data suggests that the amount of retelling is related to the type of text. The mean retelling of narrative texts ranged from 17%–41%, whereas the mean retelling of expository texts ranged from 13%–31%. The superior retelling of narrative texts was found from pre-primer through fourth-grade reading levels. Differences have also been found among sixth-grade average readers (Leslie & Cooper, 1993) and below-average readers (Leslie, unpublished).

2. What is the relationship between retelling and comprehension as measured by questions? Correlations between retelling scores (number of propositions retold that are on the retelling scoring sheet plus relevant inferences) and total number of questions correctly answered were examined on all passages with N of 10 or larger. The number of statistically significant correlations ranged across readability levels. At the pre-primer level, two out of the three correlations were significant. In "Just Like Mom," the print basically describes the actions in the pictures. There was no significant correlation between retelling and comprehension on "Just Like Mom." The non-pictured pre-primer story, "Lost and Found," is a predictable sequence of goal-directed events. There was a significant correlation $r(25) = .61$, $p < .01$, between retelling and comprehension on "Lost and Found." The expository pictured passage, "People at Work," also showed a significant correlation between retelling and comprehension, $r(28) = .60$, $p < .01$. At primer, no correlations were statistically significant on the two passages with N greater than or equal to 10. At first-grade, one out of four, at second-grade, two out of four were significant. At third- and fourth-grade, three out of six correlations were significant. At fifth- and sixth-grade levels, one out of two correlations were significant.

There were no consistent patterns by which to explain the differential results. We have concluded that retelling and comprehension share some of the same processes, but there are differences in the processes required on the tasks. It may be that characteristics of the texts influence whether retelling and comprehension are significantly correlated. For young readers, reading other than predictable text, the relationship between retelling and comprehension is not consistently strong. Many children have not been asked to retell what they have read, yet they are familiar with the question format. They probably have less well developed schema for narrative or expository text, thus cannot organize a retelling. As children spend more time reading and listening to stories, they build a schema for text (narrative and expository) and retelling and comprehension share more common properties.

3. What is the relationship between explicit and implicit comprehension?
Because there are only four or five explicit questions and zero, two, four, or five implicit questions, depending upon the level of the passages, any conclusion about a child's ability to answer these types of questions based on the administration of a single passage is unwarranted. In order to address this question with more reliable data, we examined the correlation between explicit and implicit comprehension on data from pairs of passages. In the *QRI*–II there are passages of the same type (i.e., narrative, expository) at each level above pre-primer. We collapsed data from students who read more than one of each type and examined the correlation between explicit and implicit comprehension. The correlations were significant on three of the five narrative passage sets from second grade through sixth grade, but only one of the five sets of expository passages. Only one of the correlations was greater than .60. Based on the standard error of measurement on explicit and implicit questions on two passages (that is, eight of each type of question), if a student answered three to four explicit questions and only one or no implicit questions correctly on *two or more passages at their instructional level in familiar text,* then the difference is of diagnostic significance. This figure was determined by considering the standard error of measurement of these questions. The standard error of measurement of the difference between two scores is roughly equal to the square root of the sum of the squared standard errors of both tests (Thorndike & Hagen, 1977, p. 100).

4. What are the effects of look-backs?
We examined the effects of having students look back in text to find answers to questions that they had not answered correctly. In the case of explicit questions, all they had to do was find the answer. In the case of implicit questions, they had to find text clues to support their answers. As we attempted to have beginning readers do this, we found that most of them could not skim to find answers but rather chose to re-read the entire passage. Because that was not the purpose of the look-backs, we discontinued that aspect of our pilot. However, we found that students with instructional levels at or above third grade could do this readily. At third-grade instructional level, children engaging in look-backs (N = 13) increased their explicit and implicit comprehension by an average of one item ($ps <$ .001). At fourth-grade instructional level, children who looked back (N = 16) increased their explicit comprehension by 1.25 items ($p < .001$) and implicit comprehension by .78 items ($p < .01$). At sixth-grade instructional level, students (N = 51) increased their explicit comprehension by 1.5 items ($p < .001$), and implicit comprehension by 1.3 items ($p < .001$). Note the increase in students abilities to use look-backs to improve comprehension as they increase in reading ability. This increase could be due to growing awareness of question type and the strategies to use to find answers to different types of questions (Raphael, 1986). Clearly, the real challenge is the use of text clues to answer implicit questions. Sixth graders demonstrated that they could do this very well.

In summary, we recommend that examiners use look-backs in children with third-grade instructional level and above to determine whether students can use look-backs to find answers to questions. The difference between total comprehension without access to the passage, and total comprehension with look-backs helps to distinguish between what is remembered versus what is understood with text access.

Development of the Passages

Development of the Pre-primer Passages

The pre-primer passages were written jointly by the authors and were developed because our users asked for them. We chose to write predictable texts because our examination of reading materials for emergent readers illustrated the use of predictable text with heavy picture support. We decided to include both narrative and expository text, and pictured and non-pictured passages at the pre-primer level to allow users to compare students' abilities with a variety of text types with and without pictures. The variability in performance from the children in our pilot sample supported the decisions. All comparisons described below are based on within-subject comparisons. That is, students read both forms of the passages. A comparison of word-recognition accuracy in pictured vs. non-pictured narratives found that the narrative with pictures, "Just Like Mom," was read more accurately than the narrative without pictures, "Lost and Found," whether total accuracy (means = 90.4% vs. 83.2%), $F(1,11) = 11.92$, $p < .005$, or acceptable accuracy (mean = 91.8% vs. 86%), $F(1,11) = 6.75$, $p < .05$ was measured. However, there were no statistically significant differences in retelling (means = 38% vs. 25%) or comprehension (means = 63% vs. 73%). It appears that the lower word-recognition accuracy on "Lost and Found" did not interfere with general comprehension of the story. The accuracy percentages on these pre-primer stories suggest that word-recognition accuracy below 90% can be associated with instructional-level comprehension at pre-primer level.

A comparison between the pre-primer narrative and expository pictured passages, found a higher total word accuracy on the narrative text (means = 90.5% vs. 78.14%), $F(1,13) = 14.60$), higher acceptable accuracy on the narrative text (means = 92.14% vs. 80.57%), $F(1,13) = 13.02$, $p < .01$, and higher reading rates (means = 31.50wpm vs. 24.93), $F(1,13) = 13.07$, $p < .01$. In addition, retelling of the narrative text was higher than of the expository text (means = 40% vs. 15%), $F(1, 14) = 14.13$, $p < .01$, despite higher conceptual knowledge scores on the expository text (means = 56% vs. 74%), $F(1,14)$, = 7.30, $p < .05$. The differences in comprehension favored narrative text (means = 53% vs. 32%), although the differences were not statistically significant, $F(1,14) = 3.47$, $p < .08$.

In summary, the pictured narrative text was easier for children to read and retell than the pictured expository text, in spite of their having higher conceptual knowledge scores on the expository text. It was the experience of one of the authors (LL) that the pictures on the expository text did not facilitate word identification as readily as those on the narrative text. This difference allows for examination of children's reading ability in different contexts.

Development of the Primer Through Junior High Passages

The primer through third-grade passages were written by one author. In order to determine concepts which were familiar to children reading at these levels, we examined basal readers and content area (science and social studies) textbooks. We took ideas for content of the passages from these books and other children's books, and we used the length of passages included in basal readers at the primer and first-grade levels to control the length of our passages. Our passages are purposely longer than the passages on most inventories to provide enough content to assess comprehension without asking questions on unimportant information. However, no passage is longer than the average passage in a basal reader at that level. The fourth-grade through junior-high passages were taken from social studies and science materials published by Scott, Foresman and Company; Silver Burdett & Ginn; and Holt, Rinehart & Winston, Inc. We made minor changes in order to improve their coherence.

Although there is debate about the utility of readability formulae for judging the comprehensibility of text (Davison & Kantor, 1982), we needed some indication that our texts were of increasing difficulty prior to empirical validation. Thus, we estimated the difficulty of our passages through an examination of the difficulty of vocabulary as measured by word frequency or number of syllables and average sentence length. While we agree that these factors do not, in and of themselves, *cause* reading difficulties, they are good *indices* of difficulty (Klare, 1974–75).

We used three or four formulae to measure the readability levels of all passages. For primer-level passages, we used the Spache Readability Formula (Spache, 1974), Harris-Jacobson (Harris & Sipay, 1985), and Wheeler and Smith formula (1954) to estimate level. We used agreement between two of the three formulae to estimate level. Passages at the first through third grade were estimated through the Spache Readability Formula (Spache, 1974), Harris-Jacobson (Harris & Sipay, 1985), Fry Readability Graph (Fry, 1977), and Wheeler and Smith formula (1954). The Fry and Wheeler-Smith were estimated by the computer program, "Readability Estimator" (Hardy & Jerman, 1985). We used agreement between three of the four formulae, using one standard error of measurement, to estimate level. Because the Wheeler-Smith formula counts the number of syllables per word and the Fry formula determines readability using average number of syllables per word and average sentence length, these two were in agreement most often. The Spache and Harris-Jacobson use average sentence length; they also look for the particular word on their word lists. Thus, content-area materials which contain less familiar words would sometimes be considered more difficult using the Spache and Harris-Jacobson formulae. This was a problem on the first-grade passage, "What You Eat," and the third-grade passage, "Wool: From Sheep to You," where two formulae estimated the passages at one level and the other formulae at one level higher.

For passages at the fourth-grade through junior-high level, we estimated readability levels using the Dale-Chall formula (1948) and Fry Readability Graph (1977) through the use of the computer program, "Readability Estimator" (Hardy & Jerman, 1985). The Harris-Jacobson was calculated by hand. We used agreement on two of the three formulae to estimate level. We modified the Dale-Chall formula according to the following criteria: if a key concept contained in the title of the passage was repeated throughout the passage and was not on the Dale List, we counted it only once (we did not count repetitions as unfamiliar words). If a word that was not on the Dale list was defined in the text, we did not count it as an unfamiliar word *after its initial appearance*. These modifications are the same as those recommended for use with the Harris-Jacobson. With these modifications of the formula, the Dale-Chall and the Fry Index were the most similar in their estimate of the readability of the passages. On most of the passages, all three formulae agreed; when discrepancies existed, all were within one grade level of the other formulae.

Development of Pictured Passages at the Primer, First, and Second Levels

We chose to design pictures to accompany one of the narratives at each of the primer, first, and second levels included in the original *QRI*. At these levels, pictures were designed to support the *ideas* in text, but because of the number of words in the stories, children could not read the text by reading the pictures, as was possible with one story at the pre-primer level. We compared the word-recognition accuracy, retelling, and comprehension of students who read the original *QRI* passages with students who read the pictured passages in the *QRI*–II. At the primer level, there were no significant differences on any measure, and except for the retelling mean, the other means were identical. At the first-grade level, comprehension of "Bear and Rabbit" was significantly higher with pictures than without, $t(30) = 2.71$, $p < .01$. The mean increased from 61% correct to 74% correct for an effect size of .68. There were no other significant differences on "Bear and Rabbit." At the second-grade level, retelling of "Father's New Game" was significantly higher on the pictured passage, $t(30) = 4.73$, $p < .001$. The proportion retold increased from .13 to .39 for an effect size of 1.2. Although comprehension increased by 5%, the difference was not statistically significant.

In conclusion, the role of pictures depends upon several factors. At the pre-primer level, pictures helped children "read" words that they were not able to read otherwise. Above that level, pictures did not provide as much word-recognition support, but rather assisted retelling or comprehension.

Empirical Validation

1. Are the passages of increasing difficulty? We assessed the difficulty of passages by comparing the performance of students reading passages of increasing readability. Specifically, we conducted multivariate analyses of variance with readability as the within-subjects factor, and total comprehension, retelling, and reading rate as the dependent measures. Also, we designated total oral reading accuracy and acceptable accuracy as dependent measures in analyses through sixth grade. We conducted separate analyses for different text types (goal-based narrative, and expository) because data indicated differences in comprehension among these text types (see page 306 for a discussion of these results). We conducted sets of analyses on adjacent levels, which we will refer to as P–1, 1–2, 2–3, 3–4, 4–5, 5–6, and 6–junior high.

Our results showed significant differences at each level. On P–1 narratives, we found differences on all measures: total comprehension, retelling, rate, total oral reading accuracy, and acceptable accuracy. In all cases, students performed better on the primer than first-level passages. On the P–1 expository passages, we found differences illustrating the greater difficulty of the first-level passages on all measures except rate. On the 1–2 goal-based narratives, total oral reading accuracy, acceptable accuracy, and comprehension of first-level passages were higher than on second level. We found no significant differences on exposition, where only eight students had read first- and second-level expository passages. Mean differences illustrated that second level was harder than first.

On the 2–3 narratives, total oral reading accuracy and total comprehension were significantly higher on second-level material. We found no differences on exposition, where only ten students had read second- and third-grade expository passages. On the 3–4 narratives, comprehension, retelling, and rate were higher on third than fourth, although total or acceptable miscues did not differ. Thus, although the students could decode the texts equally well, they read the fourth-grade narratives more slowly and retold them and comprehended them less well. On the 3–4 expository passages, we found significant differences on all dependent measures.

On the 4–5 narratives, comprehension of fourth-grade passages was higher than of fifth-grade passages. There were no other significant differences. Again, although the students could decode these materials similarly, they comprehended the fourth-grade materials better. On the 4–5 exposition, total oral reading accuracy, acceptable accuracy, and comprehension was higher on fourth- than fifth-grade materials. On the 5–6 narrative and expository passages, we found no significant differences. Means illustrated higher comprehension on fifth than sixth ($ps < .10$).

On the 6 through junior-high narratives, comprehension and total retelling were higher on the 6 than junior-high passages. On the exposition for these levels, comprehension was significantly higher on the sixth-grade passages.

We believe there is sufficient data to indicate that the passages are of increasing difficulty. In all passage comparisons, the comprehension of the lower passage was one to two questions higher than the higher passage. In addition, on passages through third grade, children read with greater accuracy on the passages of lower readability. On expository passage comparisons of levels 3–4 and 4–5, students read with greater accuracy and greater acceptable accuracy on the lower passage.

2. Are there comprehension differences on different text types?
One of the theoretical foundations of the *QRI*–II was that it should find comprehension differences between narrative and expository passages. We conducted multivariate analyses of variance comparing conceptual-knowledge scores, retelling, and comprehension for children who read at least one narrative and expository text at a readability level. Because each student read both a narrative and an expository text, passage type was a within-subjects factor.

Results of these analyses differed according to the readability of the passages. Table 16.3 presents the means and standard deviations of proportion correct score on conceptual knowledge, retelling, and comprehension as a function of readability and text type. Significant effects of passage type were found at all levels except primer, fifth, and sixth. At the pre-primer level, students retold, $F(1,14) = 17.10$, $p < .001$, and comprehended, $F(1,14) = 5.78$, $p < .05$, more on narrative texts despite having higher knowledge scores on the expository text, $F(1,14) = 8.96$, $p < .01$. At the primer level, no significant differences were found, and as Table 16.3 illustrates, all means were very close. At first-grade level, students had more conceptual knowledge, retold more and comprehended more on narrative text than on expository, $Fs(1,31) = 16.56, 24.16,$ and 22.07, $ps < .001$. A multivariate analysis of covariance that removed the variance due to conceptual knowledge (*Beta* = .32), still found higher retelling and comprehension on narrative text, $Fs(1,30) = 9.23$ and 9.50, $p < .01$. At second-grade level, students retold and comprehended more of the narrative text, $Fs(1,18) = 45.60$ and 11.53, $p < .001$ and $.01$, respectively, than of the expository text despite almost identical conceptual knowledge scores. At third-grade level, students retold and comprehended more of the narrative than expository texts, $Fs(1,25) = 21.31$ and 12.32, $ps < .001$, and $.01$, respectively, despite similar conceptual knowledge scores. At the fourth-grade level, students retold more of the narrative text, $F(1,16) = 5.29$, $p < .05$, but differences between comprehension and conceptual-knowledge scores were not statistically significant. At fifth- and sixth-grade levels, there were no statistically significant differences on any measure, however, it should be noted that the number of students in these analyses were small (≤ 12). Leslie and Cooper (1993) found that average sixth-grade readers retold more of the narrative text, $F(1,53) = 12.85$, $p < .001$, than expository text despite showing more prior knowledge of the expository text, $F(1,53) = 68.13$, $p < .001$. No differences in comprehension were found. These findings corroborate those found with sixth-level readers on the original *QRI*.

In summary, an examination of the above findings, in addition to those on the original *QRI*, suggests that students recall more from narrative than expository text through sixth-grade reading level. Comprehension differences appear through third-grade reading level at least. It should be noted that these differences are likely subject to instructional modification. That is, in schools where

TABLE 16.3   Means and Standard Deviation of Proportion Correct Score on Conceptual Knowledge, Retelling and Comprehension on Narrative and Expository Text as a Function of Readability Level

Readability Level	Conceptual Knowledge	Retelling	Comprehension
Pre-primer (n = 15)			
Narrative	.54**	.35*	.57**
	(.14)	(.16)	(.33)
Expository	.74	.15	.31
	(.23)	(.13)	(.18)
Primer (n = 13)			
Narrative	.58	.29	.72
	(.19)	(.16)	(.23)
Expository	.62	.33	.68
	(.11)	(.17)	(.16)
First (n = 32)			
Narrative	.67**	.26**	.76**
	(.14)	(.13)	(.12)
Expository	.54	.15	.50
	(.19)	(.13)	(.26)
Second (n = 19)			
Narrative	.69	.43**	.82**
	(.15)	(.18)	(.17)
Expository	.68	.22	.61
	(.19)	(.13)	(.19)
Third (n = 26)			
Narrative	.69	.34**	.77**
	(.16)	(.18)	(.16)
Expository	.66	.19	.58
	(.13)	(.11)	(.22)
Fourth (n = 17)			
Narrative	.46	.34*	.65
	(.29)	(.15)	(.20)
Expository	.47	.27	.71
	(.21)	(.13)	(.18)
Fifth (n = 12)			
Narrative	.52	.27	.74
	(.31)	(.13)	(.19)
Expository	.57	.24	.62
	(.20)	(.18)	(.21)
Sixth (n = 13)			
Narrative	.47	.28	.73
	(.21)	(.15)	(.15)
Expository	.40	.27	.62
	(.18)	(.13)	(.22)

$*p$ .05
$**p$ .01

more emphasis is placed on reading expository material, the differences should be less pronounced, or ameliorated. Such may be the case in our current fourth-level readers compared to the fourth-level readers in our original sample.

3. Is comprehension affected by interest in the topic? We piloted an interest measure to assess the effect of interest on retelling or comprehension. Prior to reading the student was asked, "If the title of the passage is '____', how interested are you to read about '____'." A four-point Likert scale was used: "very interested," "a little interested," "not very interested," and "not at all interested." Again, after students finished reading the selection, and before retelling, we asked them to rate, on the same scale, how interesting the passage had been to them. Results indicated that the two interest measures were highly correlated with each other at all levels, thus establishing the reliability of the measure. Interest predicted retelling or comprehension on three out of four passages at the first and second reading level. It only correlated with retelling or comprehension once at the fourth level, and twice at the sixth level. Because of the inconsistency of these results we chose not to include the interest measure on the *QRI*–II. It should be noted that interest was more likely to correlate with retelling than comprehension, thus may be a measure of motivation to retell. Further research should be done to investigate this possibility.

4. Is comprehension affected by sex of character and sex of reader? The narratives above third-grade level are biographies. The name of the person was the title of the passage and one of the concepts assessed in the prior knowledge measure. Some of the biographies were about males, others about females. There was concern that students' interest in the characters might affect their comprehension and that the interest might be sex-related. We conducted a multivariate analysis of variance on the fifth-grade data because there were two biographies of males and two of females. The reader's sex was the between-subjects factor and the character's sex was the within-subjects factor. The dependent measures were comprehension as measured by questions and total retelling. There were no significant effects of either of these factors, or their interaction, on comprehension.

5. Are there differences in instructional levels obtained in familiar and unfamiliar text? We have used the same criteria for determining instructional level in familiar vs. unfamiliar material. To ascertain whether students' instructional level in familiar material was different than their instructional level in unfamiliar material, we performed analyses of variance with instructional level in familiar and unfamiliar material as the within-subject variable at all grades above third. We did not use the lower levels because many of these children did not have an instructional level in unfamiliar material (all the material was relatively familiar to them). We found significant differences between the levels for the children at all grade levels between fourth and junior high. At all readability levels, the mean instructional level in familiar material was one-half year higher than in unfamiliar material.

An examination of the percentage of students whose familiar instructional level was either the same or one or more levels higher than their instructional level in unfamiliar material showed differences depending upon readability level. At the third-grade and junior-high levels most students had instructional levels which were equal in familiar and unfamiliar material. In contrast, at all other levels, 67% showed an instructional level in familiar material one or more levels higher than in unfamiliar material.

This finding supports the use of materials of varying familiarity on the *QRI*–II. Because students will vary in their familiarity with material, a teacher or assessment specialist needs to be aware that students' instructional level may vary as a function of the familiarity of the material.

Rationale for Scoring Oral Reading Miscues

We recommend examiners to score miscues in two ways: (1) to find the total number of miscues and convert it to oral reading accuracy in percentage; (2) to determine the percentage of uncorrected miscues which change the authors' meanings. Studies by Leslie (1980), Leslie and Osol (1978), and Bristow and Leslie (1988) indicate that changes in miscue quality occur as the total number of miscues increases. Specifically, as the total number of miscues increases, the number of miscues that change the authors' meaning and are not corrected also increases. Research indicates that these changes may occur as the child reads with less than 95% accuracy (supporting the traditional criteria for instructional level), but these changes certainly occur if the student reads with less than 90% accuracy. The one exception to this finding occurs for children at the pre-primer instructional level. Data describing this exception are presented below.

1. What is the relationship between oral-reading accuracy and retelling or comprehension? The correlation between oral reading accuracy and retelling and comprehension was examined at each readability level. At the pre-primer level, there were significant correlations between oral-reading accuracy and both retelling and comprehension (rs ranged from .38–.83). At the primer level, significant correlations were found only on one passage, "Trip." At the first-grade level significant correlations were found on three out of the four passages (rs ranged from .36–.66). There were no statistically significant correlations at the second-grade level. Above second-grade level, fewer subjects read orally, thus the number of students upon which the correlations are based is small, contributing to the lack of statistically significant correlations at those levels.

2. How accurate does oral reading need to be for instructional level comprehension? The traditional oral-reading accuracy scores used to determine instructional level have been between 90%–95%. We analyzed our pilot data to determine the level of accuracy related to instructional-level comprehension (70%). In other words, how accurately does one need to read to comprehend, or how much meaning construction needs to occur for accurate oral reading?

Discriminant function analyses were conducted on pre-primer, primer, and first-grade level passages and showed significant correlations between either total accuracy or acceptable accuracy and either retelling or comprehension. From the classification function coefficients, we determined the accuracy level that best predicted instructional-level comprehension (80% at pre-primer, 67% at primer and first-grade level). At pre-primer, a total accuracy score of 85% best predicted instructional-level comprehension on "Just Like Mom," whereas a total accuracy score of 80% best predicted instructional-level comprehension of "Lost and Found." This difference in accuracy level was expected from the mean accuracy differences between the two stories. Why was 80% comprehension associated with 85% accuracy on one story but with only 80% accuracy on the other? There are two obvious differences between the stories: picture vs. no pictures, and predictability of text. "Just Like Mom" had pictures, and "Lost and Found" didn't. One would expect if pictures supported comprehension that the accuracy percent associated with instructional-level comprehension would be lower on the pictured than on the non-pictured passages. Given that the opposite was found, the "picture–no pictures" difference does not seem a likely explanation. Alternatively, the questions on "Just Like Mom" appear to be more open-ended and thus, children with less accurate reading may have given answers from their knowledge base because they weren't able to construct enough meaning from the text or the picture. One author (LL) who gathered 90% of the pre-primer data observed such responses. In contrast, on "Lost and Found," the questions did not elicit responses from prior knowledge, but rather tapped key words which the children appeared likely to recognize in the predictable text (e.g., cat, dog, bed, table). Thus, if the children read these words correctly, they could comprehend at instructional level, even though they could not read other words in the story correctly.

An analysis of the accuracy score related to retelling of at least 20% indicated that on both pre-primer narratives, 88% acceptable accuracy was related to a retelling of at least 20% of the text. At the primer level, 87% total accuracy was related to a retelling of at least 20%. At first-grade level, the accuracy percent increased: 93% total accuracy was related to instructional level comprehension, and 96% acceptable accuracy was related to a retelling of at least 20%.

In conclusion, at the pre-primer and primer levels, children may read with less than 90% accuracy and still achieve instructional-level comprehension. Whether it would be instructionally beneficial for children to spend a lot of time reading such challenging material is an empirical question. It would likely depend upon teacher support, picture support, interest, and other factors. At the first-grade level, however, the traditional criteria of at least 90% total accuracy and 95% acceptable accuracy were supported.

Reliability and Validity

An informal reading inventory should meet the requirements presented in the *Standards for educational and psychological testing* (1985) written by the American Educational Research Association, American Psychological Association, and National Council on Measurement in Education. According to the *Standards,* a test is an instrument which evaluates some ability, and an inventory obtains data upon which no evaluation is made (such as a personality inventory). Thus, informal reading inventories are tests, not inventories. We acknowledge this, but we call our instrument an inventory because it is structurally similar to other IRIs, however misnamed historically. No matter what you call this instrument, there are basic standards of any instrument which must be met. Following is a discussion of reliability and validity issues as they pertain to the uses of our instrument.

Issues of Reliability of an Informal Reading Inventory

Cross and Paris (1987) present an analysis of the relationship between test purposes and the statistical evidence necessary to document the reliability and validity of the test. Perhaps the most important contribution of this work is the illustration that evidence important to one kind of test may be irrelevant or detrimental to another type of test. The purpose of the instrument should guide the author and user to determine the relevant reliability and validity data for the instrument's purposes.

Because we designed the *QRI*–II for mastery (that is, determination of an instructional level) and diagnostic purposes, the essential test properties, according to Cross and Paris, are consistency, construct representation, and penetration. Consistency is a reliability property of a test that refers to the replicability of scores for a single individual. A score is consistent if, in the absence of growth or learning, an individual repeatedly obtains the same score. The *QRI*–II measures consistency of scores in three ways: interscorer reliability, internal consistency reliability, and alternate-form reliability. Construct representation and penetration are validity properties and are discussed in the validity section.

Interjudge Reliability (Consistency) of Scoring. Aside from the purposes for which an instrument is used, one must have evidence that the test is scored consistently across examiners. Whenever there is a judgment, lack of consistency can develop. In our analysis of scoring reliability of the *QRI*–II, we examined the reliability of judges' scores on total percent of miscues, percent of meaning change miscues, prior knowledge concept score, total explicit comprehension score and total implicit comprehension score, and the propositional analysis of recall. All examiners had the same scoring manual to judge these scores. However, our expert scorers (N = 3) were reading teachers or specialists who had a master's degree. Thus, our reliability estimates compare persons without extensive training by the test developers to those with training by the test developers. It should be noted that the experts did not receive their master's degrees from the program of either test author, but one test author trained the experts in the scoring of the *QRI*–II. We did not have two judges listen to the tapes of the children's oral reading unless the examiner was an undergraduate student. Thus we assumed that the transcription of the total number of miscues was correct. Hood (1975–76) reports the reliability of two judges recording total miscues from tape to be .98+.

Estimates of the inter-scorer reliability of the new conceptual-knowledge questions found agreement upon 299 of the 304 concepts sampled, for a 98% agreement. Scorers used the scoring instructions and examples found in Section Eight. Estimates of inter-scorer reliability of total miscues, acceptable miscues, explicit and implicit comprehension were assessed by examining data from 122 readings. These data were gathered across all readability levels and both types of text. Of the 122 readings, 49 were conducted orally. Thus the estimate of reliability for total miscues and acceptable miscues is based on 49 observations. The estimates of inter-scorer reliability was found using Cronbach's alpha (Cronbach, 1951). Alpha reliability estimates were .99 for total miscues, .99 for meaning-change miscues, .98 for explicit comprehension, and .98 for implicit comprehension. These reliability estimates indicated a high degree of consistency between scorers. Thus, an examiner should be able to score the *QRI*–II reliably without extensive training.

We used a sample of 393 passages to estimate the reliability of scoring the list of propositions for each passage. Again, all levels and types of text were represented. The alpha estimate of interjudge reliability was .94. This indicates that the proposition data from which we built our passage maps were scored reliably.

Internal Consistency Reliability. This form of reliability examines how reliable the score is as an estimate of the true score. For example, when we measure total comprehension, how reliable is the score as an estimate of the student's true comprehension score?

The standard error of measurement of the total comprehension score was estimated through an analysis of variance with items (1–5; 1–6; 1–8; 1–10) as the within-subjects factor and subjects as the between-subjects factor. Crocker and Algina (1986) recommended the use of the standard error of measurement rather than a correlational estimate of reliability for criterion-referenced tests where there is reduced variability in subject's performance. Remember that a correlation is based, in part, on variability. In our case, we did not give harder passages to students who frustrated on easier material, and so we reduced variability. Thus, a traditional correlational measure of reliability would not accurately reflect the reliability of the scores. Similarly, because the alpha coefficient is based on variability, it is subject to the same restrictions. Crocker and Algina (1986, p. 196) illustrate that the standard error of a criterion-referenced test can be very low (such as .001) indicating a highly reliable score, yet the reliability, expressed as a generalizability coefficient, could be very low .00. This happens when there is no variability in the data. Because we have restricted variability, we chose to use the standard error of measurement. The formula for determining the standard error of measurement from analysis of variance data is:

$$\text{standard error of measurement} = \sqrt{\frac{\frac{(MS_i - MS_r) + MS_r}{n_p}}{n_i}}$$

where MS_i = Mean square for items
MS_r = Mean square residual
n_i = number of items
n_p = number of persons

According to Crocker and Algina (1986, p. 196), the standard error must be between .00 and $\sqrt{.25/(n_i - 1)}$; the lower, the better. This maximum value is obtained by considering the maximum variance possible with a set of items. For example, if all examinees get half the items correct and the other half incorrect, we have the maximum item variance, which works out mathematically to be $\sqrt{.25/n_i - 1}$. There were five comprehension questions on the Pre-primer passages. For the primer and first-grade passages, there were six comprehension questions; for second- to sixth-grade passages there were eight; and for junior high there were ten. As the formula above illustrates, the more items, the more reliable the test will be, because you are dividing by n_i. Also, the more items, the less the SEM will affect instructional level decisions.

Table 16.4 presents the mean, standard deviation, and the standard error of measurement (SEM) of the proportion correct total comprehension score for all passages. Consider the highest SEM for an eight-item test, .18 for "Wool: From Sheep to You" and "Sequoyah." A student with a score of 75% has a true score between 57% and 93%, 68% of the time. Because of the relatively large SEMs on any single passage, we recommend that an examiner give passages of the same type (such as narrative or expository) with which the student is familiar when attempting to estimate true score. When the examiner uses two passages, the percent correct is determined from sixteen items. The standard error is based on sixteen items and is reduced substantially. When we pooled data from children who read "The Trip to the Zoo" and "The Surprise," the SEM for sixteen items was 10. Thus, a child with a total score of 75% has a true score which lies between 65% to 85%, 68% of the time; a much more reliable estimate of true score than their separate SEMs on .15 and .14 based on eight items.

For similar reasons, we cannot recommend that users interpret scores for explicit and implicit comprehension on a single passage. First, these subtests do not contain enough items to be reliable indicators of the children's true scores in these areas if only one passage is used. Even when the examiner uses two passages, and the total number of explicit items from both passages is compared to the total number of implicit from both passages, large differences are needed for reliable diagnostic conclusions. When we pooled explicit items from "The Trip to the Zoo" and "The Surprise," we obtained a SEM of .13; the standard error for implicit items was .15. The standard error of the *difference* between these two is .20. (The formula is SEMdiff = the square root of the sum of the two squared SEMs.)

Thus, only if a student received scores of 75% to 100% correct on explicit questions and 0 to 25% correct on implicit questions, can we be 95% sure that these scores do not overlap. If a student consistently receives scores which differ by as much as 50%, then conclusions that a student is better in answering one type of question than the other are reliable.

TABLE 16.4 Standard Error of Measurement (Proportion Correct) for Total Comprehension Scores for Passages

Passage Level and Name	Mean	S.D.	N	SEM
Pre-primer				
Just Like Mom	.65	.25	48	.22
Lost and Found	.72	.29	25	.19
People at Work	.30	.20	28	.20
Primer				
A Trip	.81	.21	12	.15
The Pig Who Learned to Read	.67	.23	19	.18
Who Lives Near Lakes?	.67	.19	12	.19
Living and Not Living*	.58	.17	25	.21
First Grade				
The Bear and the Rabbit	.72	.20	33	.18
Mouse in a House	.66	.19	14	.20
Air	.55	.27	18	.19
What You Eat	.40	.25	15	.19
Second Grade				
What Can I Get for My Toy?	.82	.15	19	.13
Father's New Game	.73	.26	18	.14
Whales and Fish	.68	.18	17	.17
Seasons	.50	.22	13	.17
Third Grade				
The Trip to the Zoo	.76	.18	22	.15
The Surprise	.78	.21	10	.14
The Friend	.71	.19	20	.16
Cats: Lions and Tigers in Your House	.69	.21	20	.16
Where Do People Live?	.47	.30	11	.15
Wool: From Sheep to You	.45	.19	12	.18
Fourth Grade				
Johnny Appleseed	.81	.22	9	.13
Amelia Earhart	.67	.15	11	.17
Sequoyah	.53	.17	9	.18
The Busy Beaver	.71	.13	9	.17
The City of Cahokia	.74	.25	10	.15
Saudi Arabia	.75	.16	10	.15
Fifth Grade*				
Martin Luther King, Jr.	.65	.21	32	.17
Christopher Columbus	.63	.24	31	.16
Margaret Mead	.66	.18	23	.16
Getting Rid of Trash	.59	.21	38	.17
Octopus	.66	.19	32	.16
Laser Light	.54	.20	36	.17
Sixth Grade				
Pele	.71	.17	57	.16
Abraham Lincoln	.75	.17	16	.16
Andrew Carnegie	.47	.20	57	.17
Computers	.70	.15	57	.16
Predicting Earthquakes	.61	.22	20	.16
Ultrasound	.58	.24	19	.16
Junior High*				
Lewis and Clark	.63	.21	36	.14
Ferdinand Magellan	.64	.19	28	.15
Peter the Great	.40	.25	21	.14
Fireworks	.71	.18	34	.14
Diamonds	.64	.16	20	.15
The City of Constantine	.54	.21	29	.15

*based on original piloting of the *QRI*.

Alternate-Form Reliability (Consistency) of Placement Decisions.   If the major purpose is to determine an instructional level, then it is important to have consistency in that level. Thus, the reliability issue becomes, "If I find an instructional level of fifth grade on this test, would I find an instructional level of fifth grade if I gave the test tomorrow or next week?" This type of reliability is called *test-retest reliability.* The interest is in the consistency of test results over time or conditions. As many test developers have learned, there is a problem in giving exactly the same test over two time periods in order to assess test-retest reliability, because the student may learn something in the first administration that raises his or her score on the second administration.

An alternative method of estimating level reliability is to examine performance on two passages similar in design; this method is called *alternate-form reliability* (Crocker & Algina, 1986). In the *QRI*–II, this means that we would examine performance on two similar passage types (such as narratives or familiar expository). If performance on these indicates the same instructional level, we have evidence for alternate-form reliability.

In order to obtain the best estimate of alternate-form reliability of level, we examined the reliability of the total comprehension score to estimate instructional level across passages of the same type. The procedure used to estimate alternate form reliability of criterion-referenced tests was Livingston's (1972) K^2. This index reflects the magnitude of the discrepancy of misclassification in judging the reliability of the decision. In our case, the question is, "How close are the two comprehension scores to the cutoff of 70% for instructional level?" The formula for K^2 may be found in Crocker and Algina (1986, p. 203).

The reliabilities of our instructional level decisions based on comprehension scores were all above .80; 75% were greater than or equal to .90. In addition, we examined whether the same instructional level would be ascertained on the basis of the comprehension scores on each passage. Across the readability levels, 71% to 84% of the time the same instructional level would be found on both passages. Specifically, at the primer level, 71%; first, 86%; second, 78%; third, 80%; fourth, 80%; fifth, 75%; sixth, 77%; and junior high, 81% of the time the same instructional level would be identified.

Reliability (Consistency) of Diagnostic Profiles.   The pertinent reliability data are somewhat different if the purpose for giving the test is diagnostic. In this case the examiner seeks consistency in conclusions regarding the child's strength and weaknesses in reading. For example, if the child's major reading problems appear to be in decoding words, support for that conclusion should come from several sections of the test. One should expect that the child will score low on word lists at or below grade level and have low oral reading accuracy scores on passages at or below grade placement. Thus, consistency should exist between total accuracy in oral reading on a passage and performance on the word list at the comparable level of readability. This same child should comprehend material generally well if he or she is within instructional range on oral reading accuracy, or if material is read to him/her.

In another case, a child might have consistently high scores on oral reading accuracy but might have difficulty comprehending material at his or her grade level. Or perhaps a child will comprehend narrative material for which she has prior knowledge but has difficulty with expository material.

Two judges examined test results from 108 children to assess the reliability of diagnostic judgments. The child's grade level, percent accuracy on word lists, percent or oral reading accuracy on all passages read orally, and comprehension on all passages were available. In addition, the level and types of passages (such as narrative) were given. The two judges independently classified the student's abilities according to word recognition and comprehension. A sample judgment would be, "word recognition—excellent; has trouble comprehending in all types of material." Or, "word recognition problems at grade level, comprehension good when word recognition is within instructional range." Or, "word recognition good, comprehension okay in narrative material, but problems in expository material beginning at fourth-grade level." The judges agreed on the diagnostic category for the student's abilities 87% of the time. An examination of misclassifications showed that in most cases lack of agreement came on cases where the pattern of strengths and weaknesses were not clear. In other cases one judge had a more stringent criteria than the other for word identification difficulties.

Sensitivity to Change.   Sensitivity to change refers to the responsiveness of a test to change or difference on the underlying construct being measured. We have conducted research on two aspects of the *QRI* which should be sensitive to change.

Regner (1992) used the *QRI* to compared progress made by two groups of children who were experiencing reading difficulties. One group has been identified as learning disabled, and the other group, while not significantly different in reading, as measured by the *QRI* and the *Woodcock Reading Mastery Test-Revised* (Woodcock, 1987), or intelligence, had not been so identified. Regner (1992) followed the children for four months examining their reading instruction. Pre-test and post-test performance in reading as measured by the above instruments showed significant gains for both groups but no difference between the groups. Thus, the *QRI* was capable of measuring change in word recognition and comprehension over a four-month period. It should be noted that such change was assessed by weighting the word recognition and comprehension scores. For example, the total score on a word list was multiplied by its level (primer = .5, first = 1, etc.) and added to a word-recognition accuracy score in context weighted in the same manner. Comprehension was weighted by multiplying the percent correct by the readability of the passage. The passage chosen for this procedure was the highest-level narrative passage at the student's instructional level. This weighting made the measurements more precise, and sensitive to change, then simply an instructional level.

Glass (1989) examined whether students' comprehension of two first- and second-level passages would be increased if they participated in a personal, analogical discussion related to themes in the story. For example, on "Bear and Rabbit," the researcher engaged students in a discussion of why people are afraid of real bears, why animals would like to have friends, and why people become friends. These concepts are related to the theme of the passage and directly related to the most difficult comprehension question, "Why did the bear and the rabbit become friends?" Two groups of second-grade students participated: sixteen average and sixteen below-average readers, reading the second- and first-level passages, respectively. Students' prior knowledge of concepts was assessed on two passages, and the analog discussion was held on one passage, and not on the other. Whether the discussion was held on the first or second story was counterbalanced across students. Results showed significant improvement in comprehension when students participated in the analog discussion on a story (effect sizes were greater than 1 for students at each readability level). These results suggest that instruction directed toward the conceptual knowledge judged as important to comprehending stories can enhance comprehension on the lower level *QRI*–II passages.

These findings suggest that the passages on the *QRI*–II are sensitive to immediate change (Glass, 1989) and long-term (four month) instructional interventions (Regner, 1992). Thus, researchers may use the *QRI*–II as outcome measures of instructional research.

Issues of Validity of an Informal Reading Inventory

Content Validity. Content validity is the degree to which the sample of items, tasks or questions on a test are representative of some domain of content (*Standard for educational and psychological testing,* 1985, p. 10). This type of validity is usually judged by experts in the content field. In our case, the research literature describe in Section Two, served as the basis for test development. Thus, to review our conclusions, we sought to represent the domain of reading more systematically than other IRIs. We chose narrative and expository material to represent the reading abilities from pre-primer through junior high. We included passages with pictures at the pre-primer through second-grade level to more fully represent the type of materials children encounter in and out of school. Passages were varied in their familiarity. In addition to presenting children with a variety of materials, we chose to measure their reading abilities in ways that reflect research findings and classroom practice.

Research suggests the powerful effects of prior knowledge, so we included a measure of prior knowledge. Oral reading research suggests that in addition to finding total miscues examiners should attend to the proportion of uncorrected miscues which change the meaning of the passage; thus, we score oral reading accuracy in these two ways. Because of findings that comprehension may be measured by examining whether children can make inferences, remember information stated directly in text, and retain information in memory, we chose to include three ways of measuring comprehension: answers to implicit questions, answers to explicit questions, and retelling. On the word lists we included words which can be decoded using the rules of English and those which must be memorized because their spelling is irregular. We measured children's rate of word recognition, in addition to their accuracy.

Whether we have succeeded in our attempts to present the domain of reading depends, in part, upon one's view of the importance of the factors listed above. In addition, examinations of the pilot data provided us evidence of the construct representation and penetration which we have achieved. Validity data for each part of the *QRI*–II are presented in the previous parts of this section called "Development of the. . . " (e.g., Word Identification Tests). In addition, we have presented evidence of overall test validity below.

Criterion-Related Validity. Criterion-related validity demonstrates that test scores are related to one or more outcome criteria (*Standards for educational and psychological tests,* 1985, p. 11). There are two types of criterion-related validity: *predictive* (where the test is used to predict future criterion behavior) and *concurrent* (where the test results are compared to a current criterion). According to the *Standards* (1985), "concurrent evidence is usually preferable for achievement tests, tests used for certification, diagnostic clinical tests or for tests used as measures of a specified construct" (p. 11). Thus, concurrent validity is needed for the *QRI*–II.

We examined the correlation (within a grade) between the instructional level in familiar material obtained from the *QRI*–II and the student's NCE for Total Reading on either the California Achievement Test or Iowa Test of Basic Skills. We conducted an analysis whenever we obtained data on at least fifteen children at a grade level. Table 16.5 presents the correlations between instructional level in familiar material and NCE.

At all grade levels where we had sufficient data there were significant correlations between a student's instructional level in familiar material and NCE. Results from the original *QRI* reached the same conclusions at grades 3, 5, 6, 7 and high school. Taken together, the results indicate that the instructional

TABLE 16.5 Correlations Between Instructional Level in Familiar Material and NCE as a Function of Grade

Grade	Correlation	N
1	.86*	41
2	.65*	32
4	.66*	31

*$p < .01$

levels obtained on the *QRI*–II and NCE obtained on standardized achievement tests are measuring some common factors and support the validity of the instructional levels obtained on the *QRI*–II.

Regner (1992) found that weighted word-recognition scores from the *QRI* correlated .90 with a combined Word-Identification and Word-Attack scale score from the *Woodcock Reading Mastery Test-Revised* (WMRT-R, 1987). Similarly, weighted *QRI* comprehension scores (% correct on the highest instructional level in narrative text × the readability level of the passage) correlated .75 ($p < .01$) with Passage Comprehension from the WMRT-R (1987). Thus, when *QRI* scores are weighted to reflect the difficulty of the words or passages they correlate quite highly with results from the WRMT-R (1987).

Construct Validity.   Evidence of construct validity focuses on the test scores as a measure of the psychological characteristics, or construct, of interest. The conceptual framework specifies the meaning of the construct, distinguishes it from other constructs and indicates how measures of the construct should relate to other variables (*Standards for educational and psychological testing,* 1985, p. 10). At the most general level, the *QRI*–II measures word-recognition ability and comprehension. Depending upon the stage of reading development, we should find different patterns of intercorrelations. Among beginning readers, we should find greater interrelatedness among word identification on word lists, oral-reading accuracy in context, and reading rate than among those factors and comprehension. On the other hand, after students have achieved some degree of automaticity of word recognition, we expect correlations between our prior-knowledge measures and retelling and comprehension.

1. Correlations among factors on the *QRI*–II.   We found support for the interrelatedness and uniqueness of several factors on the *QRI*–II. The inter-correlations among word identification on the word lists, total oral-reading accuracy in context, acceptable accuracy in context, and rate of reading were consistently highly correlated, particularly among beginning readers (those with instructional levels at or below second grade). Word identification was also significantly correlated to retelling or comprehension through first-grade level. Thus, there is evidence for a word-identification factor in early reading.

The other construct in evidence was illustrated by the intercorrelations among conceptual knowledge scores, and prediction, with retelling and comprehension. Evidence for the role of prior knowledge in predicting retelling or comprehension began at first-grade level (in expository text) and held through junior high. At some levels, conceptual-knowledge scores correlated most highly with retelling or comprehension, at other levels (e.g., third-grade), prediction was most highly correlated. Certainly we have evidence that the *QRI*–II measures at least two constructs which theorists have posited to be central to the reading process: word recognition and comprehension (Gough & Tunmer, 1986).

2. Are there diagnostic categories of reading (dis)abilities? To determine if different factors predict comprehension of beginning readers compared to comprehension of more advanced readers, or students with good vs. poor word-identification scores, we divided our sample into three groups, organized by their instructional levels in familiar text. Group 1 comprised children with pre-primer, primer, or first-grade instructional levels. Group 2 included children with second- or third-grade instructional levels, and Group 3 included students with fourth- through sixth-grade instructional levels. Next, within each group, children were further divided into two groups based on their word-identification score on the word list at their instructional level. Note that word-list scores are not used to judge instructional level. Those with scores on the word list at their instructional level of under 70% correct were called *poor word identifiers,* and those identifying 70% of more of the words correctly, were called *good word identifiers.*

At each instructional-level grouping, stepwise regression analyses were conducted with acceptable miscues, rate, prior conceptual knowledge, and text type (whether the text read was narrative or expository) as the predictor variables and total comprehension (on questions) as the dependent variable. We conducted the same analyses without acceptable miscues on the silent reading data. The summary below describes the variables that entered the regression equation and the amount of variance accounted for by the entering variables.

For children with instructional levels of pre-primer, primer, and first-grade levels, and poor word-identification skills nothing predicted comprehension (the number of students with such low word-identification scores, yet instructional levels within this range was only 13). For children within these same instructional level and who had good word-identification skills, acceptable miscues accounted for 16% of the variance in oral comprehension (n = 83 passages), and text type explained an additional 7% of the comprehension variance. For students with instructional levels at the second- and third-grade levels, and poor word-identification skills, nothing predicted oral or silent reading comprehension, but again few subjects fit this category (n = 17). For students at the same instructional levels with good word-identification skills, text type accounted for 26% and 16% of the variance in oral and silent comprehension, respectively. For students with instructional levels at fourth-, fifth-, or sixth-grade level, prior knowledge accounted for 34% and 23%, respectively of the oral and silent reading comprehension of good word identifiers. Again small samples of students at these instructional levels with poor word-identification skills on the word list at their instructional level precluded accounting for variance in their comprehension scores.

In summary, at beginning reading levels, students' comprehension is best predicted by the percent of miscues which retain meaning and whether they are reading a narrative or expository text. At the upper levels, comprehension is best predicted by conceptual knowledge that the reader possessed before reading the text.

Using the *QRI*–II to Guide Instruction

In addition to the type of construct validity presented above, Cross and Paris (1987) describe how a diagnostic test must represent specific constructs to be of use to teachers. Construct representation assessed how well a construct is contained in the items. Construct representation is often uncertain because one test score is the result of many cognitive processes. Often achievement test scores have not been able to provide educators with direction for instruction. This inability is related to the fact that construct representation does not usually occur in a one-to-one relationship between a score on a test and a single cognitive process responsible for the performance on that item (Cross & Paris, 1987).

We have attempted to provide construct representation by providing the examiner with a set of passages that vary according to type of text and familiarity to the reader. In this way an examiner can determine why a child might comprehend one type of material well but not another. In addition, we have assessed comprehension in several ways: retelling, answers to questions with the text absent, and answers to the questions with the text present. Thus, an examiner can separate what a student remembers from a text from what the student comprehends with access to the text. Furthermore, on the word lists, we have represented the construct of word identification by measuring student's rate of identification and by including words which vary in their decodability.

In order to assess whether we have been successful at providing an examiner with information useful to guide instruction, called *penetration* by Cross and Paris (1987), a small instructional study was conducted in 1991. Sixth graders from a single classroom were given the *QRI*. Although all students were taught, only the data from students reading at a sixth-grade instructional level in narrative text (n = 16) were used in the analyses. The mean pre-test scores showed that students retold more information from narrative than expository text, $F(1,15) = 15.71$, $p < .001$, although there were no differences in comprehension, $F < 1$, and the prior conceptual knowledge scores were higher for *expository* text, $F(1,15) = 14.64$, $p < .01$. The teacher then taught four text structures to the students: cause–effect, problem–solution, sequence, and compare–contrast. The text structure instruction occurred over one month, and was integrated within a unit on Greek and Roman governments, which was particularly useful in teaching the compare–contrast structure. The instruction was composed of direct instruction of text structures, modeling how to determine structures in text, guided-practice of finding structures in text, independent assessment of knowledge gained, and an application project. Post-testing with the *QRI* was conducted two months after the formal instruction had ended. Students read new (not used at pre-test) sixth-grade narrative and expository texts. We also asked students to identify text structures of the expository texts. Although there were no differences between pre-test and post-test in students abilities to identify different text structures, increases in their ability to recall expository texts were found, $F(1,15) = 12.79$, $p < .01$. Mean retelling scores on expository text increased from .20 at pre-test to .30 at post-test, which made it non-significantly different from the retelling of narrative text (mean = .33). We cannot conclude that the instruction on text structures resulted in the improvement in retelling ability. Rather the effect could have been a more general one. It may have been that the greater emphasis on constructing meaning in expository text was the factor. The students certainly liked the unit, as we learned when one teacher came and asked what we were doing in social studies. Students had reported to her an excitement in the subject that she had not seen before. Although our results were less than conclusive, others have found that instruction in text structures can improve students' recall and comprehension of expository text (Armbruster, Anderson & Ostertag, 1987; Richgels, McGee, Lomax & Sheard, 1987).

References

Alvermann, D.E., Smith, L.C., and Readance, J.E. (1985). Prior knowledge activation and the comprehension of compatible and incompatible text. *Reading Research Quarterly, 20,* 420–436.

Anderson, R.C., Reynolds, R.E., Schallert, D.L., and Goetz, E.T. (1977). Frameworks for comprehending discourse. *American Educational Research Journal, 14,* 367–382.

Armbruster, B.B., Anderson, T.H., and Ostertag, J. (1987). Does text structure/summarization instruction facilitate learning from expository text? *Reading Research Quarterly, 22,* 331–346.

August, D.L., Flavell, J.H., and Clift, R. (1984). Comparisons of comprehension monitoring of skilled and less-skilled readers. *Reading Research Quarterly, 20,* 39–53.

Baker, L. and Brown, A.L. (1984). Metacognitive skills and reading. In P.D. Pearson, M. Kamil, R. Barr, and P. Mosenthal (eds.), *Handbook of Reading Research* (vol. I, pp. 353–394). White Plains, NY: Longman.

Becoming a nation of readers: The Report of the Commission on Reading. (1985). Washington, DC: The National Institute of Education.

Berkowitz, S. and Taylor, B.M. (1981). The effects of text type and familiarity on the nature of information recalled by readers. In M. Kamil (ed.), *Directions in Reading: Research and Instruction* (pp. 157–161). Washington, D.C.: National Reading Conference.

Betts, F. (1946). *Foundations of reading instruction.* New York: American Book.

Blanchard, J.S., Borthwick, P., and Hall, A. (1983). Determining instructional reading level: Standardized multiple choice versus IRI improved recall questions. *Journal of Reading, 26,* 684–689.

Brennan, A.D., Bridge, C., and Winograd, P. (1986). The effects of structural variation on children's recall of basal readers stories. *Reading Research Quarterly, 21,* 91–104.

Bristow, P.S. (1985). Are poor readers passive readers? Some evidence, possible explanations, and potential solutions. *The Reading Teacher, 39,* 318–325.

Bristow, P. and Leslie, L. (1988). Indicators of reading difficulty: Discrimination between instructional and frustration range performance of functionally illiterate adults. *Reading Research Quarterly, 23,* 200–218.

Brown, C.S. and Lytle, S.L. (1988). Merging assessment and instruction: Protocols in the classroom. In S.M. Glazer, L.W. Searfoss, and L.M. Gentile (eds.), *Reexamining reading diagnoses: New trends and practices.* Newark, DE: International Reading Association.

Burge, P.D. (1983). Comprehension and rate: Oral vs. silent reading for low achievers. *Reading Horizons, 23,* 201–206.

Caldwell, J. (1985). A new look at the old informal reading inventory. *The Reading Teacher, 39,* 168–173.

Carroll, J.B., Davies, P., and Richman, B. (1971). *The word frequency book.* New York: American Heritage Publishing.

Carver, R.P. (1990). *Reading rate: A review of research and theory.* San Diego: Academic.

Chall, J.S. (1983). *Stages of reading development.* New York: McGraw-Hill.

Chrystal, C. (1991). Assessing prior knowledge across cultures. Unpublished doctoral dissertation, Marquette University.

Clark, H.H. and Clark. E.V. (1977). *Psychology and language.* New York: Harcourt.

Clay, M.M. (1985). The early detection of reading difficulties (3rd ed.). Portsmouth, NH: Heinemann.

Crocker, L. and Algina, J. (1986). *Introduction to classical and modern test theory.* New York: Holt, Rinehart and Winston.

Cronbach, L.J. (1951). Coefficient alpha and the internal structure of tests. *Psychometrika, 16,* 297–334.

Cross, D. and Paris, S. (1987). Assessment of reading comprehension: Matching test purposes and test properties. *Educational Psychologist, 22,* 313–332.

Dale, E. and Chall, J.S. (1948). Formula for predicting readability. *Educational Research Bulletin, 27,* 11–20.

Davison, A. and Kantor, R.N. (1982). On the failure of readability formulas to define readable texts: A case study from adaptations. *Reading Research Quarterly, 27,* 187–209.

Durkin, D. (1978–79). What classroom observations reveal about reading comprehension instruction. *Reading Research Quarterly, 14,* 481–533.

Durkin, D. (1981). Reading comprehension instruction in five basal reader series. *Reading Research Quarterly, 16,* 515–544.

Ehri, L.C. and Wilce, L.S. (1979). Does word training increase or decrease interference in a stroop task? *Journal of Experimental Child Psychology, 27,* 352–364.

Ehri, L.C. (1991). Development of the ability to read words. In R. Barr, M.L. Kamil, P. Mosenthal, and P.D. Pearson (eds.), *Handbook of Reading Research* (vol. II, pp. 383–417). White Plains, NY: Longman.

Ehri, L.C. (1992). Reconceptualizing the development of sight word reading and its relationship to recoding. In P.B. Gough, L.C. Ehri and R. Treiman (Eds.), *Reading Acquisition,* (pp. 107–143). Hillsdale, NJ: Erlbaum.

Englert, C.S. and Hiebert, E.H. (1984). Children's developing awareness of text structures in expository material. *Journal of Educational Psychology, 76,* 65–74.

Fry, E. (1977). Fry's readability graph: Clarifications, validity and extension to level 17. *Journal of Reading, 21,* 242–252.

Garner, R. and Reis, R. (1981). Monitoring and resolving comprehension obstacles: An investigation of spontaneous text lookbacks among upper grade good and poor readers. *Reading Research Quarterly, 16,* 569–582.

Garner, R., Hare, V.C., Alexander, P., Haynes, J., and Winograd, P. (1984). Inducing use of a text lookback strategy among unsuccessful readers. *American Educational Research Journal, 21,* 789–798.

Glass, S. (1989). The effect of prior knowledge on reading miscues and comprehension of narrative text. Unpublished master's thesis, Marquette University.

Goodman, K.S. (1969). Analysis of reading miscues: Applied psycholinguistics. *Reading Research Quarterly, 5,* 9–30.

Gough, P.B. & Juel, C. (1991). The first stages of word recognition. In L. Rieben & C.A. Perfetti (Eds.), *Learning to Read: Basic Research and its Implications* (pp. 47–56). Hillsdale, NJ: Erlbaum.

Gough, P.B. & Tunmer, W.E. (1986). Decoding, reading and reading disability. *Remedial and Special Education, 7,* 6–10.

Graesser, A.C. and Goodman, S.M. (1985). Implicit knowledge, question answering and the representation of expository text. In B.K. Britton, and J.B. Black (eds.), *Understanding Expository Text* (pp. 109–171). Hillsdale, NJ: L. Erlbaum.

Graesser, A., Golding, J.M., and Long, D.L. (1991). Narrative representation and comprehension. In R. Barr, M.L. Kamil, P. Mosenthal, and P.D. Pearson (eds.), *Handbook of Reading Research* (vol. II, pp. 171–205). White Plains, NY: Longman.

Hardy, N.D., & Jerman, M.E. (1985). *Readability estimator.* Seattle, WA: Berta-Max Inc.

Hare, V.C. (1982). Preassessment of topical knowledge: A validation and extension. *Journal of Reading Behavior, 15,* 77–86.

Harris, A.J. and Sipay, E. (1985). *How to increase reading ability: A guide to developmental and remedial methods* (8th ed). New York: Longman.

Holmes, B.C. and Roser, N.L. (1987). Five ways to assess readers' prior knowledge. *The Reading Teacher, 40,* 646–649.

Hood, J. (1975–76). Qualitative analysis of oral reading errors: The inter-judge reliability of scores. *Reading Research Quarterly, 11,* 577–598.

Hood, J. (1984). Stages of reading. In E. Forell (ed.), *Manual for student teachers: Children's Reading Clinic* (pp. 14–23). Iowa City: University of Iowa.

Huey, E.B. (1968). *The psychology and pedagogy of reading.* Boston, MA: The MIT Press. (Originally published by Macmillan in 1908).

Jett-Simpson, M. and Leslie, L. (1994). *Ecological Assessment: Under Construction.* Schofield, WI: Wisconsin State Reading Association.

Johnson, N.S. and Mandler, J.M. (1980). A tale of two structures: Underlying and surface forms in stories. *Poetics, 9,* 51–86.

Johnson, P.H. (1984). Prior knowledge and reading comprehension test bias. *Reading Research Quarterly, 19,* 219–239.

Kintsch, E. (1990). Macroprocesses and microprocesses in the development of summarization skills. *Cognition and Instruction, 7,* 161–195.

Klare, G.R. (1974–75). Assessing readability. *Reading Research Quarterly, 10,* 62–102.

Kletzien, S.B. (1991). Strategy used by good and poor comprehenders reading expository text of differing levels. *Reading Research Quarterly, 26,* 67–86.

Langer, J. (1984). Examining background knowledge and text comprehension. *Reading Research Quarterly, 14,* 468–481.

Leslie, L. (1980). The use of graphic and contextual information by average and below average readers. *Journal of Reading Behavior, 12,* 139–149.

Leslie, L. (1993). A developmental-interactive approach to reading assessment. *Reading and Writing Quarterly, 9,* 5–30.

Leslie, L. Recall and comprehension of narrative vs. expository text. Unpublished manuscript. Marquette University.

Leslie, L. and Osol, P. (1978). Changes in oral reading strategies as a function of quantities of miscues. *Journal of Reading Behavior, 10,* 442–445.

Leslie, L. & Caldwell, J. (1990). *Qualitative Reading Inventory.* NY: HarperCollins.

Leslie, L. and Caldwell, J. (1989). The Qualitive Reading Inventory: Issues in the development of a diagnostic reading test. In S. McCormick and J. Zutell (eds.), *Cognitive and social perspectives for literacy: Research and instruction* (pp. 413–419). Chicago, IL: National Reading Conference.

Leslie, L. and Cooper, J. (1993). Assessing the predictive validity of prior-knowledge assessment. In D.J. Leu, and C.K. Kinzer (eds.), *Examining central issues in literacy research, theory and practice* (pp. 93–100). Chicago, IL: National Reading Conference.

Lipson, M.Y. (1983). The influence of religious affiliation on children's memory for test information. *Reading Research Quarterly, 18,* 448–457.

Livingston, S.A. (1972). Criterion-referenced applications of classical test theory. *Journal of Educational Measurement, 9,* 13–26.

McCracken, R. (1966). *Standard Reading Inventory.* Klamath, OR: Klamath Printing.

Mandler, J.M. and DeForest, M. (1979). Is there more than one way to recall a story? *Child Development, 50,* 886–889.

Mandler, J.M. (1984). *Stories, scripts and scenes: Aspects of schema theory.* Hillsdale, NJ: Erlbaum.

Markman, E.M. (1977). Realizing that you don't understand: A preliminary investigation. *Child Development, 48,* 986–992.

Markman, E.M. (1979). Realizing you don't understand: Elementary school children's awareness of inconsistencies. *Child Development, 50,* 643–655.

Meyer, B.J.F. and Rice, G.E. (1984). The structure of text. In P.D. Pearson, R. Barr, M.L. Kamil, and P. Mosenthal (eds.),

Handbook of Reading Research (vol. I, pp. 319–352). White Plains, NY: Longman.

Meyers, M. and Paris, S.G. (1978). Children's metacognitive knowledge about reading. *Journal of Educational Psychology, 70,* 680–690.

Miller, J. and Leslie, L. Story content and structure in children's recall and comprehension. Unpublished manuscript Marquette University.

Mulcahy, P.I. and Samuels, S.J. (1987). Problem solving schemata for text types: A comparison of narrative and expository text structures. *Reading Psychology, 8,* 247–256.

Nelson, K.E. (1986). *Event knowledge: Structure and function in development.* Hillsdale, NJ: Erlbaum.

Nicholson, T., Lillas, C., and Rozoskama, M.A. (1988). Have we been misled by miscues? *The Reading Teacher, 42,* 6–10.

Paris, S.G., Wasik, B.A., and Turner, J.C. (1991). The development of strategic readers. In R. Barr, M.L. Kamil, P. Mosenthal, and P.D. Pearson (eds.), *Handbook of Reading Research* (vol. II, pp. 609–640). White Plains, NY: Longman.

Pearson, P.D., Hansen, J., and Gordon, C. (1979). The effect of background knowledge on young children's comprehension of explicit and implicit information, *Journal of Reading Behavior, 11,* 201–209.

Pearson, P.D. and Johnson, D.D. (1978). *Teaching reading comprehension.* New York: Holt, Rinehart & Wintson.

Perfetti, C.A. (1985). *Reading ability.* New York: Oxford University Press.

Perfetti, C.A. (1991). Representations and awareness of the acquisition of reading competence. In L. Rieben and C.A. Perfetti (eds.), *Learning to Read: Basic Research and its Implications* (pp. 33–44). Hillsdale, NJ: Erlbaum.

Perfetti, C.A. (1988). Verbal efficiency in reading ability. In M. Daneman, G.E. MacKinnon, and T.G. Waller (eds.), *Reading Research: Advances in theory and practice* (vol. 6, 109–143). New York: Academic.

Pinter, R. (1913). Oral and silent reading of fourth grade pupils. *Journal of Educational Psychology, 4,* 330–337.

Pinter, R. and Gilliland, A.R. (1916). Oral and silent reading. *Journal of Educational Psychology, 7,* 201–212.

Raphael, T. (1986). Teaching question–answer relationships, revisited. *The Reading Teacher, 39,* 516–522.

Recht, D. (1986). The effect of prior knowledge on the spatial performance, verbal short-term memory and verbal long-term memory of good and poor readers. Unpublished doctoral dissertation, Marquette University.

Recht, D.R. and Leslie, L. (1988). The effects of prior knowledge on good and poor readers' memory for text. *Journal of Educational Psychology, 80,* 16–20.

Regner, M. (1992). Predicting growth in reading in regular and special education. Unpublished doctoral dissertation, Marquette University.

Richgels, D.J., McGee, L.M., Lomax, R.G., and Sheard, C. (1987). Awareness of four text structures: Effects on recall of expository text. *Reading Research Quarterly, 22,* 177–196.

Rowell, E.H. (1976). Do elementary students read better orally or silently? *The Reading Teacher, 29,* 367–370.

Rumelhart, D. (1977). Toward an interactive model of reading. In S. Dornic (Ed.), *Attention and Performance* VI (pp. 573–603). Hillsdale, N.J.: Erlbaum.

Schmidt, M.B. (1990). A questionnaire to measure children's awareness of strategic reading processes. *The Reading Teacher, 43,* 454–461.

Smith, W.E. and Beck, M.B. (1980). Determining instructional reading level with 1978 Metropolitan Achievement Test. *The Reading Teacher, 34,* 313–319.

Spache, G.D. (1974). *Good reading for poor readers* (rev. 9th ed.). Champaign, IL: Garrard Publishing.

Spache, G.D. (1981). *Diagnosing and correcting reading disabilities.* Boston: Allyn and Bacon.

Standards for education and psychological testing. (1985). Washington, D.C.: American Psychological Association.

Stanovich, K.E. (1980). Toward an interactive compensatory model of individual differences in the development of reading fluency. *Reading Research Quarterly, 16,* 32–71.

Stanovich, K.E. (1991). Discrepancy definitions of reading disability: Has intelligence led us astray? *Reading Research Quarterly, 26,* 7–29.

Stanovich, K.E., Cunningham, A.E., and West, R.F. (1981). A longitudinal study of the development of automatic recognition skills in first graders. *Journal of Reading Behavior, 13,* 57–73.

Stein, N.L. (1979). How children understand stories. A developmental analysis. In L. Katz (ed.), *Current topics in early childhood education* (vol. 2, pp. 261–290) Norwood, NJ: Ablex.

Stein, N.L. and Glenn, C. (1979). An analysis of story comprehension in elementary school children. In R.O. Freedle (ed.), *Advances in discourse processes* (vol. 2): *New directions in discourse processes* (pp. 53–120). Norwood, NJ: Ablex.

Stevens, K.C. (1980). The effect of background knowledge on the reading comprehension of ninth graders. *Journal of Reading Behavior, 12,* 151–154.

Sulzby, E. and Teale, W. (1991). Emergent literacy. In R. Barr, M.L. Kamil, P. Mosenthal, and P.D. Pearson (eds.), *Handbook of Reading Research* (vol. II, pp. 727–758). White Plains, NY: Longman.

Swalm, J.E. (1972). A comparison of oral reading, silent reading, and listening comprehension. *Education, 92,* 111–115.

Taft, M.L. and Leslie, L. (1985). The effects of prior knowledge and oral reading accuracy on miscues and comprehension. *Journal of Reading Behavior, 17,* 163–179.

Taylor, B. (1979). Good and poor readers' recall of familiar and unfamiliar text. *Journal of Reading Behavior, 11,* 375–380.

Taylor, B.M. (1982). Text structure and children's comprehension and memory for expository material. *Journal of Educational Psychology, 74,* 323–340.

Thorndike, R.L. and Hagen, E. (1977). *Measurement and evaluation in psychology and education.* New York: Wiley.

Valencia, S.W. and Stallman, A.C. (1989). Multiple measures of prior knowledge: Comparative predictive validity. In S. McCormick and J. Zutell (eds.), *Cognitive and social perspectives for literacy: Research and instruction* (pp. 427–436). Chicago, IL: National Reading Conference.

Valencia, S.W., Stallman, A.C., Commeyras, M., Pearson, P.D., and Hartman, D.K. (1991). Four measures of topical knowledge: A study of construct validity. *Reading Research Quarterly, 26,* 204–233.

Vosniadou, S., Pearson, P.D., and Rogers, T. (1988). What causes children's failures to detect inconsistencies in text? Representation versus comparison difficulties. *Journal of Educational Psychology, 80,* 27–39.

Weaver, C.A. and Kintsch, W. (1991). Expository test. In R. Barr, M.L. Kamil, P. Mosenthal, and P.D. Pearson (eds.), *Handbook of Reading Research* (vol. II, pp. 230–245). White Plains, NY: Longman.

Wheeler, L.R. and Smith, E.H. (1954). A practical readability formula for the classroom teacher in the elementary grades. *Elementary English, 31,* 397–399.

Wisconsin Department of Public Instruction (1986). A guide to curriculum planning in reading. Madison, WI.

Woodcock, R.W. (1987). *Woodcock Reading Mastery Test-Revised,* Circle Pines, MN: American Guidance Service.

Zabrucky, K. and Ratner, H.H. (1992). Effects of passage type on comprehension monitoring and recall in good and poor readers. *Journal of Reading Behavior, 24,* 373–391.

BASAL REFERENCES

Heath Reading (1991). Lexington, MA: D.C. Heath.

Houghton Mifflin Reading (1991). Boston, MA: Houghton Mifflin.

Scott, Foresman Reading: An American Tradition (1987). Glenview, IL: Scott, Foresman and Co.

Silver Burdett-Ginn Reading Program (1991). Lexington, MA: Ginn and Co.

VIDEOTAPES WILL BE AVAILABLE
TO ACCOMPANY THE *QRI*–II

The Instructional Media Center at Marquette University is producing a 40-minute VHS color videotape. The tape demonstrates how to assess a beginning reader in the primary grades and a more advanced reader in the intermediate grades.

ESTIMATED DATE: April 1, 1995

Cost: $50.00 for each 1/2″ VHS tape

I wish to order:

____videotapes @ $50 each $ _____total

+ _____**5.5% sales tax**
for WI residents only

$ _____**TOTAL ENCLOSED**

....

NOTE: A check or money order payable to Marquette University must accompany your order. If a purchase order is attached, a $5.00 shipping and handling fee will be added to the total billed.

....

Name _____

School _____

Address _____

City _____ **State**_____ **Zip Code**_____

MAIL ORDER FORM TO:
Lauren Leslie, Ph. D.
School of Education
Marquette University
Milwaukee, WI 53233
ATTN: Video Order